Cocoon
Kim Davis

COCOON
A Journey of Transformation

KIM DAVIS

Belleville, Ontario, Canada

COCOON
Copyright © 2009, Kim Davis

All Rights Reserved. No part of this publication may be reproduced, stored in a retrieval system or transmitted in any form or by any means—electronic, mechanical, photocopy, recording or any other—except for brief quotations in printed reviews, without the prior permission of the author.

All Scripture quotations, unless otherwise specified, are taken from the HOLY BIBLE, NEW INTERNATIONAL VERSION ®. Copyright © 1973, 1978, 1984 by International Bible Society. Used by permission of Zondervan Publishing House. All rights reserved. • Scripture taken from *The Holy Bible, King James Version*. Copyright © 1977, 1984, Thomas Nelson Inc., Publishers. • Scripture quotations marked NKJV are taken from the New King James Version. Copyright © 1979, 1980, 1982. Thomas Nelson Inc., Publishers. • Scripture taken from *The Message*, copyright © by Eugene H. Peterson, 1993, 1994, 1995. Used by permission of NavPress Publishing Group.

Library and Archives Canada Cataloguing in Publication

Davis, Kim, 1955-
    Cocoon / Kim Davis.

Includes bibliographical references.
ISBN 978-1-55452-365-8

    1. Faith development. 2. Christian life. I. Title.
BV4501.3.D3756 2009   248.4   C2009-901216-2

**For more information or
to order additional copies, please contact:**

Kim Davis
6214 Moore Road
Nashville, NC 27856

Guardian Books is an imprint of *Essence Publishing,* a Christian Book Publisher dedicated to furthering the work of Christ through the written word. For more information, contact:
20 Hanna Court, Belleville, Ontario, Canada K8P 5J2
Phone: 1-800-238-6376 • Fax: (613) 962-3055
E-mail: info@essence-publishing.com
Web site: www.essence-publishing.com

Dedication

To all those who have been a part of my life from its beginning and will be throughout the rest of it. You have helped and will help me to know the Lord as I see in you a revelation of Him, as you are being transformed into His image. Particularly, I thank my wonderful husband, Kenny, who is loving me throughout this journey and has helped me see the LORD in awesome ways!

Acknowledgements

A special thanks to my brother, Buddy, for giving of his editing expertise and viewing this project from a different perspective. You have been extremely helpful! Also, a special thanks to an anonymous donor who confirmed God's Word to me to write this book and enabled me to purchase a computer to work on this project. Thank you, Kenny Davis Ministries board members—you have been so encouraging throughout this entire process! Last but certainly not least, a very special thank you to all of my family—immediate and both sides—who continue to show much grace as I am undergoing this transformation in my cocoon and have provided me with a lot of this material.

Table of Contents

Introduction 11
Preface 13
Part One: Becoming 15
Chapter One: Metamorphosis 17
Chapter Two: Spinning the Cocoon 23
Chapter Three: Our Dwelling Place 35
Chapter Four: The Mirror 41
Chapter Five: The Rhythm of the Process 49
Part Two: Under the Shadow 63
Chapter Six: See, A Son 71
Chapter Seven: One Who Hears 103
Chapter Eight: Attached 115
Chapter Nine: Praise 129
Chapter Ten: He Has Vindicated 137
Chapter Eleven: My Struggle 155
Chapter Twelve: Good Fortune, or a Troop 177
Chapter Thirteen: Happy 213
Chapter Fourteen: Reward 231

Chapter Fifteen: Honor 253
Chapter Sixteen: Justice 269
Chapter Seventeen: May He Add 289
Chapter Eighteen: Son of My Right Hand 299
Chapter Nineteen: The Butterfly 305
Bibliography 311

Introduction

For in him we live and move and have our being (Acts 17:28).

There have been so many books that I have read throughout my life that have had a tremendous impact on my life. The primary one has been the Bible, God's love letter to man, a record of His dealings with man and His revelation of Himself. Other books have pulled out portions of *The Book* and applied a magnifying glass to these portions. They have helped shine further light on the subjects they have addressed, but even more significantly—actually of primary importance—they have helped me see the ONE whom *The Book* and these other books were written about. They have not just been *information* but *revelation* of Him. And the Him to whom I refer is Elohim, creator of heaven and earth, Yahweh of old, who revealed Himself to man as the I AM, in whose image we were created.

My prayer for you is that this book helps you see Him in even clearer focus than you have before. I pray that He will reveal Himself to you as you ponder these thoughts, scriptures and revelations that I have experienced and am herein sharing with you. Indeed, our revelation of God is a progressive revelation throughout our lifetime as we walk through this journey of life with Him. He is far more than words on a page or thoughts in a book or an ominous power at work in the universe. He is the real life force of all, the essence of life and all it contains, who invites us to draw near Him to know Him intimately and experience vitally His life in us. As we see Him and know Him in this intimate, vital way, we are transformed into His image once again, having fallen and marred that image with our sin. The only begotten Son of the Father, our Savior, Jesus Christ, Yeshua the Messiah, has paid the penalty for our sin and enabled us to connect once again to our loving heavenly Father. In Him we see the Father and engage in the journey to wholeness.

This process of transformation is likened to the process by which the caterpillar becomes a butterfly. In the transition, the caterpillar rests within a cocoon, in which the transformation takes place. On our journey to wholeness, where is our cocoon and how do we enter in? Come explore this with me in the pages of this book. I believe we can experience an exciting and enlightening journey together. As with any revelation, as the apostle Paul reminds us, *"we see through a glass dimly."* I do not profess to see the total picture, but I share what I do see to help thrust you forward on your journey, and I ask Him to help you know Him more and more.

The path of the righteous is like the first gleam of dawn, shining ever brighter till the full light of day (Proverbs 4:18).

Preface

A few words of instruction are necessary for you to get the most out of this book. It is written in two parts. The first part should be read straight through as it gives the overall process of the metamorphosis that we are experiencing as new creatures in Christ.

The second part of this book must be digested a little more slowly. It contains twelve different views of the Lord as we look to Him in our cocoon. I believe that these twelve views help us to become established in twelve foundational areas so that we can grow as children of God and be transformed into the image of His Son. As we get a hold of each of these twelve foundations, we are being formed into the beautiful butterflies God has designed us to be. The twelve foundations are based on the meanings of the names of each of the twelve sons of Jacob and on that same truth illuminated by each one of Jesus' twelve apostles. The twelve sons of Jacob are the fathers of the twelve tribes of Israel. Jacob had a daughter also. I believe that there is something to be said to the women in the Body of Christ in this also, and so I have included a chapter on the meaning of her name as well. The final chapter releases the new creation.

At the beginning of each of these twelve chapters in the second part of the book, a narrative is written with Moses speaking to the representatives from each of the tribes. Within this section, you will notice that each time *God* is mentioned it is written as *G_d*, leaving out the vowel. I did this in honor of the Jewish people who believe that the name of God is too sacred to pronounce. God is worthy of all reverence and honor, regardless of whether we pronounce His name or not. We can learn much from the Jewish people, our ancestral roots within our Christian faith.

Within each of the chapters of the second part of this book, there are forty days of your cocoon. To best experience each day's journey, I would suggest that you read only one day's journey at a time and respond to what has been shared by recording your experiences in a journal. Your response is an integral part of your journey. As faith comes from your hearing, it also needs expression. *Faith by itself, if it is not accompanied by action, is dead* (James 2:17).

I really desire that you have an awesome journey and want to do everything I can to help get you started. I know that there is a beautiful butterfly in you that is being formed even now. I can't wait to see all the beautiful colors and see just how high you can fly!

Part One

Becoming

Yet to all who received him, to those who believed in his name, he gave the right to become children of God (John 1:12).

One of the most common excuses for not coming to Jesus is that what some people see as the church is to them just a big bunch of hypocrites. They hear a little about Jesus but don't see those who claim to know Him as being much like their vision of who He is. Sometimes we as believers do act hypocritical, just like the Pharisees of old. But I believe a large number of us who believe in Jesus are sincerely wanting to live the life He gives but find it very difficult to do so. We are caught in the space between the beginning of the journey and the end of it. We are in process. You see, what we don't understand as much as we need to is that this Christian life we have in Jesus is a journey. When we recognize Jesus as our Savior and apply His work on Calvary to our lives, receiving the paid penalty for our sins and the resultant freedom to new life, we are born again that very instant. We have been taken out of the kingdom of darkness and put into the kingdom of light through Christ. *For he has rescued us from the dominion of darkness and brought us into the kingdom of the Son he loves* (Colossians 1:13).

However, as the above verse from John 1:12 states, in this new life that we have been given, we are still *becoming* the children of

God. This is certainly not to say that the sacrifice of Christ was not enough to completely save us! On the contrary!! *Therefore he is able to save completely those who come to God through him, because he always lives to intercede for them* (Hebrews 7:25). And I am also not saying that once we are born again we have to make the life of Christ real in us by our own efforts. We cannot accomplish that feat with our own strength. I know; I have tried at times! *Are you so foolish? After beginning with the Spirit, are you now trying to attain your goal by human effort* (Galatians 3:3)? What I *am* saying is that the Christian life is a progressive journey. Everything we need to make the journey is deposited within us when we're born again. We just have to learn to release it in our lives and walk out the reality of it.

Actually, our journey is a deep one, into our own spirit where we connect with the Spirit of God. A former pastor, Scotty Todd, used to teach us about the difference of what is legally ours and what is vitally ours. Legally, we have it all because of the finished work of Christ, but we must vitally experience the reality of all that is ours in Him to see it at work in our lives.

I've been on this journey for quite some time now. But I know I have only just begun. My journey has been so exasperating at times and so exhilarating at other times. All in all, as the old song goes, "I wouldn't take nothing for my journey now!" I've learned a lot, and I'm still learning. Maybe some of what I've learned could help you along your journey. That is my desire. Come on. Let's look a little more closely.

Chapter 1
Metamorphosis

I declare to you, brothers, that flesh and blood cannot inherit the kingdom of God, nor does the perishable inherit the imperishable. Listen, I tell you a mystery: We will not all sleep, but we will all be changed (1 Corinthians 15:50,51).

When you look up the word *metamorphosis* in any dictionary, one key word immediately jumps out: *change!* Change can be good or it can be bad. It is the *process* of change that is usually difficult. My husband and I have moved a number of times to different homes. He tells me that I am a woman of vision and able to look at a house and see its possibilities. He, on the other hand, has frequently been ready to make another choice, to move on to something that didn't require so much work! But as we spent time and effort painting, wallpapering, cleaning, planting—and the list goes on—we ended up with a very special place to call home that reflected our own personalities and lifestyles at the time.

Change requires us to have a different perspective. During most of our married life, Kenny traveled a great deal in ministry. He would joke that if he came home late at night, he would certainly turn on the light to find his way through the house so that he wouldn't trip over anything. I was always rearranging the furniture for a different look or better function. (I would make the changes

 Cocoon

while he was gone to get past the first obstacle of change involving a lot of work—for him anyway!) Even after the change had been made, it would take some time to get used to. Kenny used to do a lot of changing in his physical appearance. For a while, he would be clean shaven. Then he would wear a mustache for a season. And when he'd get tired of that, he'd grow a beard and wear that for a while. It was always hard for me to get used to him when he shaved his beard. I liked it.

We human beings can be real creatures of habit. We like things a certain way and want them to stay that way. There is a certain comfort in things being the same—we know what to expect. It is quite interesting that people who grow up in abusive situations, for example, often put themselves in those type of situations over and over again. It may not be pleasant, but for them, it is their concept of normal and they have learned to live this lifestyle. It is said that animals such as ponies or elephants that have been chained and led around in a circle day after day will still continue to travel that path even if loosed from their chains. Continuing to travel in the same path over and over can only make a very big rut!

Another difficulty with change is the transition. To get from point A to point B, there is a space in between. It can be difficult sometimes, especially if the process is a long one, to see what is ahead but not be there yet. Cleo, a good friend, had a saying about having to "go through to get to." We can certainly see this in the Israelites. They were released from the slavery of Egypt, but to get to the Promised Land, they had to go through the wilderness. This "in-between" is what this book is all about.

The Butterfly

Butterflies are found all over the world but are primarily in abundance in tropical Central and South America. Costa Rica has over 1,300 species.[1] Certainly, the butterfly is one of God's most beautiful creations. Its glory shines from its brilliantly colored wings as it flits from flower to flower in the garden. But it hasn't always been this beautiful. It is truly amazing to realize that this beautiful creature was once worm-like.

Butterflies and moths both belong to a family of insects called Lepidoptera. All moths and butterflies have tiny three-dimensional structures on their wings. These scales reflect light differently, producing the many color variations that are seen. The scales also help to repel water. Both moths and butterflies go through the same life-cycle stages—egg, larva, pupa, and adult.

There are several characteristics of moths and butterflies that are different. Butterflies usually fly in the daytime, while moths usually fly at night. Butterflies have a feeding mechanism (proboscis). Moths often do not because they do not eat as adults. They have "filled up," so to speak, as larvae. Butterflies usually rest with their wings closed. Moths rest with their wings open. Butterflies form a hanging chrysalis, produced by a single butterfly without silk. Moths form a cocoon, usually on the ground and surrounded by silk. Butterflies have straight, club-like antennae, while moths have shorter feathery antennae. For our purposes, we will use the word *cocoon* in reference to the butterfly because of people's familiarity with it. The purpose of the chrysalis and the cocoon is the same, that of transformation from one form to another.

Let's look at the life cycle of the butterfly. A female butterfly releases her perfume, pheromones, into the air. A male butterfly's antenna can detect the pheromones over a mile away. Some perfume, huh?! He finds the female and mates with her. As the butterflies mate, semen from the male enters a small storage pouch in the abdomen of the female. After mating, the female has about 100 eggs inside her and this pouch of spermatozoa. The female finds a host-plant, which will be food for the hatched larvae, and deposits an egg on it. She's already setting up her child in a pad of his own,

completely stocked. What a mama! As the egg is passing out, it passes the pouch. One spermatozoa will fertilize the egg and determine its sex. Some species lay their eggs in clusters. Others scatter the eggs on various plants. And so the "little butterfly" begins its life as a tiny egg.

The egg hatches and out comes a larva (caterpillar). This is the second stage in the butterfly's life cycle. The larva is an eating machine extraordinaire! "Some caterpillars eat twenty times their weight a day in food. If a human baby grew as fast as some species of caterpillars, it would weigh eight tons when it was only two weeks old."[2] Now you know why mama sends out junior to fend for himself! The larva has mandibles for crushing the leaves and chewing them. The largest segment of the larva is its abdomen, which contains the "giant stomach." The abdomen can make up as much as 80 per cent of the size of the larva. As the larva continues to eat and grow, it sheds its skin four different times until it finally reaches its full size. This sure beats having to buy a whole new wardrobe each time! Can you imagine having to find the perfect fit when you're constantly growing?! *Within the larva are all the parts of the butterfly.* The larva just has additional parts—suction feet, strong mandibles, and a big stomach—to help with its function as a caterpillar. The only stage in which the butterfly actually grows is in its larval stage. The larva is consumed with eating, growing, and gathering energy needed to transform into an adult while it will be in the pupa.

Once the larva reaches its full size, it enters the pre-pupa stage. It stops eating, empties its stomach, and finds an ideal spot, a new "hangout," to begin its pupa stage. In this spot, the larva will hang upside down, attached to the tree by a small ball of silk, called a cremaster. As it hangs, two things happen: one, it slowly begins to condense its body and, two, the last molting forms the pupa beneath it. Ugh! A crash diet!

The pupa stage is where the serious transformation takes place. This happens in the "cocoon," if you will, or chrysalis. The larva becomes the adult butterfly. In place of its "big mouth" (mandibles), the proboscis begins to form. This new feature will serve the adult as it consumes its new liquid diet. Wings begin to form, protruding from the thorax. Parts of the head change drastically in appearance. "Visible changes on the outer layer of the pupa can be noticed as the butterfly begins to develop within."[3] The organism consumes the "giant stomach," releasing energy throughout this stage. (Aerobic exercise?)

As the pupa stage comes to an end, out comes a butterfly. Its wings and body are small and limp at first, having been confined to the "cocoon." (Because of the crash-and-burn diet?) As it continues to hang upside down, the butterfly sends liquid down through the veins of its wings. (Gatorade, perhaps?) Within half an hour, it will fully extend its wings. A lamination will begin to harden and strengthen them, preparing them for flight. Then, it's time for takeoff! The caterpillar has become the butterfly; an awesome transformation has taken place.

The cycle then begins again. "The only goal in life for an adult butterfly is to reproduce."[4]

Just as the caterpillar contains all the parts of the butterfly within but must undergo the process of transformation to exhibit all the characteristics of the butterfly, so we who have come to Christ and experienced regeneration—the new birth—must undergo the process of transformation to exhibit all the characteristics of our new nature. We have come to point A, a new beginning for us. We see in the Word that we are a new creature in Christ (2 Corinthians 5:17), and indeed we are. We begin to see who Christ is in us and who we are in Him, but are we really walking in the reality of that truth? We have left the slavery of Egypt, but are we living in the Promised Land? Many of us come to Christ and

are born again like the little butterfly egg on the leaf. We devour God's Word and its lessons taught by many various teachers along the way (and rightly so—we have much to learn!), but our needed knowledge is not *about* God; rather the knowledge we so desperately need is *of* God, a relational knowledge of who He is. We grow and grow, getting fatter and fatter, and then what happens? I believe that we must spin our cocoon and await the transformation to emerge as an adult butterfly who is ready and able to reproduce.

> *So God created man in his own image, in the image of God he created him; male and female he created them. God blessed them and said to them, "Be fruitful and increase in number; fill the earth and subdue it"* (Genesis 1:27,28).

Chapter 2
Spinning the Cocoon

Christ redeemed us from the curse of the law by becoming a curse for us, for it is written: "Cursed is everyone who is hung on a tree" (Galatians 3:13).

First, let's back up and see why we need this metamorphosis, this transformation, this change. God had originally created us as beautiful butterflies. Okay, we can only take this analogy so far; we were not really literal butterflies, but He did create man in His own image, the crowning touch of creation. And that is even more beautiful than the butterfly! He breathed into man His breath of life. He placed man, male and female, in a perfect environment that He had created especially for them. He told them to be fruitful and multiply and replenish the earth.

Being made in God's image, man is a three-part being, just as God, the "three in one," is Father, Son and Spirit. These three parts are particularly spelled out in 1 Thessalonians 5:23, which says, *May God himself, the God of peace, sanctify you through and through. May your whole spirit, soul, and body be kept blameless at the coming of our Lord Jesus Christ.* Now let's remember that God is the three in one. Even though there are three parts to His person, these three are in total agreement. These three parts function as one. And that is God's desire for us, as well, that our spirit, soul and body would also, even though it exists in three parts, function as one. So we do not differentiate between these three parts of man to divide and scatter our being but rather to understand the function of each and then to allow for them to come together in complete unity and oneness.

The first two chapters of the book of Genesis tell us of the creation of the earth and mankind created to inhabit it. Genesis 2:7 says, *And the LORD God formed the man from the dust of the ground and breathed into his nostrils the breath of life, and the man became a living being.* To this we compare John 20:21-23, where Jesus appears to His disciples following the resurrection.

> *So Jesus said to them again, "Peace be with you! As the Father has sent me, I am sending you." And with that he breathed on them, and said, "Receive the Holy Spirit. If you forgive anyone his sins, they are forgiven; if you do not forgive anyone their sins, they are not forgiven."*

The Tree of the Knowledge of Good and Evil

In the garden, God had instructed the man not to eat of one certain tree, the tree of the knowledge of good and evil. He told the man that when he ate of it, he would surely die. God's Word is true, whether or not we believe it or understand it. When the man and the woman ate of this tree, they died. Their bodies did not die. They went and hid in the garden. Their souls did not die. They still talked and reasoned and acted on that reasoning. But something happened to them: they died spiritually. I guess you could say that they had the "breath knocked out of them." The glory of God ceased to cover them so that they saw their nakedness and were ashamed. The man and the woman ceased to live out of their spirits, as in the image of their Creator, who is a spirit, and they had to make judgments based on their own reasoning, understanding

Spinning the Cocoon

and feelings. Wade Taylor says, "The tree of life (spirit) represents our utter dependence upon and trust in the outworking of His purpose and provision for us. The tree of the knowledge of good and evil (soul) represents our desire to be independent and choose for ourselves what is right or wrong."[5] Life was on a whole different plane, a lower plane than it had been before. Romans 3:23 tells us that *all have sinned and **fall short** of the glory of God* (emphasis added). Their physical bodies were affected too. Genesis 2:16,17 records God's instruction to the man concerning that tree:

And the LORD God commanded the man, saying, "Of every tree of the garden you may freely eat; but of the tree of the knowledge of good and evil you shall not eat, for in the day that you eat of it you shall surely die" (NKJV).

The margin of the *Spirit-Filled Life Bible* notes that the literal translation of this last phrase, *"you shall surely die"* is "dying you shall die."[6] The spiritual death introduced death into the body as well. Even though the body continued to live on, the process of death began its work and eventually the man and woman died physically.

Sin is ugly! Instead of the beautiful "butterfly," here was an ugly worm. The caterpillar actually hides motionless in corners of its host-plant throughout the daytime so that its predators will not see it and attack and consume it. Then it comes out under the cover of the darkness of night and voraciously eats the leaves of the plant on which it lives.

In the garden, when the man and woman sinned, their eyes were immediately opened to the ugliness of sin. They tried to cover their ugliness with fig leaves, and they hid themselves among the trees. Their Creator, in whose image and likeness the man and the woman were made, came into the garden to talk with them, as was His custom, but could not find the "beautiful butterflies." He called out to them, "Where are you?" Adam and Eve crawled out from behind the trees. There, in full view, cowered the lowly worms. And God, in His great mercy and grace, looked at the man and the woman, seeing what they could not see deep within. Covered over with the ugliness of sin lay a dead butterfly in each of them. That butterfly needed resurrection, but first the caterpillar must be dealt with. Seeing the ugly caterpillars only brought God pain. He chose, instead, to remember the vision of the beautiful butterflies. God made a covering for the ugliness of the sin. He killed animals, a blood sacrifice, and took the skin of the animals and made clothing to cover the nakedness of the man and the woman. This death, dealt by God's own hands, was a redemptive death, as it covered the sin of the man and woman, if only temporarily. Death had taken place in the beautiful butterflies. They needed life imparted to them once again.

The Tree of Life

There was another tree in the garden, the tree of life. God, once again in His mercy and grace, knew that He needed to hide the way to the tree of life so that this man and woman would not eat of this tree in this "dead butterfly" state and live forever as the lowly worm. There must be a slow and complete transformation that would not be easily lost. So God cast the man and the woman out of the garden. Adam and Eve began their journey to try and recover what had been lost. Their journey was not a hopeless one, for God had given them a glimmer of light even as He spoke to them of the curse they had entered into.

Let me just break into the story at this point and address what I believe are three very important issues. First, a lot of folks want to get mad at God and ask why He even allowed the tree of the knowledge of good and evil in the garden, knowing man like He does and how he would respond. But remember, the primary character of God is love: *God is love* (1 John 4:8). Love does not confine and demand, manipulate and control. Rather, love frees its object to make choices. Love desires and believes the best. Just look at the description of love given to us in 1 Corinthians 13:4-8:

> *Love is patient, love is kind. It does not envy, it does not boast, it is not proud. It is not rude, it is not self-seeking, it is not easily angered, it keeps no record of wrongs. Love does not delight in evil but rejoices with the truth. It always protects, always trusts, always hopes, always perseveres. Love never fails.*

God, love that He is, gave man a choice. He clearly communicated to the man that the best choice for him was to not eat of the tree of the knowledge of good and evil. He warned man of the consequence of eating of that tree. But man chose to eat anyway. *Love never fails.* God, in His great love, always makes a way. We must choose to respond to Him in love as we take the way that He has given.

Second, many folks see God as an angry God, and indeed, throughout the Old Testament we see His anger. But what is He angry about? With whom is He angry? I believe that He is angry because of the hurt and pain the beautiful butterfly experienced in dying. I believe that He is angry at sin and the one who had chosen rebellion himself, Lucifer, who was now trying to deceive His creation. God's anger is different from ours. His anger is wholly righteous and out of love. His anger is that of a loving Father desiring to protect His child from all harm, to embrace this child in His care and yet free him to love Him in return. Our anger, on the other hand, is often self-centered and self-seeking, about what we want, to please and exalt ourselves.

Third, God did not curse the man, but rather spoke to him the results of what he had chosen. In Genesis 3, as God was speaking these curses, He made it very clear, I believe, that the curses were coming because of what they had done. The New Testament gives us even clearer revelation on this in 2 Peter 3:9: *The Lord is not slow in keeping his promise, as some understand slowness. He is patient with you, not wanting anyone to perish, but everyone to come to repentance.* And what is repentance but change that we are talking about. Repentance has to do with going in one direction and then turning to go in an opposite direction because of a change of mind. The direction man was going after eating of the forbidden fruit was leading to death via sin and sickness. He needed to turn around and go in the opposite direction, to find the very opposite—life. God, in His justice, also set certain laws or processes in motion from the very beginning. If we violate those laws, we reap the consequences. Even as God is perfect love, He is also perfect justice. As author Rufus Mosely put it in his book entitled *Perfect Everything*, He is "perfect everything!"

Okay, let's get back to our story. The curse that the man and woman had entered into (of their own choice) had been spoken to them by God. But even in this curse, there was a word of hope. As God spoke to the serpent, *And I will put enmity between you and the woman, and between your offspring (or seed) and hers; he will crush (strike) your head, and you will strike his heel* (Genesis 3:15). There arose a flicker within their souls. This was the promise. They didn't understand it all but knew this spoke of a Redeemer who would put things right once again. Man had yielded authority to "the serpent" rather than to God in that he chose to heed the voice of the deceitful serpent rather than the voice of all-wise God. But here in this word to the serpent, God was speaking of the "seed of the woman" who would crush the head (authority) of the serpent, even as the serpent would strike his heel. The man (male) is the one who carries the seed in the natural. Only in the virgin Mary was there no seed from a man. Rather, the Spirit of God, the *Ruach HaKodesh* (breath of God, Holy Spirit) impregnated Mary with His seed. The "seed of the woman," indeed the seed of faith in receiving God's Word to her, is Jesus Christ, our Redeemer, the One birthed into the earth who was not infested with sin, a real "butterfly," if you will.

Jesus Christ, though a butterfly, put on a worm suit, or an "earth suit" as our pastor Howard would call it, to come to earth and redeem fallen man. Philippians 2:6-11 says of Him,

> *Who, being in very nature God, did not consider equality with God something to be grasped, but made himself nothing, taking the very nature of a servant, being made in human likeness. And being found in appearance as a man, he humbled himself and became obedient to death—even death on a cross! Therefore God exalted him to the highest place and gave him the name that is above every name, that at the name of Jesus every knee should bow, in heaven and on earth and under the earth, and every tongue confess that Jesus Christ is Lord, to the glory of God the Father.*

Now remember that in the garden, when man had sinned, God killed the animals, a blood sacrifice, and made a covering for the man and woman. This was just a temporary fix. You see, God tells us in Leviticus 17:1 that *the life of every creature is its blood.* The blood of Adam and Eve passed on the sinful nature to all of mankind. Jesus Christ did not have that sinful nature, but rather the nature of the Father God. Instead of being infested with the sin that had transformed us into the ugly worm, Jesus Christ, who had no sin, took our sin upon Himself and gave His life, shed His blood, as a sin offering (2 Corinthians 5:21). He was the perfect spotless Lamb who gave Himself for us. He had become flesh and blood, but His flesh was not infected with sin. As He gave His life, His blood cleansed our sin.

Legally, our sin has been atoned for. But once again, just as in the garden with Adam and Eve, a choice has to be made. You see, there are still two trees from which we can choose to eat. We can still choose to eat of the tree of the knowledge of good and evil and continue to die, or we can choose to eat of the tree of life, yielding its fruit of eternal life. Life is found only in Christ. When the penalty for our sin had been paid, there remained life in Christ Himself. Death could not hold Him. He rose from the grave, victorious over the claims of sin and death. He could then impart that resurrection life to us. As we choose to eat of Him, our "butterfly" is resurrected to newness of life as Christ Jesus breathes life into our spirits once again.

> *Jesus said to them, "I tell you the truth, unless you eat the flesh of the Son of Man and drink His blood, you have no life in you. Whoever eats my flesh and drinks my blood has eternal life, and I will raise him up at the last day. For my flesh is real food and my blood is real drink. Whoever eats my flesh and drinks my blood remains in me, and I in him. Just as the living Father sent me and I live because of the Father, so the one who feeds on me will live because of me. This is the bread that came down from heaven. Your forefathers ate manna and died, but he who feeds on this bread will live forever"* (John 6:53-58).

> *That if you confess with your mouth, "Jesus is Lord," and believe in your heart that God raised him from the dead, you will be saved. For it is with your heart that you believe and are justified, and it is with your mouth that you confess and are saved…For, "Everyone who calls on the name of the Lord will be saved"* (Romans 10:9,10,13).

And so, we eat of Christ, of the fruit of His death, burial and resurrection, and enter the cocoon of transformation, the caterpillar becoming the butterfly. *Yet to all who received him, to those who believed in his name, he gave the right to become children of God—children born not of natural descent, nor of human decision or a husband's will, but born of God* (John 1:12,13). That life brings healing and fills our recreated spirits and then flows out into our souls and our bodies as well for the transformation to be complete. We are indeed *born again* and are *becoming* the children of God as was our original created intention.

As Adam and Eve left the garden that day, they felt a tremendous void. They had been flying high in fellowship with their Creator, flitting from flower to flower in the beautiful garden prepared by Him for them. Now their bodies shivered with the coldness of the deep emptiness they felt. And yet, deep within them stirred once again that flicker of hope. As they clung to each other in their desperation, yearning for that "something missing" to be restored, the man and the woman began their journey to find redemption. The woman conceived and brought forth children, experiencing the pain that God had foretold. The man worked with all his might to provide food and shelter for his family. And the caterpillars' appetites grew and grew. There was a deep hunger within them that nothing seemed to fill. The food outside the garden did not satisfy their hunger. They had each other, but something had changed even in their relationship. There was a longing for deeper intimacy, but instead they began to feel jealousy, greed, worry and fear. The atmosphere of peace that had once enveloped them was pushed aside by storm clouds of strife. Life so precious, so wonderful, so glorious now lay spilled on the ground in death. Its deafening roar grew louder and louder. Where was this Redeemer?

We have already climbed the hill of Calvary. Our view is vastly different from the view of Adam and Eve as they left the garden that day. Perhaps their view can be seen as shown in a poem written by my brother, called *Beginnings*:

 Cocoon

Adam stands—
Drooping by the river
With an apple on one limb
And a snake on the other—
Watching the hole
In the Earth
That God dug
When he was formed.

Eve stands—
Drooping in the garden
With a snake on one limb
And an apple core on the other—
Watching the hole
In the Earth
That God dug
To make her
Form from Adam.

Eden stands—
Drooping in the wind
With stones rolling
Down its hills
And mosquitoes skimming
Across its ponds—
Watching the hole
In the Earth
That God left behind.

God stands—
Drooping in the stars
With Eden in one hand
And another Earth in the other—

*Watching the hole
In the other Earth
From which Eden was dug*
(Buddy West, 1978)

In the "hole in the Earth," God planted a seed. The seed would come forth and bear fruit in the fullness of time. Man would reach his destination, the tree of life. Have you found that tree? Isaiah foretold of this tree: *A shoot will come up from the stump of Jesse; from his roots a Branch will bear fruit* (Isaiah 11:1). Will you eat of the fruit of this tree?

> *Who has believed our message and to whom has the arm of the Lord been revealed? He grew up before him like a tender shoot, and like a root out of dry ground. He had no beauty or majesty to attract us to him, nothing in his appearance that we should desire him. He was despised and rejected by men, a man of sorrows, and familiar with suffering. Like one from whom men hide their faces he was despised, and we esteemed him not. Surely he took up our infirmities and carried our sorrows, yet we considered him stricken by God, smitten by him, and afflicted. But he was pierced for our transgressions, he was crushed for our iniquities; the punishment that brought us peace was upon him, and by his wounds we are healed. We all, like sheep, have gone astray, each of us has turned to his own way; and the Lord has laid on him the iniquity of us all. He was oppressed and afflicted, yet he did not open his mouth; he was led like a lamb to the slaughter, and as a sheep before her shearers is silent, so he did not open his mouth. By oppression and judgment he was taken away. And who can speak of his descendants? For he was cut off from the land of the living; for the transgression of my people he was stricken. He was assigned a grave with the wicked, and with*

the rich in his death, though he had done no violence, nor was any deceit in his mouth. Yet it was the Lord's will to crush him and cause him to suffer, and though the Lord makes his life a guilt offering, he will see his offspring and prolong his days, and the will of the Lord will prosper in his hand. After the suffering of his soul, he will see the light of life and be satisfied; by his knowledge my righteous servant will justify many, and he will bear their iniquities. Therefore I will give him a portion among the great, and he will divide the spoils with the strong, because he poured out his life unto death, and was numbered with the transgressors. For he bore the sin of many, and made intercession for the transgressors (Isaiah 53).

My prayer is that you eat voraciously like the caterpillar of the leaves of the tree of life and experience your healing and that you find a nice spot and spin a cocoon in which your total transformation will be realized. Where does that cocoon come from?

The mystery that has been kept hidden for ages and generations, but is now disclosed to the saints…Which is Christ in you, the hope of glory (Colossians 1:26,27).

Chapter 3
Our Dwelling Place

My lover spoke and said to me, "Arise, my darling, my beautiful one, and come with me. See! The winter is past; the rains are over and gone. Flowers appear on the earth; the season of singing has come, the cooing of doves is heard in our land. The fig tree forms its early fruit; the blossoming vines spread their fragrance. Arise, come, my darling; my beautiful one, come with me" (Song of Songs 2:10-13).

An amazing and awesome thing happens when we are born again by the Spirit of God. God imparts to us new life through Jesus Christ. Jesus tells us, *Now this is eternal life: that they may know you, the only true God, and Jesus Christ, whom you have sent* (John 17:3). So the key here is not what we do or don't do, but rather *who we know*. Jesus *is* the lover of our souls and only in union with Him can we experience true life and be who we really were created to be. As *The Message* puts it, He invites us to *Live in me. Make your home in me just as I do in you* (John 15:4). Psalm 90, a prayer of Moses, states, *Lord, you have been our dwelling place throughout all generations.* Psalm 91 gives us a beautiful picture of the blessing and safety of dwelling in the shelter of the Most High. And the most amazing thing about this is that it is a place of rest, a house that God builds. *Unless the LORD builds the house, its builders labor in vain* (Psalm 127:1). Jesus' invitation extends to each of us, *Come to me, all you who are weary and burdened, and I will give you rest. Take my yoke upon you and learn from me, for I am gentle and humble in heart, and you will find rest for your souls. For my yoke is easy and my burden is light* (Matthew 11:28-30).

Resting in the Lord is a very crucial issue determining whether or not we experience life in the Kingdom. Resting in the Lord is not about being inactive and doing nothing, but rather about our attitude, our state of mind in all we do. Our mind is resting from carrying the weight of life and working it out. We are trusting in God, completely confident in Him and His flow of life in us and through us. As Jesus says in this passage, *You will find rest for your souls.* Our souls can rest from the struggle to lead us as this was not the purpose for which our souls were designed. *His* yoke is easy and *His* burden is light. We are yoked together with Him, Spirit to spirit, and our soul is yoked to our spirit, carried along as our spirit takes its rightful place. It's like driving a car with transmission problems stuck in first or second gear. It's going, but it takes a lot of time and effort to get to the destination. Move on into fourth gear and you'll get where you want to go a whole lot faster and with far greater ease. Our souls can never lead us into that place of spiritual rest.

Hebrews 4:1-11 talks about this rest also and how the children of Israel who did not enter into the Promised Land did not enter this rest because of their unbelief. Let us heed the warning here:

> *Therefore, since the promise of entering his rest still stands, let us be careful that none of you be found to have fallen short of it. For we also have had the gospel preached to us, just as they did; but the message they heard was of no value to them, because those who heard did not combine it with faith. Now we who have believed enter that rest, just as God has said, "So I declared on oath in my anger, 'They shall never enter my*

> rest.'" *And yet his work has been finished since the creation of the world... There remains, then, a Sabbath-rest for the people of God; for anyone who enters God's rest also rests from his own work, just as God did from his. Let us, therefore, make every effort to enter that rest, so that no one will fall by following their example of disobedience.*

(It is very interesting here that this word *disobedience* in the NIV is rendered *unbelief* in the KJV. I suggest that the two are inextricably mixed, belief or unbelief producing the consequent action.)

When we think of our dwelling place, we think of a place where we can find rest, a place where we can go to relax and be ourselves, our little spot for peace and tranquility. Many people in the world today do not have such a place in our natural physical world. Just visit the crowded streets of Calcutta, filled with folks who have no place to call home except the dirty streets. Walk through the back alleys of major metropolitan areas all over the world and see the homeless curled in some tiny corner, covered with discarded newspapers, trying to find just a little warmth in which to rest their weary bodies. All day long they have traversed the endless sidewalks not even remembering what they are seeking, just constantly moving forward until their weariness consumes them and they find yet another dark corner in which to rest their exhausted bones. And these are those who have no physical homes. There are countless others, some living in meager circumstances, others in lavish beautiful mansions, who although they have the physical provision of a home, live in internal anguish and unrest in their own minds. Others exist in cold marriages or families where they should be experiencing intimate connection and contentment but instead live as virtual strangers, just going through the motions of one more day, escaping through bottle after bottle of booze or pills or endless hours of work or some other means. Yes, we all need rest for our bodies, our souls, and our spirits.

God hears the cries of our hearts, even when we don't really understand our deep need ourselves. He made us and knows us. He heard our cries, just like He heard the cries of the Israelites while enslaved in Egypt. They had labored for the Egyptians for 400 years and began to cry out to their maker. God heard their cry and sent a deliverer, Moses, to speak to the Pharaoh to let His people go. Through many plagues, which were judgments on the false gods of the world, God led His people out of Egypt, and they began their journey toward a land He had promised to their ancestor, Abraham, many years earlier.

The journey started off with a bang. God led them into what seemed a trap for them but was in reality a trap for their enemies. He had them camp at the edge of the desert, by the Red Sea. Pharaoh again changed his mind about wanting to release the Israelites and started pursuing them. When the Israelites looked up, there on the one side was the Egyptian army armed for battle to recapture them and on the other side was the Red Sea. What were they to do? **You could say that they were "out on a limb."** They could not do a thing. God miraculously parted the sea as Moses lifted the rod of God over it. The people went through on dry land. When the Egyptians pursued, the waters crashed down on them, drowning Israel's enemies. They definitely did a victory dance on the far side of the Red Sea.

The children of Israel stayed out on that limb for the rest of their journey. But that limb was a great place to be. God was taking His people on a journey. The journey was long and difficult, and they had to rely on their God. They were getting to know Him as they traveled. He went with them every step of the way. He led them with a cloud by day and fire by night. And the interesting thing is that God Himself was seeking a resting place as much as the Israelites were.[7] He gave Moses the plans for a tabernacle, His dwelling place among them. Every facet of that tabernacle was a

Our Dwelling Place

type and shadow of Jesus Christ who was to come, who had always been the *Lamb slain before the foundation of the world*. John 1:14 tells us, *The Word became flesh and made his dwelling among us*. The *Interpreter's Bible*, Volume 8, expounds on this verse as follows: "The clause *and dwelt among us* may imply more than the English verb suggests. The Greek word, derived from the noun for *tent*, is often used without any reference to its etymology. But so allusive a writer as the Fourth Evangelist may well have been thinking of the tabernacle in the wilderness where the Lord dwelt with Israel (Exodus 25:8-9; 40:34), and more particularly of that pillar of cloud above the tent of meeting, typifying the visible dwelling of the Lord among His people."[8]

I believe that as we observe these two settings we can see the cocoon that the Lord would have us to live in as we journey through life. Under the Old Covenant, we see God living among His people in the wilderness tabernacle and the cloud. The tabernacle provided a way for the priest to come into the presence of God, by the blood of the sacrifices, the washing of the water, into the Holy Place of the Table of Shewbread, the Golden Lampstand, and the Altar of Incense, and then finally into the Most Holy Place with the Ark of the Covenant covered by the Mercy Seat, the resting place of God as He dwelt among them. Jesus Christ, according to the writer of Hebrews, has opened up for each of us, a priesthood of believers (1 Peter 2:5), a way into the very presence of God.

> *Therefore, brothers, since we have confidence to enter the Most Holy Place by the blood of Jesus, by a new and living way opened for us through the curtain, that is, his body, and since we have a great priest over the house of God, let us draw near to God with a sincere heart in full assurance of faith, having our hearts sprinkled to cleanse us from a guilty conscience and having our bodies washed with pure water* (Hebrews 10:19-22).

 *Cocoon*

I would submit to you that ***Jesus Christ is our cocoon.*** When we are born again by the Spirit of God, by believing in Jesus and receiving His life, His breath upon us, Christ comes in and makes His home in us by His Spirit. We live in Him and He in us. That's the abiding that He talks about in John 15. Then we can get back to God's original creation and purpose for our lives, to bear good fruit. *I am the vine; you are the branches. If a man remains in me and I in him, he will bear much fruit; apart from me you can do nothing* (John 15:5). We can experience the glory of God once again, the manifest presence of God, just like Adam and Eve in the garden, in ever increasing increments until we experience His fullness forever.

> *On each side of the river stood the tree of life, bearing twelve crops of fruit, yielding its fruit every month. And the leaves of the tree are for the healing of the nations. No longer will there be any curse. The throne of God and of the Lamb will be in the city, and his servants will serve him. They will see his face, and his name will be on their foreheads. There will be no more night. They will not need the light of a lamp or the light of the sun, for the Lord God will give them light. And they will reign for ever and ever* (Revelation 22:2-5).

So, hang on to that limb. Spin that cocoon in experiencing life daily with the Lord. Let's look at the journey of the twelve tribes of Israel as they lived in His presence in the wilderness and at the journey of the twelve disciples of Jesus as they lived in His presence, as He became flesh and lived among them, for inspiration for our own journey. Keep hangin'!

> *Take me away with you—let us hurry! Let the king bring me into his chambers* (Song of Songs 1:4).

Chapter 4
The Mirror

But we all, with open face beholding as in a glass the glory of the Lord, are changed into the same image from glory to glory, even as by the Spirit of the Lord (2 Corinthians 3:18).

As we hang out in the cocoon, we are being changed from the lowly worm to the beautiful butterfly! I believe that there are two basic agents of change in our lives, the Word of God and the Spirit of God. In the midst of all the experiences of our lives, these two are at work bringing forth the transformation we need to experience the full glory of God for which we were intended. The Word of God is a mirror we look into to see who we are, and the Holy Spirit is the One holding the mirror at just the right angle to enhance our view.

The Word of God

Back in Hebrews 4, where we were reading earlier about the rest of God, we find an interesting statement about the Word of God. At first glance, it seems that the writer suddenly changes focus in mid-stream, but by looking closer, we see that as the Lord is encouraging us to *make every effort to enter that rest,* He is actually showing us the means by which we do that.

> *For the word of God is living and active. Sharper than any double-edged sword, it penetrates even to dividing soul and spirit, joints and marrow; it judges the thoughts and attitudes of the heart. Nothing in all creation is hidden from God's sight. Everything is uncovered and laid bare before the eyes of Him to whom we must give account* (Hebrews 4:12,13).

In this scripture, we find a key to this new life in Christ. We find here that it is the Word of God that divides soul and spirit. That was the problem in the garden that led to our sin. The soul rose up and tried to lead. The soul is not equipped to lead. It ran us off the road, crashing into that deadly tree.

> *When the woman saw the fruit of the tree was good for food and pleasing to the eye, and also desirable for gaining wisdom, she took some and ate it. She also gave some to her husband, who was with her and he ate it* (Genesis 3:6).

The soul judges by what things seem to be through reasoning, what things look like, to satisfy its own desires. Man was created as a spiritual being, made in the image of God. Our spirits were designed to lead us. That is God's intention. Our spirits have the capacity to relate to God who is a spirit. Only God can reveal to us the truth beyond what things may look like. When we are born again, our dead spirits are resurrected, but we have been so accustomed to being led by our soul that a transfer of leadership must take place. The Word of God helps us to discern spirit and soul and get our spirit back into its rightful place of leadership, connected to our God who made us.

Let's not forget **who** the Word of God is:

> *In the beginning was the Word, and the Word was with God, and the Word was God…Through him all things were made; without him nothing was made that has been made. In him*

The Mirror

was life, and that life was the light of men. The light shines in the darkness, but the darkness has not understood [or, overcome] *it…The Word became flesh and made his dwelling among us. We have seen his glory, the glory of the One and Only, who came from the Father, full of grace and truth* (John 1:1-5,14).

Jesus Christ is the Word—the Living Word! *For you have been born again, not of perishable seed, but of imperishable, through the living and enduring word of God* (1 Peter 1:23).

May God himself, the God of peace, sanctify you through and through. May your whole spirit, soul and body be kept blameless at the coming of our Lord Jesus Christ. The one who calls you is faithful and he will do it (1 Thessalonians 5:23,24).

Therefore, get rid of all moral filth and the evil that is so prevalent and humbly accept the word planted in you, which can save you. Do not merely listen to the word, and so deceive yourselves. Do what it says. Anyone who listens to the word but does not do what it says is like a man who looks at his face in a mirror and, after looking at himself, goes away and immediately forgets what he looks like. But the man who looks intently into the perfect law that gives freedom, and continues to do this, not forgetting what he has heard, but doing it—he will be blessed in what he does (James 1:21-25).

Jesus Christ, the Living Word, is within us to release the power to bring about the change we need to be shaped once again in His image. Notice, in this passage from James, that it is in *doing* the Word, not just *hearing* it, that we are blessed and changed. The potential is there, but we must yield to it (Him), we must come into agreement with it (Him). Remember, as we already mentioned before, there is a direct correlation between what we really *believe* and what we *do*. We can say we believe something, but if we aren't willing to act on it and live it out in our lives, do we really believe? Jesus, the Living Word, lived a life in union with the Father. *I and the Father are one,* He said (John 10:30). *I tell you the truth, the Son can do nothing by himself; he can do only what he sees his Father doing, because whatever the Father does the Son also does* (John 5:19).

The Spirit of God

As Jesus releases the power of His Word in our lives, His Spirit is at work in us as well. Jesus told His disciples,

> *And I will ask the Father, and he will give you another Counselor to be with you forever—the Spirit of truth. The world cannot accept him, because it neither sees him nor knows him. But you know him, for he lives with you and will be in you* (John 14:16, 17).

> *I have much more to say to you, more than you can now bear. But when he, the Spirit of truth, comes, he will guide you into all truth. He will not speak on his own; he will speak only what he hears, and he will tell you what is yet to come. He will bring glory to me by taking from what is mine and making it known to you. All that belongs to the Father is mine. That is why I said the Spirit will take from what is mine and make it known to you* (John 16:12-15).

The seed of the Word of God is watered by the Spirit of God. New spirit life comes forth. The Spirit of God is within us to reconnect us to our Father.

> *The Spirit searches all things, even the deep things of God. For who among men knows the thoughts of a man except the man's spirit within him? In the same way no one knows the thoughts of God except the Spirit of God. We have not received*

the spirit of the world but the Spirit who is from God, that we may understand what God has freely given us (1 Corinthians 2:10-12).

Jesus invites us, just as He did the woman at the well in Samaria, to drink deeply of the water of His Spirit. *Whoever drinks the water I give him will never thirst. Indeed the water I give him will become in him a spring of water welling up to eternal life* (John 4:14).

> *On the last and greatest day of the Feast* [of Tabernacles!], *Jesus stood and said in a loud voice, "If anyone is thirsty, let him come to me and drink. Whoever believes in me, as the Scripture has said, streams of living water will flow from within him." By this he meant the Spirit, whom those who believed in him were later to receive. Up to that time the Spirit had not been given, since Jesus had not yet been glorified* (John 7:37-39).

After Jesus' resurrection, on the Day of Pentecost, the Spirit was poured out, just as promised, and is still available today to all who believe and receive.

Romans 8 further shows us the work of the Spirit in our lives:

> *I consider that our present sufferings are not worth comparing with the glory that will be revealed in us…We know that the whole creation has been groaning as in the pains of childbirth right up to the present time. Not only so, but we ourselves, who have the first fruits of the Spirit, groan inwardly as we wait eagerly for our adoption as sons, the redemption of our bodies…In the same way, the Spirit helps us in our weakness. We do not know what we ought to pray for, but the Spirit himself intercedes for us with groans that words cannot express. And he who searches our hearts knows the mind of the Spirit, because the Spirit intercedes for the saints in accordance with God's will* (Romans 8:18,22,23,26,27).

This same chapter also encourages us that Christ Jesus, the Living Word, *is at the right hand of God and is also interceding for us* (Romans 8:34).

A House of Mirrors

When we look to someone, desiring to pattern after them because we admire them or extol their qualities as being good and to be sought after, we continue our gaze to know all there is to know about them. We look into the living water to see our reflection. *Let us fix our eyes on Jesus, the author and perfecter of our faith, who for the joy set before him endured the cross, scorning its shame, and sat down at the right hand of the throne of God* (Hebrews 12:2). As the writer of the Song of Songs says of Him, *he is altogether lovely* (Song of Songs 5:16). You might say that our cocoon is a "house of mirrors." As we fix our gaze on Jesus, the light from His countenance etches that same image into our own being.

Have you ever been in one of the funhouses at a fair? There are many mirrors to look into. Some of the mirrors elongate your frame so that you look very tall and thin. Other mirrors cause you to appear short and fat. Still others distort your image in a variety of ways that can be truly hilarious. Even the standard mirror over the bathroom sink shows us far too many flaws as we look into it. We can be our own worst critics as we see that person staring back at us. And think about the image that we have of ourselves from the way that others speak to us, relate to us or treat us. Very seldom does that reflect who we really are. The mirror of the living Word is a much better place to look to find out who we are. Any other mirror is false and deceptive. I love the song written by Jonathan Helser, "I've Seen I AM." Here are the words to this song:

I looked into the eyes of a Lion;
I felt the courage in His gaze.

The Mirror

I heard Him roar my name with passion
As I buried my tears in His mane.

I looked into the eyes of a Lamb,
I saw love face to face,
I felt grace destroy my sin
As mercy flowed from His veins.

(chorus)
I've seen I AM; now I know that I am loved.
I've seen I AM; now I know who I am.
I've seen I AM; now I know that I am loved.
I've seen I AM; now I know who I am.

I looked into the eyes of a King;
I saw the beauty of holiness.
I heard the voice of many waters
As worship poured from my lips.

I looked into the eyes of a Savior,
I saw love stronger than death.
I kissed the scars that bought my freedom
As I laid my head on His chest.

Lined with Grace

So, in this cocoon, this house of mirrors, we are being changed. A metamorphosis is taking place. Come with me into this cocoon. Let's get a vision of this new creature that is taking shape. If you look at this outward shell, you may not fully see what is taking place inside. It is indeed a work in progress. Gratefully, the shell is lined with grace. This grace is an extension of favor that is freely given. It always blows me away to remember that God, so rich in mercy toward us, chose to do what we could not do for ourselves in doing away with sin's penalty and its power in our lives. In Jesus

Christ, God, our Father, has provided everything necessary to bring about this metamorphosis to enable us to live forever in His glorious kingdom where love truly reigns.

What do you see in that mirror? Why, I think you're looking more and more like Jesus. You are a beautiful creation!

> *Therefore, since we have been justified through faith, we have peace with God through our Lord Jesus Christ, through whom we have gained access by faith into this grace in which we now stand. And we rejoice in the hope of the glory of God* (Romans 5:1,2).

Chapter 5
The Rhythm of the Process

Peter replied, "Repent and be baptized, every one of you, in the name of Jesus Christ for the forgiveness of your sins. And you will receive the gift of the Holy Spirit" (Acts 2:38).

It was a beautiful Sunday morning, set aside as a Sabbath to worship the Lord and seek His face. We had gathered at the little church, turned on some worship music and each of us found a spot and began to seek the Lord. As I sat in the pew, my eyes were drawn to a bucket filled with brightly colored slips of material attached to small dowels to be used for flags to wave in worship. As I looked at the various colors and shapes, the Lord began to speak to me concerning how those flags were made. He likened the flags to our lives and began to share with me that our lives of worship are made as we take the things of our old lives, yield them to Him, and allow those things that once were areas of hindrances, of trials, of temptations to become testimonies of His grace and salvation. They are forever part of our lives, not in defeat to show what terrible people we have been, but in victory to show the power, the love, the grace of God in our lives to enable us to be victorious overcomers in Him. And isn't that just like the butterfly we have been speaking of? God creates the new creature out of the old. As the caterpillar finds its spot, attaches to and hangs from the tree, it begins to con-

dense its body. As the body is being condensed, the larva is also forming the outer layer of the pupa underneath it. When the larva sheds its skin for the last time, the pupa, its "cocoon," is formed.

In the beginning, the earth was just one big chaotic mess! Out of the waters, as God spoke, the earth began to take shape, day by day.

In its beginning, the nation of Israel was a big chaotic mess! Enslaved in Egypt, they had lost sight of who they were supposed to be. God began to speak to them and remind them of the covenant He had made with their ancestor, Abraham. He began to reacquaint them with Himself. And as He led them out of Egypt, God took them through the waters of the Red Sea to begin their journey to the Promised Land. I like the way *The Message* paraphrase reads in 1 Corinthians 10:1,2: *Remember our history, friends, and be warned. All our ancestors were led by the providential cloud and taken miraculously through the Sea. They went through the waters, in a baptism like ours, as Moses led them from enslaving death to salvation life.* Out of these waters came a new nation.

Throughout the history of the nation of Israel, we see them over and over again turning away from their God and once again becoming enslaved—to the Babylonians, the Assyrians, the Romans. While under Roman rule, there appeared on the scene yet another prophet calling for repentance. He was a different sort of fellow who lived in the desert, who ate locusts and wild honey, who dressed in camel's hair with a leather belt around his waist. John the Baptist (or the Baptizer) stood in the waters of the Jordan River, immersing folks who were responding to his message of repentance. This baptism portrayed that repentance, a surrender to God, choosing to turn from living their own way to living God's way. He gave the people new hope as he told them that the Kingdom of God was at hand, that there was a Messiah who was coming who would baptize not with water, but with the Spirit of God and fire.

The Rhythm of the Process

Day after day, John carried out his God-given mission to prepare the way of the Lord. And then, the moment he had been waiting for arrived. There before him stood the Messiah. Jesus came to John to be baptized by him. As Jesus approached him, John proclaimed, *Look, the Lamb of God, who takes away the sin of the world* (John 1:29). He continued by saying, *I myself did not know him, but the reason I came baptizing with water was that he might be revealed to Israel* (John 1:31). Here was John's cousin, and John says that he did not know Him. He was seeing his cousin in a different light, as if the curtain was pulled back and he saw for the first time who He really was—the Lamb of God. There was something hugely monumental taking place in the Jordan that day. Jesus didn't have any sin to wash away. He was already walking in unbroken fellowship with His Father. Why was Jesus being baptized? Matthew's Gospel tells us that John tried to tell Jesus that he was the one needing to be baptized by Him instead of him baptizing Jesus. Jesus' reply was *"Let it be so now; it is proper for us to do this to fulfill all righteousness." Then John consented* (Matthew 3:15).

This baptism was taking place in the Jordan River. If you look throughout scripture, you will find that the Jordan is a place of *change*. As the children of Israel were passing from the wilderness into the Promised Land, they had to cross the Jordan River. As Jesus was being baptized in the Jordan River, there was a big change taking place. A Messianic Jew, Dick Rueben, enlightened me on this as he taught on the priesthood from the Old and New Testaments.[9]

John was a member of the house of Levi, of the priestly tribe, of the order of Aaron (Aaron being the first High Priest to serve as God called this tribe to priestly service). You may remember the story of his birth, how his father Zachariah had been performing his temple service when an angel appeared to him and told him of the child's miraculous birth to he and his barren wife, leaving him speechless until John was born. The Levitical Priesthood served as priests to the children of Israel. In all actuality, John the Baptist, who was baptizing Jesus in the Jordan River, was in line to be the High Priest. He was not serving, however, because under Roman rule, the Romans had appointed another man to serve as High Priest, Caiaphas. They wanted someone they could hold under their thumb, to be submissive to their control.

Prior to the Levitical Priesthood, we see another priest who was apparently a priest to the Gentiles. The Jewish nation had not yet been birthed. Abram was still Abram. He had not made a covenant with God at this point. Abram was a Gentile before he became Abraham, the father of the Jewish nation (God changed his name when he entered into covenant with Him). After defeating several kings who had captured his nephew Lot, Abram paid tithes to *Melchizedek king of Salem, priest of God Most High, and he blessed Abram* (Genesis 14:18,19). Melchizedek is made up of two words, one meaning king, and the other meaning righteousness—king of righteousness.

The book of Hebrews has much to say about Jesus being our Great High Priest, after the order of Melchizedek. Jesus was of the tribe of Judah, not the Levitical tribe. Jesus had no right to the office of High Priest as a descendant of Aaron of the tribe of Levi, but Jesus is our King of Righteousness, a Great High Priest after the order of Melchizedek. *God made him who had no sin to be sin* [or a sin offering] *for us, so that in him we might become the righteousness of God* (2 Corinthians 5:21). The Lamb of God who takes away the sin of the world! There was a change of priesthood taking place at Jesus' baptism. One High Priest passed the mantle to the next High Priest by water immersion. This is how it was done. Jesus went down into the water as the *King of the Jews* (Matthew 2:2). He came up out of the water as the *King of Righteousness, our Great High Priest after the order of Melchizedek!*

The Rhythm of the Process

Even though Caiaphas was not the God-ordained choice for High Priest, as he served as the one appointed to this position, he carried the authority of the office. At the trial of Jesus, Caiaphas tore his garment because he was so upset. When a High Priest tore his garment, he was nullifying his priesthood. The High Priest's duty each day was to preside over the sacrifice of two lambs, three lambs on the day of Passover. The next day was Passover. With Caiaphas' annulment of his priesthood, there would be no High Priest to preside over the offering for the next day. However, Jesus, our Great High Priest, fulfilled those duties as the perfect spotless Passover Lamb and the High Priest who offered it. *For Christ, our Passover Lamb, has been sacrificed* (1 Corinthians 5:7). When the High Priest saw that the sacrifice was done just as required, he would then raise his hands and say, "It is finished." He stood until these sacrifices were done. Then he sat down.

Day after day every priest stands and performs his religious duties; again and again he offers the same sacrifices, which can never take away sins. But when this priest had offered for all time one sacrifice for sins, he sat down at the right hand of God (Hebrews 10:11,12).

A priest must have an altar. The first altar in the Tabernacle was made of wood covered in bronze. Jesus' cross was made of wood. Archaeologists have uncovered nails made of bronze that were used during this time by the Romans. The Romans could harden bronze to enable it to hold heavy weights.

In the book of Leviticus, chapter 8 shows us the consecration ceremony for the priests. Blood was placed on the ear, the hand and the foot. On the cross, Jesus wore a crown of thorns. The thorns cut into His scalp, and the blood ran down onto His ears. The nails were driven in His hands and feet, causing blood to flow on them. Also, as the priests were consecrated, anointing oil was sprinkled on

them. Mary poured fragrant oil from an alabaster box upon Jesus to prepare Him for His death.

During His crucifixion, the soldiers divided Jesus' clothes. His tunic, however, was not torn. His Priesthood was not nullified. His heart, however, was torn for us. *Rend your heart and not your garments* (Joel 2:13). As you recall, there were two others who were crucified on either side of Jesus that day. The day following Jesus' crucifixion was to be a special Sabbath, and the Jews didn't want the bodies still hanging on the crosses. To speed up the death process, the Jews asked Pilate to have the legs of those being crucified broken and their bodies taken down from the crosses. When the soldiers came to Jesus, they found He was already dead and did not break His legs as had been prophesied. Instead, a soldier pierced Jesus' side. Out flowed blood and water. Every Jew seeing this would immediately think of "sacrifice." As animals were brought to the priests to sacrifice, they were first killed and the blood sprinkled and then washed in the laver of water as the sacrifice was offered to the Lord.

There is no doubt. Jesus is our Passover Lamb and our Great High Priest. He has made intercession for the transgressors. *By one sacrifice he has made perfect forever those who are being made holy* (Hebrews 10:14).

As Jesus was baptized by John the Baptist in the Jordan River, there was a change in the priesthood. Jesus carried out the duties of our Great High Priest as He offered Himself as our supreme sacrifice upon the altar of His cross. Jew and Gentile alike now have a Great High Priest who has offered the supreme sacrifice and enables us to be changed as we come to Him.

> *Therefore, since we have a great high priest who has gone through the heavens, Jesus, the Son of God, let us hold firmly to the faith we profess. For we do not have a high priest who is unable to sympathize with our weaknesses, but we have one who has been tempted in every way, just as we are—yet was*

without sin. Let us then approach the throne of grace with confidence, so that we may receive mercy and find grace to help us in our time of need (Hebrews 4:14-16).

In Christ Jesus, our cocoon, we, too, are washed with the waters of baptism to come forth as a new creation. Let's look at the process. As the cocoon hangs from the tree, not much seems to be happening. But if you look closer, changes are definitely taking place within the sac. The worm is losing its giant stomach. The mandibles once needed to chew its big diet of leaves are no longer necessary. They disappear, and instead the proboscis begins to form for the new liquid diet of the adult. Wings form off the thorax. Parts of the head change in appearance as well. There is a real transformation taking place. The parts that were once vital to the caterpillar would only weigh down the butterfly so that it would be hindered in its flight. The new parts being formed enable the butterfly to soar way into the atmosphere. With the newly formed streamlined body and feather-light wings, the butterfly can land and take off time and time again with little effort.

This is exactly what is happening to us as new creatures in Christ. A real transformation is taking place. However, unlike the transformation of the worm into the butterfly, we cannot fit our transformation so neatly into a certain season of the work being done. Our lives are much more complicated than that of the butterfly. There are many changes taking place, and God in His mercy is very patient and deliberate in working all these out. So as not to overwhelm us, He works on primarily one area at a time and gives us "breathers" along the journey.

The Rhythm of Baptism

Recently, in one of our Thursday night meetings, Amie dropped a phrase, "the rhythm of baptism." Something exploded in me. This is such a great term to describe what is happening in

 Cocoon

our lives as we rest in our cocoon. It is like the ebb and flow of the ocean's waves crashing into the shore only to be pulled back out into the deep once again over and over. It is like the pendulum of the clock swinging first far to the left, and then far to the right to proclaim the tick-tock of time. Romans 6 really tells us what baptism is all about.

> *What shall we say, then? Shall we go on sinning so that grace may increase? By no means! We died to sin; how can we live in it any longer? Or don't you know that all of us who were baptized into Christ Jesus were baptized into his death? We were therefore buried with him through baptism into death in order that, just as Christ was raised from the dead through the glory of the Father, we too may live a new life.*
>
> *If we have been united with him like this in his death, we will certainly also be united with him in his resurrection. For we know that our old self was crucified with him so that the body of sin might be done away with, that we should no longer be slaves to sin—because anyone who has died has been freed from sin.*
>
> *Now if we died with Christ, we believe that we will also live with him. For we know that since Christ was raised from the dead, he cannot die again; death no longer has mastery over him. The death he died, he died to sin once for all; but the life he lives, he lives to God.*
>
> *In the same way, count yourselves dead to sin but alive to God in Christ Jesus* (Romans 6:1-8).

This is the baptism we have entered into—death to the old man and life unto God. This is just like the death to the caterpillar and life to the butterfly. Our spirits have been given new life as Christ has breathed on us. Everything needed to experience this new life is there for us in our spirit. But that new life must be released into

The Rhythm of the Process

our total being as well, and this is the process we are in, as if we were in a cocoon and the transformation were slowly taking place. In our cocoon, as the transformation is taking place, we continually experience the rhythm of baptism. Residue of the old man continues to try to rise up and take control. Here again, Romans 6 speaks to us:

> *Don't you know that when you offer yourselves to someone to obey him as slaves, you are slaves to the one whom you obey— whether you are slaves to sin, which leads to death, or to obedience, which leads to righteousness? But thanks be to God that, though you used to be slaves to sin, you wholeheartedly obeyed the form of teaching to which you were entrusted. You have been set free from sin and have become slaves to righteousness* (Romans 6:16-18).

So, when sin speaks to us, trying to get us to yield to it and obey it (like it did to Adam and Eve in the garden), we can choose to turn to God instead and obey Him. Because of the cross of Christ, sin no longer has power over us, if we but turn from it unto God. *For everyone who calls on the name of the Lord will be saved* (Romans 10:13). *No temptation has seized you except what is common to man. And God is faithful; he will not let you be tempted beyond what you can bear. But when you are tempted, he will also provide a way out so that you can stand up under it* (1 Corinthians 10:13). Jesus is the Way provided by God for our escape! All we have to do is call on Him!

Sometimes, as was Eve, we are deceived by sin. Sometimes, as did Adam, we choose to simply yield to it, knowing that it is wrong. Jesus is the light. When we choose to stay in fellowship with Him, He will enable us to walk in the light and not be deceived. And Jesus tells us that if we truly love Him, we will obey Him. As the light of Christ shines on the residue of the old man, we are convicted by His Spirit within us (John 16:8) but not condemned.

 *Cocoon*

> *Therefore, there is now no condemnation for those who are in Christ Jesus, because through Christ Jesus the law of the Spirit of life set me free from the law of sin and death. For what the law was powerless to do in that it was weakened by the sinful nature, God did by sending his own Son in the likeness of sinful man to be a sin offering. And so he condemned sin in sinful man, in order that the righteous requirements of the law might be fully met in us, who do not live according to the sinful nature but according to the Spirit… You, however, are controlled not by the sinful nature but by the Spirit, if the Spirit of God lives in you. And if anyone does not have the Spirit of Christ, he does not belong to Christ. But if Christ is in you, your body is dead because of sin, yet your spirit is alive because of righteousness. And if the Spirit of him who raised Jesus from the dead is living in you, he who raised Christ from the dead will also give life to your mortal bodies through his Spirit, who lives in you* (Romans 8:1-4,9-11).

When sin tries to rear its ugly head, instead of running and hiding like Adam and Eve, we can step into the light of Christ, see the sin as it is and call it what it is, simply repenting of it and turning to Him for salvation, allowing His blood to be applied and cleansing us as it releases more of His life in us in overcoming power. That is the rhythm of baptism—dead to sin but alive unto God. And that is what happens over and over in our lives, releasing more and more of the life of Christ until we are totally immersed in His life and experiencing it in all its fullness.

There is a battle going on. The serpent of sin is still calling to us, trying to trip us up, but the Lord has crushed his head!

> *For though we live in the world, we do not wage war as the world does. The weapons we fight with are not the weapons of*

the world. On the contrary, they have divine power to demolish strongholds. We demolish arguments and every pretension that sets itself up against the knowledge of God, and we take captive every thought to make it obedient to Christ (2 Corinthians 10:3-5).

In his fight against the Philistine giant Goliath, the young David picked up five smooth stones from the stream and slung one of them to slay the enemy of Israel. Perhaps the five smooth stones could be our weapons as well. One stone could be the name of the Lord. *David said to the Philistine, "You came against me with sword and spear and javelin, but I come against you in the name of the LORD Almighty, the God of the armies of Israel, whom you have defied"* (1 Samuel 17:45). Another stone might be the Word of the Lord. As Jesus faced the temptation of the devil in the wilderness, He spoke the Word of God to defeat him every time (Matthew 4:1-11). Another stone might be the blood of the Lamb. *They overcame him by the blood of the Lamb, and by the word of their testimony* (Revelation 12:11). Another stone might be the power of His Spirit. *Not by might nor by power, but by my Spirit, says the LORD Almighty* (Zechariah 4:6). A fifth stone may be the faith of the Son of God. *I am crucified with Christ: nevertheless I live; yet not I, but Christ liveth in me; and the life which I now live in the flesh I live by the faith of the son of God, who loved me and gave himself for me* (Galatians 2:20 KJV). *This is the victory that has overcome the world, even our faith* (1 John 5:4). This is but another indication of Jesus being our victory. In Romans 7, the Apostle Paul addresses this struggle with sin and comes to the same conclusion: *What a wretched man I am! Who will rescue me from this body of death? Thanks be to God—through Jesus Christ our Lord* (Romans 7:24,25).

The resurrection of Christ is proof that our sins have been atoned.

And if Christ has not been raised, your faith is futile; you are still in your sins…But Christ has indeed been raised from the dead, the first fruits of those who have fallen asleep…For as in Adam all die, so in Christ all will be made alive. But each in his own turn: Christ, the first fruits; then, when he comes, those who belong to him. Then the end will come, when he hands over the kingdom to God the Father after he has destroyed all dominion, authority and power. For he must reign until he has put all his enemies under his feet. The last enemy to be destroyed is death…The body that is sown is perishable, it is raised imperishable; it is sown in dishonor, it is raised in glory; it is sown in weakness, it is raised in power; it is sown a natural body, it is raised a spiritual body…I declare to you, brothers, that flesh and blood cannot inherit the kingdom of God, nor does the perishable inherit the imperishable. Listen, I tell you a mystery: We will not all sleep, but we will all be changed—in a flash, in the twinkling of an eye, at the last trumpet. For the trumpet will sound, the dead will be raised imperishable, and we will be changed. For the perishable must clothe itself with the imperishable, and the mortal with immortality. When the perishable has been clothed with the imperishable, and the mortal with immortality, then the saying that is written will come true: "Death has been swallowed up in victory." "Where, O death, is your victory? Where, O death, is your sting?" The sting of death is sin, and the power of sin is the law. But thanks be to God! He gives us the victory through our Lord Jesus Christ (1 Corinthians 15).

In putting everything under him, God left nothing that is not subject to him. Yet at present we do not see everything subject to him. **But we see Jesus,** *who was made a little lower than the angels, now crowned with glory and honor because he suf-*

The Rhythm of the Process

fered death…Since the children have flesh and blood, he too shared in their humanity so that by his death he might destroy him who holds the power of death—that is, the devil—and free those who all their lives were held in slavery by their fear of death (Hebrews 2:9,14,15 emphasis added).

Just as Christ had to die to experience His greatest victory, so we too will not realize the fullness of our new life until that final day of death to the old on the day of the Lord as the ashes of the kingdoms of this world give way to the beauty of the Kingdom of God. Until then, we can walk in the first fruits of this new life delivered to us by the Spirit of the Lord.

Having believed, you were marked in him with a seal, the promised Holy Spirit, who is a deposit guaranteeing our inheritance until the redemption of those who are God's possession—to the praise of his glory (Ephesians 1:13,14).

Part Two

Under the Shadow

He who dwells in the shelter of the Most High will rest in the shadow of the Almighty. I will say of the LORD, "He is my refuge and my fortress, my God, in whom I trust" (Psalm 91:1,2).

As we look at our journey to wholeness in Christ, from the caterpillar to the butterfly, and compare it to the Israelites' journey from Egypt to the Promised Land, it is interesting to note that God told them that the Promised Land would be a land *"flowing with milk and honey."* As I researched the origins of the word *butterfly*, I discovered several possible beginnings. The original word was *buterflioge*, from the two words *butere*, butter, and *fleoge*, fly. Some suggest that the word *butter* was used because many butterflies are yellow in color, like butter. Some believe it was based on a yellow excrement from the insect. Others seem to have the belief that butterflies would land in kitchens and drink milk or butter that had been left out. The German word for butterfly supports this belief also, as it is *milchdieb,* milk thief.[10] (Maybe Paula Deen, renowned Southern cook from Savannah, Georgia, really does have a hold on something here! She loves to cook with butter. She is eating of the fat of the land!)

The prophet Isaiah, in speaking of the putting off of their oppressors by the surviving remnant of Israel, had this to say: *In that day their burden will be lifted from your shoulders, their yoke from your neck; the yoke will be broken because you have grown so fat* (Isaiah 10:27). The King James Version reads, *And the yoke shall be destroyed because of the anointing.*

The priests who ministered in the wilderness Tabernacle were anointed with oil as a symbol and ceremony of their being set apart for ministry to the Lord on behalf of the people. In the New Testament, Jesus is the Christ, the Messiah, the Anointed One, who is set apart by the Father for ministry to Him on behalf of the people. Dr. Luke records that after Jesus had experienced His baptism by John and His wilderness temptation, He went to the synagogue on the Sabbath and read from Isaiah: *The Spirit of the Lord is on me, because he has anointed me to preach good news to the poor. He has sent me to proclaim freedom for the prisoners and recovery of sight for the blind, to release the oppressed, to proclaim the year of the Lord's favor* (Luke 4:18,19). Jesus proclaimed that He was fulfilling that scripture. Jesus was the Anointed One, dripping with milk and honey! I remind you that Jesus invited us to eat and drink of Him. He knocks at our heart's door and wants to come in and sup with us. Jesus is our cocoon, in which we live. As you read on, remember this. *As for you, the anointing you received from him remains in you, and you do not need anyone to teach you. But as his anointing teaches you about all things and as that anointing is real, not counterfeit—just as it has taught you, remain in him* (1 John 2:27).

According to Greta Cunningham, reporting for the Minnesota Public Radio on October 1, 2006, Steele County, Minnesota, used to be known as the butter capital of the world. Today, the Hope Creamery still churns out butter the old-fashioned way. This process is supervised by Gene Kruckeberg, having worked at the creamery since 1958. The milk brought in is pasteurized for a full day. The cream is then skimmed off the top and transferred into an old 900-gallon motorized batch churn. Well water, cream and perhaps a little salt go into the making of the butter. The churn turns quickly at first but begins to slow as the butter forms into a heavier consistency. Kruckeberg watches and listens as the churn turns. He is keenly attuned to the proper blend as the butter solidifies. Of this process, Kruckeberg says, "As soon as the water's worked in, you gotta quit rotating it; otherwise the butter gets sticky. You gotta keep an eye on it. I mean, you can't just walk away from it, let it churn and come back."[11]

As we enter into our cocoon of transformation, we are safely in the Potter's hands. He is ever attuned to what is taking place. He has given His Son, in whom we live. His Word and His Spirit are working in us. And we are abiding under His shadow during the process. I am but a tutor, bringing you to the school of Christ.

Until the time when we were mature enough to respond freely in faith to the living God, we were carefully surrounded and protected by the Mosaic law. The law was like those Greek tutors, with which you are familiar, who escort children to school and protect them from danger or distraction, making sure the children will really get to the place they set out for. But now you have arrived at your destination: By faith in Christ you are in direct relationship with God. Your baptism in Christ was not just washing you up for a fresh start. It also involved dressing you in an adult faith wardrobe—Christ's life, the fulfillment of God's original promise (Galatians 3: 23-26 The Message).

We join the Israelites on the edge of the wilderness as they began their journey to the Promised Land. There was a vast host of travelers in this caravan. God had blessed the Israelites in spite of the cruel bondage of the Egyptians. They had grown tremendously in number. In fact, that is one of the reasons the Egyptians enslaved them. Their population continued to thrive until the new pharaoh deemed them a threat. He feared they would rise and side with Egypt's enemies and overtake them. Indeed the world may try as it might, just as King Balak hired Baalam to curse the Israelites, but they discovered that no one can curse what God has blessed. And so, the cream rose to the top and needed to be skimmed off for preparation for its most noble purposes. As this vast host traveled, they must have kicked up a great deal of dust from the sandy terrain. The dust limited their vision, and as they traveled, they were filled with anxiety, insecurity and fear, though an excitement also churned deep within. Enshrouded by the dusty blanket, they began to murmur and complain.

Prodded by the cacophony of dissident voices, Moses, their leader, began to cry out to the One who had led him on this journey toward freedom. As Moses looked up toward the heavens, there was a new blanket, high above the dust, a strange cloud that pulled them forward. *By day the LORD went ahead of them in a pillar of cloud to guide them on their way and by night in a pillar of fire to give them light, so that they could travel by day or night* (Exodus 13:21).

The mysterious cloud by day and fire by night led the Israelites onward to Mount Sinai. Here, Moses once again ascended the same holy mountain on which God had appeared to him in the burning bush and had given him the commission to go back to Egypt and lead His people out of bondage. The mountain shook with quakes of thunder and danced with flashes of lightning.

> *Then Moses went up to God, and the LORD called to him from the mountain and said, "This is what you are to say to the house of Jacob and what you are to say to the house of Israel: You yourselves have seen what I did to Egypt, and how I carried you on eagles' wings and brought you to myself. Now if you obey me fully and keep my covenant, then out of all*

nations you will be my treasured possession. Although the whole earth is mine, you will be for me a kingdom of priests and a holy nation. These are the words you are to speak to the Israelites" (Exodus 19:3-6).

As Moses spoke further with God there on the mountain, God shared with him the Ten Commandments and many other laws as guidelines for living in the holiness necessary for Him to be able to live among them as He desired. As we remember, God had enjoyed fellowship with Adam and Eve in the garden. That fellowship had been broken by sin. So, here on the mountain, God set forth the holy requirements in which man could live to restore that broken fellowship. God showed Moses a heavenly pattern designed to enable man to come into His presence, a Tabernacle in which He would dwell among them. This Tabernacle was a beautiful type and shadow of our Savior, Jesus Christ (Hebrews 8).

In order to enter the Tabernacle of His Presence, God instituted a system of sacrifices to cover man's sin, and He chose a priesthood from the tribe of Levi to offer the sacrifices. You may wonder why all of this was necessary. It was necessary because of the holiness of God. God could not change His holiness, or He would cease to be God. He would become less than who He is. If we came before Him in our sin, we would be fried "extra crispy"; we could not stand before His holiness. We *must* understand that He wanted to be with us even more than we wanted to be with Him, and so He began to carry out the divine plan to reunite us to Himself, to enable us to draw near to Him and Him to draw near to us. We are the object of His divine love! The Bible is a divine love story!

God had indeed chosen the Israelites for a noble purpose, and now He was in the process of preparing them for that purpose.

> For you are a people holy to the LORD your God. The LORD your God has chosen you out of all the peoples on the face of the earth to be his people, his treasured possession. The LORD did not set his affection on you and choose you because you were more numerous than other peoples, for you were the fewest of all peoples. But it was because the LORD loved you and kept the oath he swore to your forefathers that he brought you out with a mighty hand and redeemed you from the land of slavery, from the power of Pharaoh king of Egypt (Deuteronomy 7:6-8).

Years before this, a fellow by the name of Abram responded to the call of God.

> The LORD had said to Abram, "Leave your country, your people and your father's household and go to the land I will show you. I will make you into a great nation and I will bless you; I will make your name great, and you will be a blessing. I will bless those who bless you, and whoever curses you I will curse; and **all peoples on earth will be blessed through you**" (Genesis 12:1-3 emphasis added).

Abram heard God, believed Him and started out on his own journey to the Promised Land. God entered into a covenant relationship with this man who believed Him and acted on that belief, changing his name to Abraham. And so, God was remembering His covenant with Abraham. Here were his descendants camped at the base of Mount Sinai.

This band of travelers also descended from another one from the lineage of Abraham—Jacob, with whom God had also entered into a covenant. Jacob's name, too, had been changed—to Israel. Jacob had twelve sons and a daughter. The people camped at the foot of Mount Sinai were descended from and named after the twelve sons of Jacob, or Israel—the Israelites. In interpreting scripture and learning its lessons, an importance is placed on the first mention of something in scriptures. I believe we can learn much from looking at the children of Jacob, predecessors of this holy people, our predecessors in the faith. We see the birth of these children in the book of Genesis and will look at them in the order of their birth.

The Israelites were called to be a holy nation, to bring forth the Messiah, who was the One who totally fulfilled God's righteous requirements to bring us back into fellowship with Himself. What we could not do as we tried to live up to God's laws, God enabled us to do through His Son, Jesus Christ, the only Man who has fully satisfied God's righteous requirements. Jesus Christ is Emmanuel, "God with us." Jesus actually tabernacled among the people of His day. Jesus is also the Lamb of God, who took away the sin of the world, the supreme ultimate sacrifice for sin. Jesus, as the Lion of Judah, roared from the cross of His finished work as the Lamb, *"It is finished"* (John 19:30).

Every sin had been atoned for—those that had been and those that would be. And Jesus is our Great High Priest who has opened the way for all to enter into the presence of a holy God, for we enter through His flesh, sin's atoning sacrifice. When Jesus the Messiah came, He chose twelve disciples with whom He spent most of His time, teaching them. These twelve camped around Jesus just as the twelve tribes camped around the wilderness tabernacle. The first complete listing of the twelve apostles is found in Matthew 10:2-4:

> *These are the names of the twelve apostles: first, Simon (who is called Peter) and his brother Andrew; James, son of Zebedee, and his brother John; Philip and Bartholomew; Thomas and Matthew the tax collector; James son of Alphaeus, and Thaddaeus; Simon the Zealot and Judas Iscariot, who betrayed him.*

Cocoon

Mark further clarifies Jesus' desire in calling these twelve. *He appointed twelve—designating them apostles—that they might be with him and he might send them out to preach and to have authority to drive out demons* (Mark 3:14-15).

Each of these twelve drew near to God, and God drew near to them in a cocoon of His presence. In the twelve tribes of Israel and the twelve apostles, God is bringing forth a glorious new creation transformed from a lowly worm existence brought about by the fall into beautiful "butterflies" living in the garden of His presence. I believe that in each of these twelve we can see foundational veins for our cocoon of transformation. Let's allow the Holy Spirit to teach us as we look unto Jesus, the Living Word, the Author and Finisher of our faith. Let's hang out together here on this tree. Someday soon, a beautiful butterfly is going to emerge.

Chapter 6
See, A Son

Day One

The morning sun was just peeking over the horizon. A new day was dawning. The bright sun warmed the desert ground as if it were an oven baking the morning bread. The children of the Lord went out with baskets to gather their daily bread from this earthen oven, white flakes of honey wafers they called manna. The glory cloud of the presence of the Lord hung over the tabernacle in the center of the multitude of family tents surrounding it like the smoke rising from a chimney. As the families were finishing their morning meal and engaging in their various tasks for the day, messengers strode through each camp to the tents of the leaders of each clan, summoning their appearance before Moses and Aaron. Each of the tribal leaders dropped what they were doing and gathered in front of the tent of meeting.

Moses, his face still glowing from his early morning visit with God, began to share with the twelve men the instruction of the Lord to take a census of the whole Israelite community. He spoke to the leaders, reminding them how God had formed this people and called them as His own, each of their tribes descending from one of the twelve sons of the patriarch Jacob, or Israel.

"Little did Jacob know that his band of seventy people that had entered into Egypt would become such a mighty nation here today coming out of Egypt and on its way to the land G_d has promised to our forefather Abraham," chuckled Moses. "To Jacob and his wife, Leah, was born their first child, Reuben. We know that there is so much in a name. Reuben means 'See, a son.' You all know the story of my early years. The Egyptians wanted to kill off the upcoming Hebrew generation and so began murdering the baby sons born to the Hebrews. My mother and father did a very brave thing in putting me into the river in a basket made to float along the waters. My sister Miriam watched over me as the Pharaoh's daughter drew me out of the waters. Miriam offered to get a nurse, actually my real mother, who nurtured me when I was young. Then, after I was weaned, I was taken to the palace of Pharaoh and reared as one of his own. As I grew, I discovered this deep, dark secret and chose not to continue as a son of Pharaoh's daughter, wanting to identify with my own people, this glorious rabble, instead."

All of the men laughed as they thought of this one who had grown up in Pharaoh's palace, now leading this band of nomads wandering through the desert.

Born into the Kingdom

I am aware,
As I go commonly sweeping the stair,
Doing my part of the everyday care—
Human and simple my lot and my share—
I am aware of a marvelous thing:
Voices that murmur and ethers that ring
In the far stellar spaces wherein cherubim sing.
I am aware of a passion that pours
Down channels of fire through Infinity's doors;

Forces terrific, with melody shod,
Music that mates with the pulses of God.
I am aware of the glory that runs
From the core of myself to the core of the suns…
I am aware of the splendor that ties
All the things of the earth with the things of the skies
(Angela Morgan).

In his book, *The Inner Splendor*, Lewis Dunnington shares this poem written by Angela Morgan, as well as her story of how the poem came to be published, as told to Dr. W.L. Stidger:

> *"One day an inspiration came to me. I would go to Mark Twain and see if he wouldn't help me. So one hot summer day I started for Stormfield, in Connecticut. I got off at a little way station three miles from Stormfield and walked down a dusty road. My shoes were full of dust, I was wet with sweat and my hair disheveled. But when I got in sight of Stormfield I stopped dead still in the middle of that dusty road, looked up into the blazing sun and prayed a little prayer: 'Now you Power of the universe that is back of that sun, You can do anything, and I want You to help me get Mr. Clemens to read my poem.'*
>
> *"I went up to that house full of confidence. I walked up the steps and rang the bell. Mark Twain came to the door, looked at me, smiled, and invited me to come in. I was never able to determine whether that smile was one of amusement at my looks after that three mile tramp in the heat and dust or what it was. He himself was immaculately dressed in a white summer suit. We went in and he read the poem over and then said, 'We'll have lunch first, and then you can read it to me yourself.'*
>
> *"My heart jumped a beat. But pretty soon I found myself sitting on the porch with Mark Twain and Albert Bigelow*

Paine, his biographer, eating lunch. The only thing I can remember about that lunch was that Mr. Clemens spent most of the time swatting flies. Now and then he would kill one on Mr. Paine's head. After lunch he said, 'Now we are to hear the poem.'

"It was like a command performance and I arose to it as best I could, summoning to my help that something inside of me I had been taught was there for all emergencies.

"When I had finished reading that poem, Mark Twain turned to Mr. Paine and said: 'I'm very glad! I'm very glad the Lord made her. I don't always approve of his handiwork but this time I do. And this poem must be published, Paine. You send it to the editor of Collier's Weekly and tell him that if he has any sense he will publish this poem.'

"And Mark Twain in that kind act of encouragement also released something inside of me and gave me my chance, a good deed for which I have always been grateful to his memory.

"All of us have this imprisoned splendor within us. We are like the power in an atom about which they are always talking in scientific circles these days. They talk to me in learned terms of a split electron and I do not know what they mean from a technical point of view; but I know what they mean when they talk of a hidden power, an imprisoned splendor in human beings."[12]

Dunnington goes on to expound on Jesus' statement that points to the source of this splendor within: *The kingdom of God is within you* (Luke 17:21). That is the splendor within us, the butterfly resurrected in Christ. Jesus continued to share further about the kingdom. *He called a little child and had him stand among them. And he said, "I tell you the truth, unless you change and become like little children, you will never enter the kingdom of heaven."* Unless

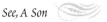

extremely traumatized or abused, a child is filled with innocence and has such a genuine realness. They are who they are, unashamed.

Jesus continues on in His preaching about the kingdom as He speaks to Nicodemus, a member of the Jewish ruling council. He instructed Nicodemus:

> *"I tell you the truth, no one can see the kingdom of God unless he is born again."*
> *"How can a man be born when he is old?" Nicodemus asked. "Surely he cannot enter a second time into his mother's womb to be born!"*
> *Jesus answered, "I tell you the truth, no one can enter the kingdom of God unless he is born of water and the Spirit. Flesh gives birth to flesh, but the Spirit gives birth to spirit. You should not be surprised at my saying, 'You must be born again.' The wind blows wherever it pleases. You hear its sound, but you cannot tell where it comes from or where it is going. So it is with everyone born of the Spirit"* (John 3:3-8).

John says of Jesus, *Yet to all who received him, to those who believed in his name, he gave the right to become children of God—children born not of natural descent, nor of human decision or a husband's will, but born of God* (John 1:11-13).

My husband, Kenny, went on a mission trip to Russia a number of years ago. On the trip, he had the opportunity to visit a music college. He was particularly thrilled since he ministers in music a great deal and is a wonderful singer. He listened to the various students give their renditions of songs for their final exams. Afterward, he had lunch with some of the folks. Kenny is a real evangelist, and as he dined, he shared Christ with several of the folks at his table. A young lady named Tatiana was particularly captivated by his message and wanted to pray with him to receive Jesus as her Savior.

 Cocoon

After the prayer, she looked at my husband and said in her broken English, "Tatiana, born from above!" and she pointed upward. She understood exactly what happened!

All of us have natural parents who birth us physically into this world. When we come to Christ, our Father God rebirths us into His kingdom. Indeed it is a rebirth, for He is the One who birthed our spirits in the very beginning of our existence. I certainly don't understand all that has taken place before we came into this world, but I do know that God is our parent who has given us life, for real life comes from Him. When we are born again, we are reconnected to Him in an awesome way. We are truly grateful to our earthly parents who birthed us. Some parents do a wonderful job in nurturing and training us and then releasing us to be who we were created to be. Other parents, with deep wounds of their own, haven't got a clue as to how to do that. I have to believe that an all-wise God has placed us in just the right home with just the right family for very good reasons to shape us into the people we become. But ultimately, we must reconnect to the One who is the real source of our life and allow Him to parent us and release us to be all we were created to be. We are born again into the household of God.

Responding:

I would like to recommend another tool I have discovered that can bless your life. It is a book titled *Blessing Your Spirit*, written by Sylvia Gunter and Arthur Burk. It contains forty days of blessings of the Father God and twenty-one days of blessings focused on the names of God. The following blessing is taken from Day 1 of this book. I would ask that in responding to today's word you would fill in your name in the blanks and read the blessing out loud to yourself.

Day 1: Identity and Legitimacy

_____, I call your spirit to attention in the name of Jesus of Nazareth. Listen with your spirit to God's Word for you. *"For you created my inmost being; you knit me together in my mother's womb. I praise you because I am fearfully and wonderfully made; your works are wonderful, I know that full well. My frame was not hidden from you when I was made in the secret place. When I was woven together in the depths of the earth, your eyes saw my unformed body. All the days ordained for me were written in your book before one of them came to be"* (Psalm 139:13-16).

_____, your Father made you special. You are a very special person, created and crafted and designed by God your Father. Before the foundation of the world, your Father planned for you. You are no accident. You did not have to exist, but your Father willed you into existence. He chose the day and the time you would start your life. He chose your parents and wove you together in your mother's womb. He planned your birth order and put you in your family. He chose every one of your twenty-three pairs of chromosomes. He chose every one of your 10,000-plus genes. He chose every part of your spiritual heritage. He reached back into your father's bloodline and your mother's bloodline, and from generations past, your heavenly Father chose different parts of your heritage. Some parts are not so beautiful, and some parts are absolutely gorgeous. Yet your Father wove it all together and gave you everything you need in the package of your life to be an overcomer, a victor, to take the negative parts of your heritage and triumph over them, to walk in the beauty of all that God has placed within you.

Your Father made you beautiful and beloved. I bless you, _____, because you are wonderfully made. God invested an incredible amount of effort and concentration in designing you. You are unique, one of a kind. There is nobody else like you. God has thought extensively about you. Every detail of your body, every organ and every cell is the result of God's thoughts. Every facet of your personality is the result of His kind intention. You are beautiful, and you are beloved. God has blessed you with His love. God smiled on the day He created you. He had been waiting for millennia for the particular point in time when you were conceived. He had great joy in His heart when His plans actually came together. He nurtures your spirit; He watches over you.

Your world needs you. You bring something to your family that no other person has. They need the gifts you bring. Your family would not be complete without you. Others in your circle need the deposit that God has placed in your life.

_____, your Father wrote your days in His book. He has already read the final chapters, although we have not had that privilege. Your life is not a random thing. He is looking forward to the chapters of the story He has already written. He designed your spiritual heritage. Your generational blessings go back a thousand generations. There is a spiritual treasure chest of generational blessings with your name on it. Those are being released to you incrementally over the course of your life at the appointed, appropriate time. All this is God's master plan. God has foreseen your pain. He promises that because of His love, His power and His blessings upon you, He causes pain and negative things to be transformed into good things before the end of the story of your life. We don't know everything about who you are going to be or what you are going to do, but you are loved, you are a blessing to your family and you are a life-giver to the world. You are special, and we celebrate God's miraculous design of who you are. I bless you in the name of Jesus of Nazareth.[13]

Journal any response you may have, and anything that the Lord would speak to you.

See, A Son

Day Two:
A Revelation of the Son of God

Remember, we are in our cocoon, which is Jesus Christ. As we look at Him, we are being transformed into His image in our "house of mirrors." The Apostle Peter received a marvelous revelation of who Jesus is.

> *When Jesus came to the region of Caesarea Philippi, he asked his disciples, "Who do people say the Son of Man is?"*
> *They replied, "Some say John the Baptist; others say Elijah; and still others, Jeremiah or one of the prophets."*
> *"But what about you?" He asked. "Who do you say I am?"*
> *Simon Peter answered,* **"You are the Christ, the Son of the living God."**
> *Jesus replied, "Blessed are you, Simon son of Jonah, for this was not revealed to you by man, but by my Father in heaven. And I tell you that you are Peter, and on this rock I will build my church and the gates of Hades will not overcome it. I will give you the keys of the kingdom of heaven; whatever you bind on earth will be bound in heaven, and whatever you loose on earth will be loosed in heaven"* (Matthew 16:13-19 emphasis added).

Peter's revelation of Christ, the Son of God, is indeed the solid-rock foundation of His Church. Peter saw a Son! Isaiah had prophesied hundreds of years earlier, *For to us a child is born, to us a son is given, and the government will be on his shoulders. And he will be called Wonderful Counselor, Mighty God, Everlasting Father, Prince of Peace* (Isaiah 9:6). In the angel's visitation to Mary before the birth of the Messiah, he told her,

> *You will be with child and give birth to a son, and you are to give him the name Jesus. He will be great and will be called*

79

the Son of the Most High… The Holy Spirit will come upon you, and the power of the Most High will overshadow you. So the Holy One to be born will be called the Son of God (Luke 1:31,32,35).

From the very beginning of His ministry, as Jesus came up out of the waters of baptism by John the Baptist, the Father affirmed the sonship of Jesus. *And a voice from heaven said, "This is my Son, whom I love; with Him I am well pleased"* (Matthew 3:17). It is imperative that we see Jesus Christ as the Son of God. *For those God foreknew he also predestined to be conformed to the likeness of his Son, that he might be the firstborn among many brethren* (Romans 8:29). Jesus is our supreme example of what a Son looks like. He gave us a picture of a Son of God. It is important here that we note that Jesus laid aside His divinity and took the form of a servant, operating as a man empowered by the Holy Spirit, looking unto His Father. As we look at Jesus, we also get a picture of who we are as children of the Most High God.

Responding:

There is new life stirring within our cocoon. We still may look pretty much like a caterpillar, but something new is happening on the inside. Just what it will be is certainly not visible yet, but the transformation process is set in motion. The seed has been awakened. The parts of this new creation begin to take shape. What will it look like? Its attributes come from its creator—in His image.

In the Word of God, there are many pictures of Jesus as the Son of God. Ask the Father to give you a revelation of Jesus, the Son. What particular attributes are more visible to you? What might the Father be saying to you? Journal what you see and hear.

Day Three:
The Father Desires to Give Us the Kingdom

Being a son speaks of a family relationship. Jesus, as the Son of God, came to reveal the Father. It is the Father who desires to give us the kingdom. *"Do not be afraid, little flock, for your Father has been pleased to give you the kingdom"* (Luke 12:32). The key to the kingdom is found in knowing the Father. We are being transformed to look more like Jesus. Jesus came showing us the Father. They are one. And He wants us to be one with them also.

> *Jesus answered, "I am the way and the truth and the life. No one comes to the Father except through me. If you really knew me, you would know my Father as well. From now on, you do know him and have seen him."*
> *Phillip said, "Lord, show us the Father and that will be enough for us."*
> *Jesus answered: "Don't you know me, Phillip, even after I have been among you such a long time? Anyone who has seen me has seen the Father. How can you say, 'Show us the Father'?"* (John 14:6-9).

This revelation of the Father was a new one. God had revealed Himself in many ways throughout His dealings with His people before He sent His Son. He was and is Elohim, the Creator of all things in the book of Genesis. He was and is El Shaddai, the Almighty God, the all-sufficient one, the many-breasted one to Abraham and Jacob. He was and is I AM THAT I AM, Jehovah God, to Moses in the burning bush. He was and is Adonai, or Lord, throughout the Old and New Testaments. He was and is all the compound names of Jehovah as revealed throughout the Old Testament in many different situations to many different people. God is all of this and much more. But His revelation to His people as Father was a new revelation that Jesus the Son came to bring. Throughout His ministry, Jesus was constantly referring to His Father who sent Him, whose will He came to do, whose Word He came to speak. Jesus went so far as to say that He could do nothing without the Father.

Arthur Burk, in his teaching on the gift of mercy, the final part in a teaching on the redemptive gifts of individuals, speaks of a "new word" released to him by God and to others in the Body of Christ in these days. That new word consists of the area of spiritual fathering. He has found 300 verses in the New Testament alone, 150 speaking of the relationship between God the Father and Jesus Christ, the Son, and 150 speaking of our relationship as believers with the Father God. He shared that as the Church is crying out as never before for the manifest presence of God, for greater intimacy with the Lord, there seemed to be something missing. As he began to contemplate that, he came to understand that we are "out of sequence."

> *"A girl is not fit to be married until she has been fathered. If she brings to her wedding day a lack of fathering, on Monday he will have to be a father, on Tuesday, a husband, on Wednesday, a father, on Thursday, a husband, etc. If he's really sharp, he can finish growing up his child bride until she's ready to become a woman and step into the role of being a wife and helpmeet. If he's not good, he'll either be neurotic or divorced in a short while. We have missed this message of spiritual fathering. We have a generation of believers who don't understand the distinction between God the Father and God the Son and in this whole theme of Bridal intimacy coming from Song of Solomon and other passages of scripture, we've been trying to go to Christ as the Bride of Christ, to have in our relationship with Christ our fathering needs met. So close and yet a little off. God is bringing a course correction into the church now for*

us to seek the face of the Father and the manifest presence of the Father and for the glory of the Father to finish repairing our dysfunctional parenting, to grow us up into our identity. Once we have established our identity, we know who we are because of a relationship with the Father, then with the King of Kings, our Lord, the Bridegroom of the Church. There is a proper, holy, wholesome intimacy there and the glory of God is able to fall upon the entire world."[14]

Even the best of families are dysfunctional to some degree. We are all imperfect people and carry that imperfection in all we do. I remember sitting on my living room floor after my youngest son was married, the wonderful day was over, and all the guests were gone. I cried to God saying, "Thank you, God. I have made so many mistakes in rearing my children, but You are faithful. Your grace and mercy have been abundant, and I can see you at work in their lives. What an awesome God you are!" Truly, what a comfort to us as parents to know that where we miss it, God takes over and redeems everything as we put it in His hands. And what a comfort for us as children also not to look to our parents for what they cannot give, for they are yet in process too, but rather to look to our Heavenly Father, who does all things well.

I remember the beginnings of my own spiritual journey. I was born again at the age of nine. I grew up in a very formal small-town Southern Baptist church. The deep wine carpet, the beautiful dark-stained wooden walls and beams, and the massive chandelier that hung from the lofty ceiling were awe inspiring as we entered the "house of the Lord." Our pastor, a usually jolly fellow who always spoke to us children and made us feel very loved and accepted in his presence, stayed with us for twenty-five years, serving to anchor the truth that God is the same yesterday, today, and forever.

I couldn't tell you what he preached on that particular Sunday morning. He always used a lot of big words that I really didn't understand. I couldn't tell you what the choir sang as its anthem that day or the hymns we sang as we followed the swelling sound of the organ. But I do remember as if it were yesterday the tugging at my heart. I knew that God was drawing me to Himself, to surrender my life to Him, to enter into a relationship with Him. And so I finally loosened my grip on the back of the pew in front of me and slipped down the aisle to go talk to Mr. Tomlinson and tell him that I wanted to ask Jesus to come into my heart. I felt as if I wanted to cry though I held back the tears. I knew something new and different was going on inside me, but I really had no clue as to exactly what it was. I took a class with some of my friends to help explain this new experience, and we were baptized on a very cold winter night. My journey had begun.

I believe that each person's journey is very unique, just like each person is unique. There are tools that can be put into our hands, encouragement along the way, and traveling companions who go with us for parts of our journey, but for the most part, we take what we have been given and then chart our own course. At least we think we are charting our course, but actually we are finding the path already laid out for us by a loving Heavenly Father who shines the light before us in the face of His Son, Jesus. It is quite interesting that even now after traveling this road for many years, I still see myself as a little child standing before the Father in need of His parenting to release misconceptions, to receive correction and healing, and to simply be affirmed in His love. What a wonderful thought that I cannot comprehend: the Creator of all things, the all-wise, all-knowing, all-filling God loves me as a Father and has a most perfect plan for my life and every provision to fulfill that plan! As I have traveled my journey, I have seen many who have experienced deep father or mother wounds in their lives that have needed healing by the Father. He is "perfect everything" and can truly supply all our needs.

Responding:

All of us have experienced negative experiences in our childhood at one time or another. These experiences, whether someone has wronged us or whether our perceptions of the experience were misconstrued, were painful to us and left wounds. Ask the Lord to reveal to you anything that He wants to deal with and heal. What memories are surfacing even now of your childhood? Ask your Father to allow His Son, our Redeemer, to come into that situation. Do you see Him? He really was there all the time. What is He doing in that situation? How does that make you feel? Allow Him to bring healing to you. Journal your response and anything that He speaks to you.

Healing us of our previous experiences will allow them to be redeemed. They are brought under the cleansing blood of Jesus. From our new birth, we are being re-fathered by a perfect Father—Father God. In this relationship, He can release into our lives true knowledge of Him and His Kingdom. Our secure home is Christ Jesus, our cocoon, where we are growing into mature sons and daughters of God.

Day Four:
Our All-Wise Father Shows Us the Path for Our Lives

I believe that we need to look at three areas of the Father/son relationship (or daughter—it is always rather funny that we as girls can be "sons of God" and men can be the "Bride of Christ!") that we can see in chapter 8 of Romans.

As a teenager, I joined the choir at our church. My dad also sang in the choir. I remember times riding with him to choir practice. My dad was always a man of few words, and when he did speak, he thought through what he was saying and usually it was worth waiting for and listening to. However, it was different when you went somewhere with him by yourself, just you and him. He always did a lot of talking. On one of our drives to choir practice, I remember him telling me that if he could have only one book out of the Bible, it would be the book of Romans. My dad taught Sunday school. I guess that's where I got my love for teaching. And I concur that Romans is full of valuable insights into our life in Christ. And if I had to choose one chapter in the Bible, I would probably choose the eighth chapter of Romans. It says so much! Take a few moments and read Romans 8. We'll be looking at it for the next few days.

First of all, we see that our all-wise Father shows us the path for our lives. He knows us even better than we know ourselves. He does know what is best for us, even though sometimes we may question that truth. One key verse is verse 14, which reads, *those who are led by the Spirit of God are sons of God.* Our butterfly, our once-dead spirit, is being resurrected in Christ as we are born again. God is a spirit and He communicates to us in our spirits that have been revived. Adam died to his spiritual life and lived out of his soul. The Lord invites us to die to our soul life and live out of the spiritual, allowing that spirit life to bring redemption to the soul to take its rightful place, being led by the Spirit.

> *However, as it is written: "No eye has seen, no ear has heard, no mind has conceived what God has prepared for those who love him" but God has revealed it to us by his Spirit. The Spirit searches all things, even the deep things of God. For who among men knows the thoughts of a man except the man's spirit within him? In the same way no one knows the thoughts of God except the Spirit of God. We have not received the spirit of the world but the Spirit who is from God, that we may understand what God has freely given us. This is what we speak, not in words taught us by human wisdom but in words taught by the Spirit, expressing spiritual truths in spir-*

> *itual words. The man without the Spirit does not accept the things that come from the Spirit of God, for they are foolishness to him, and he cannot understand them, because they are spiritually discerned. The spiritual man makes judgments about all things, but he himself is not subject to any man's judgment: 'For who has known the mind of the Lord that he may instruct him?' But we have the mind of Christ* (1 Corinthians 2:9-16).

We can communicate with God, spirit to Spirit! David spoke of this as *deep calling unto deep* (Psalm 42:7).

In this leading by our Father God, when we wander off the right path, He does not condemn us, but He does correct us. Sometimes He must discipline us to help us. We don't like the thoughts of this, but it is very necessary for our growth.

> *And you have forgotten that word of encouragement that addresses you as sons: "My son, do not make light of the Lord's discipline, and do not lose heart when he rebukes you, because the Lord disciplines those he loves, and he punishes everyone he accepts as a son."*
> *Endure hardship as discipline; God is treating you as sons. For what son is not disciplined by his father? If you are not disciplined (and everyone undergoes discipline), then you are illegitimate children and not true sons. Moreover, we have all had human fathers who disciplined us and we respected them for it. How much more should we submit to the Father of our spirits and live! Our fathers disciplined us for a little while as they thought best; but God disciplines us for our good, that we may share in his holiness. No discipline seems pleasant at the time, but painful. Later on, however, it produces a harvest of righteousness and peace for those who have been trained by it* (Hebrews 12:5-11).

Our Father has planned a wonderful journey for us. There is much to see and know. Don't miss a step of it. We all remember the classic story, *The Pilgrim's Progress*, by John Bunyan. Pilgrim learned many costly lessons as he veered off the proper path. It is so much wiser to learn the instruction of the Lord rather than learning from the teacher of experience. But rest assured, the Father will help you learn either way. Watch for the lighted pathway and stay on it as best you can. Your Father will help you find your way if you lose it. *Your word is a lamp to my feet and a light for my path* (Psalm 119:105). Godspeed, my friend!

Responding:

Kenny served as a pastor of a church in Connelly Springs, North Carolina, for almost two years. While there, he visited Bamberg, South Carolina, and took part in a series of revival meetings. A friend from seminary had started a new church there. Everyone loved Kenny and received his ministry so well that they invited him to move his family to Bamberg and become the minister of youth, education, and music. Kenny came home and we began to pray about the move. We were still learning to hear the Lord. Kenny had already sensed that it was time for him to leave the church at Connelly Springs, so he had shared this information with churches seeking a new pastor. We made the decision to go to Bamberg but prayed that if we were not to go, a pulpit committee would visit the Connelly Springs church on the following Sunday. They did. We prayed again that if we were not to go to Bamberg, this pulpit committee from another church would contact us. The men who came from Bamberg to help us pack up our belongings for the move were sitting in our living room when the call came from the pulpit committee interested in talking with Kenny about possibly serving as their pastor. "But they are already here from Bamberg," we reasoned. And so we moved to Bamberg.

See, A Son

There were some wonderful folks in Bamberg, but we were clearly out of the will of the Lord for our lives. This was not His chosen path for us and He tried to tell us that, but we just didn't listen at first. We stayed in Bamberg for about three months. The heat was almost unbearable, especially as I was expecting our second child. I was miserable. Our son, Kevin, was two years old, and we had left him with my mom and dad back in North Carolina. After we moved in and got settled, they brought him down to join us. The first night in his new home, Kevin cried and cried. He did not want to sleep in his new room in this strange place. He didn't like playing out in our backyard, contending with the sweltering heat and the myriad bugs the heat seemed to breed. We were very uncomfortable, to say the least. Soon, the pastor was taken to the hospital with a nervous breakdown. Some of the folks wanted Kenny to step into the pastor's position, but the pastor wanted to continue serving the church as their pastor. We cried out for help to those we knew would pray for us. We knew we had to get back onto God's path for our lives.

Kevin and I went home to my mom and dad's, leaving Kenny to tie up some loose ends in Bamberg and wait on the Lord for new directions, but even he had to leave before we knew where we would go next. We lived with my mom and dad until our youngest son, Kyle, was born. A wonderful friend, who owned and ran a service station and ministered locally, hired Kenny to work for him during this transition. At that time, Kenny didn't even know how to check the oil, but he learned, and he pumped a lot of gas and washed a lot of hearses. Everyday he waited for the phone to ring to hear that our baby was ready to come or to hear that a church wanted to talk with him about serving them in ministry.

One day a fellow came through who was picking up uniforms from the service station and leaving more for the employees. He worked for a company in Rocky Mount, North Carolina. It just so happened that his church was looking for a minister of youth and education. He told his pastor about Kenny, and a meeting was set for an interview with the church's search committee. He was called to the church! Our family of four moved to Rocky Mount when Kyle was one month old. We were back on God's path for us. Our journey continued with so many adventures still to come.

As you look back over your life, can you remember times you got off track and the Father brought you back? Can you remember times the Father showed you signposts to direct you on your way and keep you from falling? Thank Him for His care. Are you at a crossroads today? Are there decisions you must make about which road to take from here? Ask the Lord to give you wisdom and show you the way. Journal your response and His word to you.

Day Five:
Our Father Desires to Bring Us to Maturity

As we continue to look at Romans 8, our Father desires to bring us to maturity. One key verse here is verse 19, *The creation waits in eager expectation for the sons of God to be revealed.* It is interesting to note in this passage that *all* of creation has been affected by our fall and, consequently, *all* of creation is waiting for our full redemption to be restored to God's original intention. Mankind has been given authority and responsibility on this planet. As we move closer to the fulfillment of this, I believe that we are being called to a higher realm of commitment and relationship with the Lord and a greater awareness of the spiritual realm as we make ourselves available to the kingdom of God. As we are growing and being transformed, we drink the milk of the Word. *As newborn babes, desire the sincere milk of the word, that you may grow thereby* (1 Peter 2:2 KJV). We also eat the meat of His will as we yield ourselves to *do* His Word.

Meanwhile his disciples urged him, "Rabbi, eat something."

See, A Son

> *But he said to them, "I have food to eat that you know nothing about."*
> *Then his disciples said to each other, "Could someone have brought him food?"*
> *"My food," said Jesus, "is to do the will of him who sent me and to finish his work"* (John 4:31-34).

> *But solid food is for the mature, who by constant use have trained themselves to distinguish good from evil* (Hebrews 5:14).

> *Therefore, I urge you, brothers, in view of God's mercy, to offer your bodies as living sacrifices, holy and pleasing to God—this is your spiritual act of worship. Do not conform any longer to the pattern of this world, but be transformed by the renewing of your mind. Then you will be able to test and approve what God's will is—his good, pleasing and perfect will* (Romans 12:1,2).

His Spirit is at work within us.

> *In the same way, the Spirit helps us in our weakness. We do not know what we ought to pray for, but the Spirit Himself intercedes for us with groans that words cannot express. And he who searches our hearts knows the mind of the Spirit, because the Spirit intercedes for the saints in accordance with God's will* (Romans 8:26-27).

In addition to the Word and the Spirit, the Lord also has given gifts to the Body of Christ. As each of us finds our place in the Body of Christ and functions as he or she is called and created to function, the whole Body will be built up into the fullness of God's desire. We can receive from one another, no matter our denomination, social status, race, or any other dividing factor. We are all called to unity, and we can all learn from each other.

> *It was he who gave some to be apostles, some to be prophets, some to be evangelists, and some to be pastors and teachers, to prepare God's people for works of service, so that the body of Christ may be built up until we all reach unity in the faith and in the knowledge of the Son of God and become mature, attaining to the whole measure of the fullness of Christ.*
>
> *Then we will no longer be infants, tossed back and forth by the waves, and blown here and there by every wind of teaching and by the cunning and craftiness of men in their deceitful scheming. Instead, speaking the truth in love, we will in all things grow up into him who is the Head, that is, Christ. From him the whole body, joined and held together by every supporting ligament, grows and builds itself up in love, as each part does its work* (Ephesians 4:11-16).

The Lord is calling us to move beyond our self-centered lives into a Christ-centered life. As we do so, we will become more transparent, enabling Jesus to be seen more clearly in our lives and through our lives.

Romans 8:15 also speaks concerning this maturing as sons. *For you did not receive the spirit of bondage again to fear, but you received the Spirit of adoption by whom we cry out, Abba, Father.* The ancient Hebrew's understanding of adoption is far different from our present-day practice. Our practice of adoption involves legally taking a child born to other parents as our own. The original meaning of this word in the Greek is found in the NKJV Greek-English Interlinear New Testament: "Adoption: Greek: huiothesia. Noun, a compound noun from 'huio,' a son and 'thesia,' a placing, thus meaning adoption. The word was a legal term for the father's declaration that his natural-born child was officially a son or daughter, with all the rights and privileges that this included."[15] This makes much more sense from a Biblical perspective.

Our heavenly Father has birthed children, and they have been stolen by Satan. Our Father has reclaimed us as His own through the new birth afforded us in the redemption of Jesus Christ. Whereas once we were enslaved through the power of sin to the father of lies, as we come to Christ and receive His redemption, we are brought back to our real Father. We are freed from sin's slavery and released as sons and rightful heirs of all that belongs to our Father. As babes in Christ, we are servants in the household of God. As we mature, our Father is training us in righteousness and will release us to rule and reign with Him. *And hast redeemed us to God by thy blood out of every kindred, and tongue, and people, and nation; And hast made us unto our God kings and priests: and we shall reign on the earth* (Revelation 5:9,10 KJV).

We don't see much recorded in the Bible about Jesus' life as a young boy. The only tidbit we have of his young life is His trip to Jerusalem with His mother and father when He was twelve years old. We see that He was keenly aware of His Father even at this young age. When they lost Him among the traveling group, they found Him in the temple courts, listening to and asking questions of the teachers. *"Why were you searching for me?" He asked. "Didn't you know I had to be in My Father's house?" But they did not understand what he was saying to them. Then he went down to Nazareth with them and was obedient to them. But his mother treasured all these things in her heart. And Jesus grew in wisdom and stature, and in favor with God and men* (Luke 2:49-52).

Are you growing in like manner? Can you look back one year ago and recognize that you have grown in your life in Christ since then?

Responding:

Remember, your cocoon—the home in which you are growing—is filled with God's Word and His Spirit. You are connected to your brothers and sisters in Christ, those who are growing as children of God also.

What is a favorite Bible verse that has helped you grow?

Are you filled with the Holy Spirit? Each day we need a new infilling, but have you initially yielded your life to the Holy Spirit? John told those who had come to be baptized that he baptized with water for repentance, but that Jesus would baptize with the Holy Spirit and fire. Have you asked Jesus to baptize you in His Spirit? If not, ask Him now. He wants to empower you to live the Christian life, to bear more fruit, and to be His witness.

Who are some of the people in the Body of Christ who have touched your life in a way to help you grow in your life in Jesus? One of the people in the Rocky Mount church who took us under her wings, prayed for us, and shared encouragement was Dusty. Dusty loves butterflies. She is one. She has flitted into so many peoples' lives and shared the love and life of Christ in so many ways. Dusty would visit us on Sunday nights particularly, pour love on our children, and drop little articles, books, and testimonies to stretch us beyond where we were walking with the Lord to higher places in Him.

Dusty invited me to go with her to the Women's Aglow meetings in our town. I remember that the first speaker I heard at one of these meetings was a very vivacious Jewish lady who had been a model. Ziva was such an inspiration as she zealously worshipped Yeshua, her Messiah. On another occasion, Dusty took me to hear Gloria Phillips at one of the meetings. Gloria was also sharing at revival services at another church in town during the coming week. I went to one of the services. Kenny says that I came home that night glowing with the Spirit of the Lord. Dusty had invited him to the meetings also, so he decided he would go the next evening. He did, and really enjoyed the music and worship, but wasn't too sure how he felt about this woman speaker.

He wasn't planning to go back until the next day when he received a call from his dad telling him that his cousin's home had been broken into and his cousin had been shot. Dennis was in critical condition. They didn't know if he was going to live or what his condition would be if he did survive. We immediately called folks in our prayer chain and had them pray for Dennis. We knew the church that we had visited the night before and the ministers, including Gloria Phillips, believed strongly in healing prayer. Kenny decided we would go back to the service that night and have them pray for Dennis. At the conclusion of the service, Kenny went to the altar to ask for prayer. Gloria Phillips gently touched Kenny's elbow as he lifted his arms to the Lord. As she did, Kenny fell back, overwhelmed by the power of the Spirit of the Lord. We did not know it at the time, but his cousin had already passed away earlier that evening. Kenny was so filled with the peace of God and overflowed with His joy that it carried him throughout the coming weekend as he mourned the loss of his cousin. Despite the deep sorrow, God's presence pervaded the family gatherings. Kenny sang at the funeral. A young man shared with Kenny that he could hardly keep his eyes off of him as he sang because of such a glow of the presence of the Lord. We were yielding ourselves more and more to the Lord in our lives, experiencing His presence and His power as we were growing in our knowledge of Him.

Dusty has remained a special blessing to us through the years, continuing to pray for us, share with us, and encourage us ever onward in our walk with Jesus.

Journal what the Lord is doing and speaking to you now.

Day Six:
Our Father Loves Us

The third and final aspect of the Father/Son relationship that we can see in Romans 8 is that this relationship is centered in love.

Cocoon

The final three verses sum it all up. *No, in all these things we are more than conquerors through him who loved us. For I am convinced that neither death nor life, neither angels nor demons, neither the present nor the future, nor any powers, neither height nor depth, nor anything else in all creation, will be able to separate us from the love of God that is in Christ Jesus our Lord* (Romans 8:37-39). Even in the things that we deem bad things in our lives, the enemy of our souls who would condemn us is just a pawn in the hands of our loving Father, who causes *everything* to work together for our good as we live in His love. It's as if we're enveloped in a love bubble! It will take us a lifetime to truly know the love of God, and even then we will be just exploring the fringes of His great deep love for us. Our Father loves us extravagantly! We are the apple of His eye!

Responding:

I want to share a story with you that I heard as a recorded message given by Earl Tyson, a Methodist evangelist. In this experience with his earthly father, Earl received a revelation of the heavenly Father's great love. I join with the apostle Paul in praying for you:

> *I kneel before the Father from whom his whole family in heaven and on earth derives its name. I pray that out of his glorious riches he may strengthen you with power through his Spirit in your inner being, so that Christ may dwell in your hearts through faith. And I pray that you, being rooted and established in love, may have power, together with all the saints, to grasp how wide and long and high and deep is the love of Christ, and to know this love that surpasses knowledge—that you may be filled to the measure of all the fullness of God...Amen* (Colossians 3:14-19).

Earl was the son of Jack Tyson, a Methodist preacher. Jack and his wife had five sons and a daughter. All of his sons grew up to respond to the call of God for ministry themselves as well. Their home was in Pikeville, North Carolina.

A tent show came to Pikeville. Rusty Williams put up an old tent that would seat about 100 people. Two cowboy movies would be shown, with a stage act between the two movies. Earl and his brother Vernon wanted to go to the tent show, but their daddy forbade it. The boys were not to leave their yard.

The admission price to the tent show was ten cents, so the boys would need twenty cents. Earl had no idea where to get the two dimes, so he laid awake that night trying to come up with an idea to secure the needed funds. The idea came.

The next morning, Earl slipped out the back door and walked the three blocks to downtown Pikeville to Mr. Bass' grocery store. "What do you need, Earl?" asked Mr. Bass.

"Mama wants a dozen eggs," replied Earl. Mr. Bass got the eggs for Earl and put them in a bag. "Charge them to my daddy," said Earl. (This was before the days of the charge card, when a man's word was still good.)

Earl walked out of Mr. Bass' store and around the corner to Mr. Fleming's grocery store. "What will you give me for a dozen eggs?" asked Earl.

"Where did you get those eggs?" asked Mr. Fleming.

"My granddaddy gave 'em to me," responded Earl. "You know he lives out here in the country and he's got some chickens."

Mr. Fleming looked at the eggs and told Earl, "I'll give you twenty cents for them."

Earl took the two dimes and put them in his pocket and started walking back home. As he was walking, he heard somebody whistling. He knew the sound of that whistling. His daddy whistled quite a bit. As his daddy came around the corner, Earl hid behind an oak tree. Earl laughed to himself as he watched his daddy go by. "Old dumb thing, he can't even see me," mused Earl.

 *Cocoon*

Earl slipped out from behind the oak tree, went on back home, and he and Vernon went to school. He showed his brother the two dimes, saying "We'll go to the tent show tonight."

When Earl and Vernon got home from school that afternoon, Earl's mother told him, "Earl, your daddy said he'll be back tonight. He's going to preach. He said to tell you boys not to leave this yard. And Earl, when he gets back, he wants to talk with you."

Earl and Vernon had supper, washed the dishes, and then slipped out the back door. They ran down the street, heading to the tent show, their mama yelling, "I'm going to tell your daddy on you!"

Earl thought to himself, "You can tell anybody you want to, even God, but we're going to the tent show tonight. The devil can have tomorrow; we've got tonight." Earl and Vernon got through the tent show with great joy, but with that heaviness over their head, trying to have fun in their sin.

The boys got back to the house that night. Their daddy's car was not in the yard. As quietly as possible, they slipped into the house and tiptoed down the hallway to their bedroom. "I hear you boys," said their mama. "I'm going to tell your daddy what you've done."

Earl and Vernon crawled into bed. Within five minutes, Vernon was fast asleep, but Earl lay there wide awake. He heard his daddy drive into the yard, open the screen door, and walk into the house. Mama's soft voice drifted into his hearing, "Earl and Vernon, they did wash the dishes, but then they ran down the road and went to that tent show. They just got home a few minutes ago, Jack."

Earl thought if he snored real loud that his daddy would have sympathy on him. His daddy, however, didn't even check to see if he was asleep. He opened his door and called, "Earl, come in here."

Two chairs sat facing each other.

"Have a seat, boy," his father invited, as he pulled up his own chair and sat down. I want you to know that I love you," his father began. "Earl, I'm not going to have another Carlton in this family." (Carlton was his mother's brother and a crook. Anytime his father wanted to talk about what was going to happen if you didn't mind, Carlton was brought up.) "If the seat of your pants holds out and my belt holds out, I'm not going to have a Carlton in this family. Earl, I want to tell you something," his father continued, "and then I want to ask you a question. This morning your mother said to me, 'Jack, I need a dozen eggs.' I went down to Mr. Bass' grocery store and said, 'Mr. Bass, I'd like a dozen eggs.' Would you like to tell me what Mr. Bass said to me?"

"No sir," replied Earl.

"I'll tell you what he said, 'Mr. Tyson, Earl just got my last dozen.'"

Look at God's sense of humor. Here is this little boy, not intending to rob a bank or commit adultery, but telling a lie to get twenty cents to go to the tent show. It was the grocer's last dozen. If it had not been, perhaps he would have put the eggs in a bag, given them to Mr. Tyson, and shook his head thinking, "That preacher's family sure eats a lot of eggs." Can't we see how God arranges the events of our lives?!

"Now Earl, would you like to tell me what you did with those eggs?" asked his daddy.

"No sir," Earl once again responded.

His father, undaunted, admonished him, "Boy, you'd better tell me the truth."

"Yes sir. I sold them to Mr. Fleming."

"What'd you get for them?"

"Twenty cents."

"What'd you do with the twenty cents?"

"Me and Vernon went to the tent show."

"That's what I thought. Now come with me."

That meant a trip to the bathroom. He knew his fate. "Daddy, I'll never do it again," vowed Earl.

"Come with me," reiterated his father.

In the judgment hall, the bathroom, his father told Earl, "Unbutton those pajamas; bend over." Earl's father put Earl's head between his own legs, took out his genuine cowhide belt, and starting applying loving justice. (This is a time you want mercy instead of justice!) Earl thought his daddy was going to kill him. Finally, however, his father released the lock on his head. Earl slid down onto the cool linoleum floor, thinking, "You'll be sorry when you find me dead in the morning."

His daddy walked out into the kitchen, and then came back in. "Bend over," he told Earl. And he took a handful of lard and rubbed Earl's backside with it, then gingerly buttoned back his pajamas. He had never done that before. He reached down and helped Earl up, headed back to his room, saying to Earl, "Come back in here and sit down."

Earl thought that his daddy was going to start again and go through the whole process, and he did start by saying, "I do want you to know that I love you and I'm sorry."

Earl was sitting there, looking at the floor. He was wanting to just go back to bed, but knew he couldn't until his father gave his permission, which was with a look of the eye. Slowly he raised his head and cut his eyes toward his father, looking for that permission. His father's face was disfigured, he was biting his lower lip, his shoulders were shaking, and he was sobbing all over. Suddenly it hit Earl like a ton of bricks, "He's crying over me." The idea that his father loved him broke through his hard heart. Earl reached up, grabbed his daddy, and hugged him for the first time in his life.

After Earl had shared this story, he concluded his message by saying, "That's why Jesus came—so one day it will break through to us that God truly loves us. But He will not bless us in our sins. He's not going to change the Word to accommodate one person, but He will joyfully give forgiveness in response to confession, healing in response to our wounds, and the kingdom of heaven upon the earth all the days of our life. In that encounter with my sin, with my lie, and the love of an earthly father, which was an expression of God's grace, I came to have a new understanding, a new relationship with my earthly father and my heavenly Father. My daddy never again had to lay his belt on me; it was a delight to obey him."

Journal any responses you may have. You may want to take a few moments to thank God for His wonderful love!

We have been born again into the household of God. Jesus has prepared a place for us in Him where we can grow as God's children. We are living in that place, our cocoon.

How great is the love the Father has lavished on us, that we should be called children of God! And that is what we are! (1 John 3:1).

Chapter 7
One Who Hears

There at the foot of Mount Sinai, basking in the hot morning sun as it climbed higher in the sky, Moses continued his discourse on the sons of Jacob. "Jacob's family had just begun, and in a very short time, his wife Leah, blessed by the Lord, brought forth another son whom she named Simeon, *one who hears.*

"I'll never forget what I heard on these very mountains as I was tending my father-in-law's sheep. I first saw a strange sight, a bush that seemed to be on fire but was not being consumed. I went closer to investigate, and as I did, I heard a voice calling my name from the bush. I did not know who this could be out here in this desert place, but I answered the voice, 'Here I am.' It was the most frightening and yet the most glorious voice I had ever heard. He revealed His Name, I AM THAT I AM—may His Name be forever praised. And then He told me that He had heard your cries and wanted me to go back and bring you out of the land of Egypt and back to this holy mountain. Here we are this day." All of the men began to bow their faces to the ground in worship to the great I AM.

Day Seven:
Learning to Hear

A woman named Hannah remained childless after desiring a baby for many years. She cried out in desperation to the Lord for a child, vowing that if He would allow her to have a son, she would give him to the Lord for all the days of his life. The Lord heard her cry, and she conceived and gave birth to a son, Samuel. After the baby was weaned, he was taken to the tabernacle of the Lord in Shiloh where Eli ministered as priest, along with his two sons Hophni and Phinehas. I have always marveled at the great faith of Hannah to leave her young son in the hands of Eli, who had done a very poor job in training his own wicked sons.

> *The boy Samuel ministered before the LORD under Eli. In those days the word of the LORD was rare; there were not many visions.*
>
> *One night Eli, whose eyes were becoming so weak that he could barely see, was lying down in his usual place. The lamp of God had not yet gone out, and Samuel was lying down in the temple of the LORD, where the ark of God was. Then the LORD called Samuel.*
>
> *Samuel answered, "Here I am," and he ran to Eli and said, "Here I am; you called me."*
>
> *But Eli said, "I did not call; go back and lie down." So he went and lay down.*
>
> *Again the LORD called, "Samuel!" And Samuel got up and went to Eli and said, "Here I am; you called me."*
>
> *"My son," Eli said, "I did not call; go back and lie down."*
>
> *Now Samuel did not yet know the LORD: The word of the LORD had not yet been revealed to him.*
>
> *The LORD called Samuel a third time, and Samuel got up and went to Eli and said, "Here I am; you called me."*
>
> *Then Eli realized that the LORD was calling the boy. So Eli told Samuel, " Go and lie down, and if he calls you, say, 'Speak, LORD, for your servant is listening.'" So Samuel went and lay down in his place.*
>
> *The LORD came and stood there, calling as at the other*

One Who Hears

times, "Samuel! Samuel!" Then Samuel said, "Speak for your servant is listening" (1 Samuel 3:1-10).

God spoke to the young Samuel. Samuel developed a listening ear to hear the Lord. The end of the chapter tells us the extreme importance of Samuel hearing the word of the Lord. *The LORD was with Samuel as he grew up, and he let none of his words fall to the ground. And all Israel from Dan to Beersheba recognized that Samuel was attested as a prophet of the LORD. The LORD continued to appear at Shiloh, and there he revealed himself to Samuel through his word. And Samuel's word came to all Israel.*

You may say, "But Samuel was a prophet chosen by God for a special purpose." Yes, he was. But you are just as special to God as Samuel was. You are also His chosen vessel for whatever purposes He has created you. He wants you to hear His voice, not just so you can do His bidding, but first and foremost to be in an intimate relationship with Him. Jesus tells us in John 10:14, *"I am the good shepherd; I know my sheep and my sheep know me."* He continues on in verse 27, *"My sheep listen to my voice; I know them, and they follow me."*

Does God really speak to folks today? Yes, He definitely does! To hear, we must first listen. Attune your ear to the voice of the Lord. Ask Him to help you know His voice and hear Him. It is imperative that we hear Him. It could be a matter of life or death. Jesus told us to pray and ask God each day for our daily bread, but He also told us that *"Man does not live on bread alone, but on every word that comes from the mouth of God"* (Matthew 4:4).

Responding:

It doesn't take a baby long to recognize the voice of his parents. Even in the womb, little ears become attuned to Mom and Dad. In our cocoon, we become attuned to the voice of the Lord.

Maybe the idea of hearing the voice of the Lord is new to you, or maybe you hear the voice of the Lord very easily and very frequently. What an awesome thought to realize that God does desire to talk to us, as well as listen! A real conversation is not one way but two way. We always think of prayer as talking *to* God. *But it is even more important to listen to Him and let Him talk to us.* Take a few moments now and pour out your heart to the Lord. As you are writing in your journal, you may want to write your prayer to the Lord. Then just listen for a few moments and hear what the Lord would say to you. Record the Lord's response in your journal also. Enjoy your time with Him.

Day Eight:
Hearing Him Again

As Adam and Eve, the first son and daughter of God, were in the garden enjoying fellowship with Him, the first thing the enemy of our souls did was to question what God had said. *Now the serpent was more crafty than any of the wild animals the LORD God had made. He said to the woman,* **"Did God really say***, 'You must not eat from any tree in the garden?'"* (Genesis 3:1 emphasis added). Looking at this and the trouble that immediately ensued, I would say that it is very important to listen to God, really hear what He says, and then act on what He says.

After Adam and Eve had totally disregarded the word of God to them in the garden because of deception and disobedience, they again heard Him coming and they ran! *Then the man and his wife heard the sound of the LORD God as he was walking in the garden in the cool of the day, and they hid from the LORD God among the trees of the garden* (Genesis 3:8). In any relationship, communication is a key factor. Instead of running to God to correct the problem, Adam and Eve turned and went in the opposite direction. Repentance in the reverse runs you into the guardrail every time. Instead of drawing near to God to hear Him more clearly, they ran away and His voice became more faint.

The prophet Elijah did the same thing. He had been part of a great victory over the prophets of Baal on the mountain. God had sent down fire from heaven to consume his sacrifice. All the people fell down and worshipped the God of Elijah. Then the wicked Queen Jezebel threatened his life and away he ran like a whipped puppy. Elijah ran to Mount Horeb, went into a cave, and spent the night.

> *And the word of the LORD came to him: "What are you doing here, Elijah?"*
> *He replied, "I have been very zealous for the LORD God Almighty. The Israelites have rejected your covenant, broken down your altars, and put your prophets to death with the sword. I am the only one left, and now they are trying to kill me too."*
> *The LORD said, "Go out and stand on the mountain in the presence of the LORD, for the LORD is about to pass by."*
> *Then a great and powerful wind tore the mountains apart and shattered the rocks before the LORD, but the LORD was not in the wind. After the wind there was an earthquake, but the LORD was not in the earthquake. After the earthquake came a fire, but the LORD was not in the fire. And after the fire came a gentle whisper. When Elijah heard it, he pulled his cloak over his face and went out and stood at the mouth of the cave. The LORD said to him, "Go back the way you came, and go to the Desert of Damascus. When you get there, anoint Hazael king over Aram. Also, anoint Jehu son of Nimshi king over Israel, and anoint Elisha son of Shaphat from Abel Meholah to succeed you as prophet. Jehu will put to death any who escape the sword of Hazael, and Elisha will put to death any who escape the sword of Jehu. Yet I reserve seven thousand in Israel—all whose knees have not bowed down to Baal and all whose mouths have not kissed him"* (1 Kings 19:9-18).

 Cocoon

It was as if God used that powerful wind to clean out Elijah's ears. Elijah was shaken to get his ear tuned once again to hear the voice of the Lord. The outward roar had become so loud that he could not hear the still small voice down deep inside. God drew him near and whispered peace to him once again. He then put him back on track, giving him specific instructions as to what he was to do next.

Perhaps one of the most familiar stories of someone running away is that of Jonah. God had spoken to Jonah to send him on a mission to the wicked Ninevites to call them to repentance. Jonah boarded a ship headed in another direction. A violent storm threatened the safety of those on board the ship. The captain awakened the sleeping Jonah, asking him to cry out to God for help. The sailors then cast lots to determine who was stirring up all this trouble. The lot fell on Jonah. He confessed that he was running from the Lord and instructed them to throw him overboard so that the storm would be stilled. How's that for a solution? I suppose they must have imagined that he was in a deep depression and desired just to end his life. They tried rowing back to land but couldn't make any headway. The sea continued to churn, and the storm continued to rage. Crying out to God for forgiveness, they threw Jonah into the angry sea. At once it became calm. The Bible says that the sailors greatly feared the Lord and worshipped Him. As for Jonah, it's funny (but not usually at that moment) how we think we are jumping into a hopeless situation but find that God has a plan. *But the LORD provided a great fish to swallow Jonah, and Jonah was inside the fish three days and three nights* (Jonah 1:17).

For those three days and nights you can be assured that Jonah was crying out to the Lord. There was surely some deep calling to deep inside that fish! *And the LORD commanded the fish, and it vomited Jonah onto dry land* (Jonah 2:10). What an exit—yuck!

Now listen to what happened next. Here on the shore amid the muck and mire, *Then the word of the LORD came to Jonah a second time* (Jonah 3:1). God gave Jonah a second chance to hear His word and obey. And Jonah did. The whole city repented and turned to God. Jonah still had an attitude problem (Go figure!), but he *did* get the job done. God gives second chances! I'm so glad; how about you?

For Adam and Eve, their sin, guilt, and shame spoke so loudly. They tried to tune out the voice of the Lord. For Elijah, his fear screamed boldly. Jonah did not like what God asked him to do, so he rebelled. They all ran. They all had to be confronted by the Lord and brought back to the place where they could remember His voice to hear Him once again and continue on in their journeys. Is there anything in your life that has spoken so loudly as to crowd out the voice of the Lord? Are there things that have caused you to run away from Him rather than to Him? He asks you today, "Where are you?" And He wants you to once again hear Him. He will put you back on track just as He did Adam and Eve, Elijah, and Jonah.

Responding:

There may be something in your life that you have tried to run away from—perhaps a sin you committed and just swept under the rug, not wanting to deal with it, or perhaps a situation in your life that really scared you, paralyzing you from moving forward from that point. Maybe you knew the Lord was asking you to do something, but you just didn't want to do it. There is no better time than the present to deal with it. I believe that if you do, that faint voice that you hear in your heart will begin to get louder once again, clearer than ever. He really wants to remove all the things that come between the two of you, so just take a few moments to talk to the Lord about it now. He will remove that sin from you as far as the east is from the west. His perfect love can cast out all fear. He will give you a second chance to hear Him and obey and maybe even to understand why He wants you to do what He's asking. Record your dialogue in your journal. It will remind you in days to come that this matter has been settled by you and your Father.

Day Nine:
Deep Calls Unto Deep

No! Don't be alarmed. This is not saying that we all will have to cry out to God from the belly of a fish like Jonah. (Is this where the term "belly aching" originated?) Hopefully, if we learn to really communicate in the following manner, we won't end up in any fish bellies!

In the previous chapter, we talked about how as children of God our spirits are reborn and reconnected to God. We can commune with God spirit to Spirit. We all have those times when really deep down inside we *know* God is speaking to us and we need to listen. It touches something deep inside us, and we're compelled to respond to that word. You know what I mean. You may have heard a thousand sermons, but you probably can tell me just a few that made such an impact that they left an indelible mark in your memory. Something about that particular word was different. It actually touched you in such a way as to bring about a change in your life. And it might not have been from a sermon. It could have come from the most unusual place—a sign you read, a passage from a book, the words to a song, or even something as bizarre as something portrayed on a movie screen. It could have been spoken by a believer or an unbeliever. God has even been known to speak through such things as donkeys or angels. He might even be speaking through me to you right now. Like I said, He can speak through anything or anybody! Regardless, the Spirit of God is speaking to your spirit through whatever vessel He chooses.

One Who Hears

David wrote in Psalm 42:7, *Deep calls to deep in the roar of your waterfalls,* which also takes me to Revelation 1:15. Here, in the description of the Lord, it is said of Him, *And his voice was like the sound of rushing waters.* When we hear the Lord in our spirits, it's as if His Word churns over and over within us, continuing to speak until it has solidly taken root in our being.

Both Matthew and Mark record the same story of Andrew's becoming a disciple of Jesus Christ (Matthew 4:18-20 and Mark 1:16-18). Matthew's account reads, *As Jesus was walking beside the Sea of Galilee, he saw two brothers, Simon called Peter and his brother Andrew. They were casting a net into the lake, for they were fishermen. "Come, follow me," Jesus said, "and I will make you fishers of men." At once they left their nets and followed him.*

John tells the story a little differently. It is suggested in *The Interpreter's Bible, Volume VIII,* that "their prompt obedience [in Matthew and Mark's accounts] is explained by the earlier encounter further south, described in these verses [John 1:35-42]."[16] John tells us that Andrew had been a disciple of John the Baptist. Andrew heard John identify Jesus as the Lamb of God. When Andrew heard John, he followed Jesus.

> *Turning around, Jesus saw them following and asked, "What do you want?"*
> *They said, "Rabbi (which means Teacher), where are you staying?"*
> *"Come," He replied, "and you will see." So they went and saw where he was staying, and spent that day with him. It was about the tenth hour.*
> *Andrew, Simon Peter's brother, was one of the two who heard what John had said and who followed Jesus. The first thing Andrew did was to find his brother Simon and tell him, "We have found the Messiah" (that is, the Christ). And he brought him to Jesus* (John 1:38-42).

In both instances, *Andrew heard something that resulted in a change in his life*. He heard John say that Jesus was the Lamb of God. Immediately he was drawn to Jesus. In the time he spent with Jesus that day, he was convinced that Jesus was the Messiah. He then found his brother and took him to Jesus also. The two of them were fishermen by trade. When Jesus walked by and called them to follow Him, they heard, left their nets, and followed Him. Their lives were never the same.

Mary, Martha, and Lazarus were special friends of Jesus with whom He spent a great deal of time. Judging from various accounts in scripture, we see that particularly Mary had connected with Jesus on a deep spiritual level. As Jesus visited their home in Bethany, Mary chose to sit at Jesus' feet and hear Him rather than be about the busy preparations with her sister. The Lord applauded her heart to hear Him and know Him. Signa Bodishbaugh suggests that Mary's listening at Jesus' feet enabled her to hear the truth of what He was saying when nobody else was "getting it."

> *"Apparently at some point Mary's understanding had awakened to what Jesus had been telling His friends for days. He had said repeatedly in various ways that He was going away. He seemed so sure, though His disciples and friends argued with Him. Talk among them about what He 'really meant' had become their chief preoccupation, and they had discussed many theories in Mary's presence.*
>
> *"Suddenly all His words made sense in her heart, falling upon her like a weight. Most likely she had wanted desperately to cling to a more popular interpretation of His words, but now she quit trying to argue logically or plead with Him.*
>
> *"So Mary came to the dinner party at Simon's with her perfume bottle in hand. Hers was no spur-of-the-moment decision: Jesus had become the single most important Person in her life and she wanted to honor Him in the most mean-*

ingful way she knew. Her whole identity was wrapped up in Him and that night she knew in her heart that He was going to die. Perhaps she would not even be able to go on living without Him. She had given Him her heart completely and He had made it come alive in a way she had never dreamed possible.

"Instead of giving Jesus the gift she had brought, as perhaps she had at first intended, she broke the whole jar and spontaneously poured its contents over His head. For a Jew, it was the ultimate, symbolic gesture of anointing...

"I wonder: ***Would Mary have caught on to the real meaning of Jesus' words about 'going away' if she had not been willing to sit at His feet?"***[17]

It is important to stay responsive to the Lord first and foremost in every situation. Listen for His voice and then do what you feel He is saying. Don't be squeezed into "the world's mold" or be shaped by others' expectations or by the circumstances that call for your attention. Things aren't always what they seem and don't always call for the response or the timing that would at first seem necessary. Wait on the Lord. He is the Good Shepherd. Hear Him and obey Him as He leads. You are His sheep and can hear His voice. Yes, He's talking to you!

Responding:

I was a junior in high school and played basketball on the school team. One afternoon, I got home late from practice, ate dinner, and then went with my family to a revival meeting being held at our church. The visiting minister was a good teacher of the Word, and that night he spoke on Romans 12:1,2, about giving ourselves as a living sacrifice and being transformed by the Lord instead of being conformed to the world. Those words stuck deep in my spirit and have shaped my life over the years. Even now, yielding myself to the Lord to be transformed into His image and seeing others do the same is a passion of my heart. This book is about that very thing.

Perhaps the Lord wants to speak something deep into your heart right now, something intensely personal just to you. It may be a simple word, yet profound. Or it may be something big He's been trying to tell you if you would just be still and listen. Soak in the stillness of His presence and listen for His voice. Record His word to you and any response you may have in your journal.

Within your cocoon, your ears are becoming attuned once again to your Father's voice. His voice instructs, corrects, and comforts you as you grow.

Chapter 8
Attached

"Jacob's next son, born to him by his wife, Leah, was Levi," continued Moses. "Aaron, Miriam, and I are of the tribe of Levi. Levi means *attached*. As you can see today, we have attached ourselves to the Lord. G_d has chosen the tribe of Levi to be the priests out of all the tribes of Israel, set apart in the stead of all the firstborn, unto the Lord to minister before Him in His holy tabernacle. All of our tents surround the dwelling place of the Lord. Oh, that we would serve Him in a manner to bring glory to His holy Name!"

"We are indeed grateful for your service to the Most High G_d and to our people," said Nahshon, son of Amminadab, of the tribe of Judah. "Your zeal for the Lord challenges us to follow after Him. Even now the radiance of your countenance draws us to Him just as the fiery bush drew you to Him."

"May G_d be forever praised!" they all chorused.

Day Ten:
Our Identification: Jesus Christ

Philippians 2:7,8 tells us how Jesus identified with us, God's fallen creatures. *but made himself nothing, taking the very nature of a servant, being made in human likeness. And being found in appearance as a man, he humbled himself and became obedient to death— even death on a cross!* In His identification with us, He even went so far as to take upon Himself our sin to be able, as the sinless Lamb, to cast that sin away from us and restore us to the Father's original intention. *God made him who had no sin to be sin* [or a sin offering] *for us, so that in him we might become the righteousness of God* (2 Corinthians 5:21).

Dutch Sheets, in his book *Intercessory Prayer*, shares a very poignant illustration that portrays Christ's identification with us. Dutch paraphrases the story he had read in the book *What It Will Take To Change the World* by S.D. Gordon. The story is about a fourteen-year-old son who had lied to his parents. The son had skipped school for three days, which was discovered when the child's teacher called to find out how he was doing.

> *The parents were more upset by Steven's lies than his missing school. After praying with him about what he had done, they decided on a very unusual and severe form of punishment. Their conversation with him went something like this: "Steven, do you know how important it is that we be able to trust one another?"*
>
> *"Yes."*
>
> *"How can we ever trust each other if we don't always tell the truth? That's why lying is such a terrible thing. Not only is it sin, but it also destroys our ability to trust one another. Do you understand that?"*
>
> *"Yes, sir."*
>
> *"Your mother and I must make you understand the seriousness, not so much of skipping school, but of the lies you told. Your discipline will be that for the next three days, one for each day of your sin, you must go to the attic and stay there by yourself. You will even eat and sleep there."*
>
> *So young Steven headed off to the attic and the bed prepared for him there. It was a long evening for Steven and perhaps longer for Mom and Dad. Neither could eat, and*

for some reason when Dad tried to read the paper the words seemed foggy. Mom tried to sew, but couldn't see to thread the needle. Finally it was bedtime. About midnight as the father lay in bed thinking about how lonely and afraid Steven must be, he finally spoke to his wife, "Are you awake?"

"Yes. I can't sleep for thinking about Steven."

"Neither can I," answered Dad.

An hour later he queried again, "Are you asleep yet?"

"No," answered Mom, "I just can't sleep for thinking about Steven all alone up in the attic."

"Me neither."

Another hour passed. It was now 2:00 AM. "I can't stand this any longer!" murmured Dad as he climbed out of bed grabbing his pillow and a blanket. "I'm going to the attic."

He found Steven much as he expected: wide awake with tears in his eyes.

"Steven," said his father, "I can't take away the punishment for your lies because you must know the seriousness of what you have done. You must realize that sin, especially lying, has severe consequences. But your mother and I can't bear the thought of you being all alone here in the attic so I'm going to share your punishment with you."

Father lay down next to his son and the two put their arms around each other's necks. The tears on their cheeks mingled as they shared the same pillow and the same punishment…for three nights.[18]

This is exactly what Jesus did for us. He became a man and lived as one of us. He then took our sin and died on our cross. When He died, we died with Him (our old man), and when He rose again, we rose with Him (a new creation). He identified with us so that we could identify with Him.

And Jesus speaks this word to us just as He did to the disciples of His days of earthly visitation, *"And surely I am with you always"* (Matthew 28:20).

Rufus Mosely, while in prayer in the spring of 1926, received this word from the Lord: "I want you in Me all the time and I give you the keys." Rufus shared concerning this:

> *"I had realized, since Jesus manifested Himself and came within me and I had come out of the marvelous glory, that my great need was to take up my abode in Jesus and abide in Him without ever going out any more, just as He had taken up His abode in me to abide forever. We need to be in Him perpetually, as we need Him to be in us everlastingly. It is in the double union of Him in us and us in Him, and in the bearing of the fruit of the union, that we become like Him and joint heirs with Him in the services and in the inheritance of time and eternity. His full revelation in us and our full revelation in Him is our full salvation, redemption, and glorification.*
>
> *"I inferred rightly that His gift of the keys to me meant that He was giving me the secret of entering into and abiding in Him and in the Kingdom of Heaven, not that He was giving me authority over the church of God…I was even pulled down on my face at the feet of Jesus by the Spirit. It was while there that it was made known to me that the key to the door which is Jesus and to all doors, is love…Love is the condition and the bond of the union with Jesus. The only way you can be in the person and Kingdom of love is to be loving. If you love, you have everything. If you miss love, you miss everything. For in God's love is everything."*[19]

Jesus calls us to that place in Him, that place of love. *Remain in me, and I will remain in you. No branch can bear fruit by itself; it must remain in the vine. Neither can you bear fruit unless you remain in me* (John 15:4).

Love's Deepest Wisdom

We can learn much from the story of Solomon. At the beginning of his reign as king over all of Israel, Solomon had a dream. God appeared to him in the dream and told him to ask for whatever he wanted. The Lord was very pleased with what Solomon wanted and so gave this and much more to him. Solomon asked for a discerning heart to govern the people of God. Indeed, people came from all over the world to hear of his wisdom. Solomon ruled wisely. His kingdom experienced a time of the greatest wealth, the greatest conquest of land, the greatest commerce and civil developments, the greatest grandeur ever experienced by the nation of Israel.

After his initial blaze of glory, however, Solomon drifted far from the source of this blessing. He left the stream fed by the springs of living water and crashed into the jagged rocks along the treacherous shoreline. To his son, he left a divided kingdom, plummeting down the hillside of its former glory.

What happened?

> *King Solomon, however, loved many foreign women besides Pharaoh's daughter—Moabites, Ammonites, Edomites, Sidonians and Hittites. They were from nations about which the LORD told the Israelites, "You must not intermarry with them, because they will surely turn your hearts after their gods."* ***Nevertheless, Solomon held fast to them in love.*** *He had seven hundred wives of royal birth and three hundred concubines, and his wives turned his heart after other gods, and his heart was not fully devoted to the LORD his God, as the heart of David his father had been* (1 Kings 11:1-4 emphasis added).

Solomon *detached* from the Lord his God and *attached* to his wives. Solomon loved his wives more than he loved his God. Whatever we're attached to by our love is where we find our identification.

> *If I speak in the tongues of men and of angels, but have not love, I am only a resounding gong or a clanging cymbal. If I have the gift of prophecy and can fathom all mysteries and all knowledge, and if I have a faith that can move mountains, but have not love, I am nothing. If I give all I possess to the poor and surrender my body to the flames, but have not love, I gain nothing* (1 Corinthians 13:1-3).

The Lord praised the church in Ephesus for its hard work, good deeds, and perseverance. *Yet I hold this against you: You have forsaken your first love. Remember the height from which you have fallen! Repent and do the things you did at first. If you do not repent, I will come to you and remove your lamp stand from its place* (Revelation 2:4,5).

A lamp stand serves no purpose if it is not continuously filled with oil to burn and give off light. The fire of His presence, as we seek His face to love Him and be loved by Him, brings forth the oil of joy in knowing Him and we radiate His glory just as Moses did when He met with Him face to face in the wilderness.

Responding:

The one who loved you first and best wants to be your first love, the very center of your life to ground you and allow you to grow. Who's your first love? I hope it's the Lord. His love is perfect, pure, and powerful!

Did you ever write a love letter to a boyfriend or girlfriend? Do you remember the first "love letter" you wrote to someone when you were in elementary school? "I like you. Do you like me?" The

Bible is God's love letter to us. He is saying, "I love you! Do you love Me?"

I wrote to Kenny while he was away in college before we were married. He says that my letters were always dripping with honey. For some of us, it's easier to speak from our heart on paper. Maybe you'd like to write a love letter to the Lord today in your journal and let Him speak one back to you.

Perhaps you're a singer. Maybe you'd like to sing Him a love song. Let a song spring up from your heart. Sometimes we may express our love in a fun, playful way. At other times, we may express it with a sweet, soft melody.

Perhaps you're an artist. If so, maybe you would like to sketch or paint a picture to express your love to the Lord.

Maybe you would like to do something for someone else that would express your love to the Lord. Jesus told us that whatever we do for others, we are doing for Him.

Love without expression becomes cold, so fan the flames once again!

In our cocoon, we are discovering who we are from the one who created us and loves us with a perfect love.

Day Eleven:
Servant, Friend, Bride

Throughout the gospels, you never see James mentioned without his brother, John. The two brothers were fishermen with their father, Zebedee. When Jesus called them, together they left their father and his fishing boat to answer His call. James and John requested of Jesus that they might sit on His right and His left in His glory. Jesus, in answer to their request, taught them that the greatest in the kingdom of God was one who was a servant.

Let's look at the Philippians passage a little closer:

> *Your attitude should be the same as that of Christ Jesus: Who, being in very nature God, did not consider equality with God something to be grasped, but made himself nothing, taking the very nature of a servant, being made in human likeness. And being found in appearance as a man, he humbled himself and became obedient to death—even death on a cross! Therefore God exalted him to the highest place and gave him the name that is above every name, that at the name of Jesus every knee should bow, in heaven and on earth and under the earth, and every tongue confess that Jesus Christ is Lord, to the glory of God the Father* (Philippians 2:5-11).

Jesus humbled Himself. Jesus came as a man empowered by the Holy Spirit. Jesus came proclaiming that He could do nothing on His own but only in union with His Father, doing what He saw His Father doing and saying what He heard His Father saying. Jesus calls us to practice this same humility as we serve God and our fellow man. As Jesus humbled Himself completely, God exalted Him completely. James (not the apostle, but the brother of Jesus) instructs us to *humble yourselves before the Lord, and he will lift you up* (James 4:10). Andrew Murray defined humility as "the displacement of self by the enthronement of God."

And so, the first dimension of our attachment to the Lord is as a servant. The apostle Paul began his letter to the Romans, *Paul, a servant of Christ Jesus, called to be an apostle and set apart for the gospel of God* (Romans 1:1).

James was the first apostle to be killed for his faith. *He* [Herod] *had James, the brother of John, put to death with the sword* (Acts 12:2). Jesus said,

> "Greater love has no one than this, that he lay down his life for his friends. You are my friends if you do what I command. I no longer call you servants, because a servant does not know

his master's business. Instead, I have called you friends, for everything that I learned from my Father I have made known to you" (John 15:13-15).

When we yield to the Lord as His servants, He calls us His friends. James loved the Lord so much that he was willing to die for his friend. James was a friend of God. Abraham was another man who was called a friend of God. James laid down his life in one way, to physically die. Abraham laid down his life in another way, to believe God and follow Him to a new land that He would give to him and his descendants.

The second dimension of our attachment to the Lord is as a friend. The Lord calls us to

Offer your bodies as living sacrifices, holy and pleasing to God—this is your spiritual act of worship. Do not conform any longer to the pattern of this world, but be transformed by the renewing of your mind. Then you will be able to test and approve what God's will is—his good, pleasing and perfect will (Romans 12:1,2).

And what is God's good, pleasing and perfect will? I believe that the ultimate is to enter into the final dimension of attachment to the Lord as the Bride of Christ, one with Him forever. *"Come, I will show you the bride, the wife of the Lamb." And he carried me away in the Spirit to a mountain great and high, and showed me the Holy City, Jerusalem, coming down out of heaven from God. It shone with the glory of God, and its brilliance was like that of a very precious jewel, like a jasper, clear as crystal* (Revelation 21:9-11). John continues to describe this city, full of precious stones. I believe that we believers are the precious stones, the city of God.

Consequently, you are no longer foreigners and aliens, but fellow citizens with God's people and members of God's house-

hold, built on the foundation of the apostles and prophets, with Christ Jesus himself as the chief cornerstone. In him the whole building is joined together and rises to become a holy temple in the Lord. And in him you too are being built together to become a dwelling in which God lives by his Spirit (Ephesians 2:19-22).

We are the Lord's treasures. *For you are a people holy to the LORD your God. The LORD your God has chosen you out of all the peoples on the face of the earth to be his people, his treasured possession* (Deuteronomy 7:6). *"They will be mine,"* says the LORD Almighty, *"in the day when I make up my treasured possession"* (Malachi 3:17). *As you come to him, the living Stone —rejected by men but chosen by God and precious to him—you also, like living stones, are being built into a spiritual house to be a holy priesthood offering spiritual sacrifices acceptable to God through Jesus Christ* (1 Peter 2:4,5).

Before His crucifixion, Jesus prayed *"that all of them may be one, Father, just as you are in me and I am in you. May they also be in us so that the world may believe that you have sent me"* (John 17:21). Moses proclaimed to the children of Israel, *Hear, O Israel: The LORD your God, the LORD is one* (Deuteronomy 6:4). In the Kingdom of God, 1+1+1=1 (the Godhead). And when we join in the equation, one more added still equals one!

In John 15:5, Jesus tells us *"I am the vine; you are the branches. If a man remains in me and I in him, he will bear much fruit; apart from me you can do nothing."* Truly, *with God all things are possible.* Erin has a calling to minister to children. She and her husband have taken into their home foster children to nurture and rear as their own. They have three children of their own. One of the really neat things that Erin does is try and spend special time with each of the children. Her oldest daughter likes to sew, and so they have been spending time together making a quilt.

The Lord really spoke to me when I heard of this. In my life, it has been easier to do things *for* people rather than *with* people, and indeed there is a time for that and it is a very good thing. But there is a deeper place of fellowship in which we can do things *with* others, as well. Actually, this is real discipleship. Jesus chose his disciples *that they might be with him* (Mark 3:14) primarily, and then out of that relationship, He would send them out in ministry.

We don't leave one level of attachment and move to another, but rather each one deepens our relationship with the Lord. We always remain a servant of the Lord but become a friend also. We always remain a friend but also become a Bride.

Responding:

Only in fully abiding in the Lord can we actually find who we really are. As we lose our life in Him, we find our life. The whole premise of this book is that as we discover who Jesus is, we are changed into His likeness, who we were created to be, a son or daughter of God. In my life, I lived for many years not really knowing who I was. When I began to meditate on who God says I am in union with Him, then I began to walk in the freedom of being who He made me to be. And I'm continuing to discover that more and more each day.

Meditate on the following truths. Make them personal. Read them out loud as you proclaim the truth of God's Word.

> God is at work in me to will and to do of His good pleasure (Philippians 2:13).

> The good work that He began in me, He will carry on to completion (Philippians 1:6).

> I am crucified with Christ; nevertheless, I live, yet not I, but Christ lives in me and the life I now live, I live by the faith of the Son of God who loved me and gave Himself for me (Galatians 2:20).

God made Him who knew no sin to be sin for me, so that in Him I might become the righteousness of God (2 Corinthians 5:21).

I am a new creation in Christ; the old has gone and the new has come (2 Corinthians 5:17)!

In Him I live and move and have my being (Acts 17:28).

Christ is in me, the hope of glory (Colossians 1:27).

I am seated in heavenly places in Christ Jesus (Ephesians 2:6).

I am blessed with every spiritual blessing in Christ (Ephesians 1:3).

Nothing can separate me from God's love (Romans 8:38-39).

How great is the love the Father has lavished on me, that I should be called a child of God (1 John 3:1).

I am God's workmanship, created in Christ Jesus to do good works, which God prepared in advance for me to do (Ephesians 2:10).

I am more than a conqueror (Romans 8:37).

God always causes me to triumph in Christ (2 Corinthians 2:14).

As I look to the Lord, I am being transformed into His image, from glory to glory (2 Corinthians 3:18).

My life is now hidden with Christ in God (Colossians 3:3).

If God be for me, who can be against me? (Romans 8:31).

He is my refuge, my fortress, my God, in whom I trust (Psalm 91:2).

Unto Him be all praise and honor and glory and power, for ever and ever! (Revelation 5:13).

Does one of these truths speak to you especially today? Record it and any thoughts you may have about it in your journal.

As we are maturing in our cocoon, our relationship with the Lord continually deepens. Our union with Him provides all we need.

Chapter 9
Praise

"Nashon, yours is the tribe of Judah," continued Moses. Judah was the next son born to Leah and Jacob. Judah means *praise*, for Leah said, 'This time I will praise the Lord!' What a wise woman. Indeed the Lord had blessed her with yet another son. As we look to the east, we see the banner of Judah, the majestic lion. Yahweh has chosen the tribe of Judah to lead us as we move forward through this desert. Jacob spoke of a ruler who would come out of Judah. We look forward to that time and provision of our God."

Day Twelve:
The Lion of Judah

The male lion is truly an awesome animal recognized for its beauty and strength. It is called the king of the jungle. Its shaggy mane encircles its head like a splendid victor's wreath for a crown. One of the most distinctive features of the lion is its mighty roar. The lion's roar can be heard from a distance of up to five miles. How fitting that the insignia on the banner of the tribe of Judah, meaning *praise*, depicted the lion.

Lions live in family groups called prides. Interestingly enough, our *pride* often stands in the way of our praise. In the previous chapter, we looked at how Christ Jesus shows us the humility we need to practice as *He humbled himself and became obedient to death—even death on a cross* (Philippians 2:8). The cross of Christ stands in opposition to and in victory over our pride. The first chapter of 1 Corinthians speaks concerning this:

> *For the message of the cross is foolishness to those who are perishing, but to us who are being saved it is the power of God...But we preach Christ crucified: a stumbling block to Jews and foolishness to Gentiles, but to those whom God has called, both Jews and Greeks, Christ the power of God and the wisdom of God...Brothers, think of what you were when you were called. Not many of you were wise by human standards; not many were influential; not many were of noble birth. But God chose the foolish things of the world to shame the wise; God chose the weak things of the world to shame the strong. He chose the lowly things of this world and the despised things—and the things that are not—to nullify the things that are, so that no one may boast before him. It is because of him that you are in Christ Jesus, who has become for us wisdom from God—that is, our righteousness, holiness and redemption. Therefore, as it is written: "Let him who boasts boast in the Lord"* (1 Corinthians 1:18-31).

The gospel is the good news of the power of the cross for our lives. We rest in the power of the cross. It took our sin and gave us a Savior. It took our weakness and gave us strength. It took our poverty and gave us prosperity. It took our sickness and gave us health. It took our defeat and gave us victory. Isaiah tells us that our righteousness is as filthy rags. Christ clothes us with the garments of salvation. *For it is by grace you have been saved, through faith—and this not from yourselves, it is the gift of God—not of works, so that no one can boast. For we are God's workmanship, created in Christ Jesus to do good works, which God prepared in advance for us to do* (Ephesians 2:8-10). Our boast is not of ourselves, but in God alone. It is He who is worthy of our praise, and so we roar like the lion in praise to our God. Jesus said, *"But I, when I am lifted up from the earth, will draw all men to myself"* (John 12:32). Verse 33 explains what He was speaking of—the cross. *He said this to show the kind of death He was going to die.* Christ was lifted up on the cross. We lift Him up as we praise Him for all He has accomplished on that cross. Psalm 22:3 says, *Yet you are enthroned as the Holy One; you are the praise of Israel.* or *Yet you are holy, enthroned on the praises of Israel.*

Peter cautions us, *Be self-controlled and alert. Your enemy the devil prowls around like a roaring lion looking for someone to devour. Resist him, standing firm in the faith* (1 Peter 5:8,9). He is telling us to keep self in its proper place. Our enemy tempts us to exalt self and even tried that with Jesus as he tempted Him in the desert following His baptism. He was trying to lure Christ into taking matters into His own hands and exalting Himself rather than yielding to the Father's plan. Satan attempted to exalt himself, but it only brought his demise. The one we need to lift up is the Lord. He is the one worthy of our praise. True praise is a heart attitude of yielding to God—in everything. It is bowing our will, our understanding, our feelings to Him to exalt Him high above all. It is raising empty hands to Him that He might fill them with Himself.

The Lion Who Is the Lamb

In Revelation 4 and 5, John tells us of his vision of heaven. There around the throne are four living creatures who never cease praising the Lord and proclaiming His holiness. As the living creatures give praise to the Lord, the twenty-four elders also fall down before Him and worship Him. The one seated on the throne holds a sealed scroll. In this place filled with the glory of God, an angel calls out *"Who is worthy to break the seals and open the scroll?"* It appears that there is no one who can open the scroll and so John begins to weep. One of the elders stops him and points him to the Lion of the tribe of Judah, the Root of David. The elder proclaims the Lion's triumph and that *He* is able to open the scroll. Then, as John looks, the Lion has somehow transfigured and in its place stands a Lamb, looking as if it has been slain. All of heaven begins to worship this Lamb as He takes the scroll. The four living creatures and the twenty-four elders sing a new song: *"You are worthy to take the scroll and to open its seals, because you were slain, and with your blood you purchased men for God from every tribe and language and people and nation. You have made them to be a kingdom and priests to serve our God, and they will reign on the earth."* All of heaven joins in the singing: *"To him who sits on the throne and to the Lamb be praise and honor and glory and power, for ever and ever!"*

What seemed to be the greatest defeat, one who said He was the Son of God dying on a cross, turned out to be the greatest victory ever for all of mankind! That is the wisdom of God! And because of that victory, there is *nothing* that is hopeless, *nothing* that is impossible with God. And that is something to praise our God about. Even when we can't see the eventual outcome, when we can't perceive why things happen as they do, we can trust God. *But thanks be to God, who always leads us in triumphal procession in Christ and through us spreads everywhere the fragrance of the knowledge of him* (2 Corinthians 2:14).

Praising God actually lifts Him up in the situation and the circumstance. He stands above it. I remember a line in a song our choir sang one time: "What's over my head is under His feet." That is so true! He is worthy to be praised!

Responding:

The Lord had led us into a different experience with Him than what was accepted by the particular church in Rocky Mount where Kenny served as minister of youth and education. He submitted

Praise

his resignation, not knowing where we would go from there. This was a big fork in the road for us. We had lived in the parsonage. All of a sudden, we had no home and no job. A wonderful couple in the church offered what they had, a small tenant house on their farm. Some of our friends helped us to fix it up as much as possible, painting and cleaning, and so our family moved into it while we sought the Lord for direction for our lives. Rats and roaches were contending with us for the rights to live in the house. At night, we'd turn on some music, anything to drown out the scratching we heard in the walls. One night in particular, the Lord had a song bird sing to us outside our window. But we kept crying out to God, "Lord, get us out of this place!"

We have a tendency to be very hard on the Israelites about their murmuring and complaining but find ourselves doing the very same thing. And so, the Lord began to speak to us about thanking Him for this provision and praising Him in the midst of it. After we finally got the message and began practicing it, He opened up another house for us, an old farmhouse in the country, but a step up from where we were. He then gave Kenny a vision of a lighthouse shining onto troubled waters and called him into an evangelistic ministry to shine His healing light onto the troubled waters of people's troubled lives. What we thought was so devastating to our lives turned out to be an exciting new adventure.

Maybe there is a seemingly impossible or hopeless situation in your life or the life of someone you know. Go ahead and yield to the work of the cross in that situation. Confess any pride for trying to handle the situation in your own wisdom and strength. Give it to the Lord and begin to praise Him in it. Lift Him into the situation and watch Him work. Don't look at what you can see with your natural eyes, but look to Jesus and trust Him. All things are possible with Him.

Pour out the problem in your journal and then pour out the

praise to saturate it with the presence and power of God. This is certainly not a "magic wand" to suddenly change everything, but rather a real release to God when your praise is genuine.

Let this become a way of life to you in every situation you face. Determine to begin today to face everyday and every situation with praise.

Day Thirteen: John's Praise

It was the apostle John who seemed to be in the most intimate relationship with the Master. He spoke of himself in his gospel as *the disciple whom Jesus loved* (John 21:20) and also reminded the reader that it was he who sat closest to Jesus at their last supper and leaned back on Him to inquire of Him, *"Lord, who is going to betray you?"* Jesus had given John and his brother, James, *the name Boagernes, which means Sons of Thunder* (Mark 3:17). On one occasion, Jesus and his disciples were passing through Samaria. He sent messengers on ahead to prepare a place for them to stay, but they were not welcomed in this village. James and John wanted to *call fire down from heaven to destroy them, but Jesus rebuked them and they went to another village* (Luke 9:54,55). John was certainly passionate about His Lord!

In John's gospel, we see an awesome picture of Jesus as we hear His proclamations of Himself as the I AM. John's gospel is like a photo album in which John was sharing these snapshots of his beloved Master, glimpses he saw as he was with Him daily over the course of those three years of ministry. We see Jesus as the Bread of Life (John 6:35), the Light of the world (John 8:12), the Gate for the sheep (John 10:7), the Good Shepherd (John 10:11), the Resurrection and the Life (John 11:25), the Way, the Truth, and the Life (John 14:6), and the True Vine (John 15:1).

Even after Jesus' ascension into heaven, John continued to see

Praise

Jesus and reveal Him. John was exiled to the Isle of Patmos. There, as he continued to lean on his Master, he was transported in the spirit to see Him once again. He records the vision for us in Revelation 1:

> *I turned around to see the voice that was speaking to me. And when I turned I saw seven golden lamp stands, and among the lamp stands was someone, "like a son of man," dressed in a robe reaching down to his feet and with a golden sash around his chest. His head and hair were white like wool, as white as snow, and his eyes were like blazing fire. His feet were like bronze glowing in a furnace, and his voice was like the sound of rushing waters. In his right hand he held seven stars, and out of his mouth came a sharp double-edged sword. His face was like the sun shining in all its brilliance.*
>
> *When I saw him, I fell at his feet as though dead. Then he placed his right hand on me and said: "Do not be afraid. I am the First and the Last. I am the Living One; I was dead, and behold I am alive for ever and ever! And I hold the keys of death and Hades."*

Again, in Revelation 19, John sees Jesus and paints this picture for us to see:

> *I saw heaven standing open and there before me was a white horse, whose rider is called Faithful and True. With justice he judges and makes war. His eyes are like blazing fire, and on his head are many crowns. He has a name written on him that no one knows but he himself. He is dressed in a robe dipped in blood, and his name is the Word of God. The armies of heaven were following him, riding on white horses and dressed in fine linen, white and clean. Out of his mouth comes a sharp sword with which to strike down the nations. "He will*

rule them with an iron scepter." He treads the winepress of the fury of the wrath of God Almighty. On his robe and on his thigh he has this name written: KING OF KINGS AND LORD OF LORDS."

What an awesome picture John gives us of Jesus Christ, one that produces thunderous praise! The more that we know Him, the more praise erupts from deep within our being—toward Him and about Him. Praise is not just a type of song we sing or word we express, but praise is an attitude coming from the heart. Genuine praise comes from a heart that genuinely recognizes and celebrates who God is. Real praise is not a form, but a deep abiding faith being expressed.

Responding:

Praise comes as a natural response when we see and know Jesus for who He is. Take a few moments and look into John's gospel at the scripture surrounding each of the proclamations of who Jesus is that I stated in today's journey. Have you experienced Jesus personally in any of these aspects of who He is? You might want to remember these and note them in your journal as you praise Him once again for who He is in your life. It isn't always easy to see Jesus clearly in the dim light of a dark cocoon but He is all around us nonetheless.

I would also encourage you to read a classic book about praise, *Prison to Praise* by Merlin Corothers.

Praise becomes such a natural response as we see God in our cocoon. The more we know Him, the more we love Him and appreciate His care for us and His rule and reign over His creation.

Chapter 10
He Has Vindicated

"Ahiezer, son of Ammishaddai, come close, my son," beckoned Moses. "Your tribe of Dan seems to be the largest of the tribes. We shall see as we number them as the Lord is instructing us. But something concerns me, Ahiezer. There seems to be an unrest within your people. What do you see, my son?"

"I understand your concern, my lord," replied Ahiezer. "I, too, can see the unrest. There are certain families who tend to be easily swayed from following G_d. I make it my duty to try and persuade them in the right direction. Perhaps if you or Aaron would be inclined to speak to them on behalf of our G_d?"

"Yes, my son," replied Moses, and turning to the group, he continued to share, "Rachel saw how fruitful her sister Leah had been and she became jealous of her. She had not been able to conceive a child, so she plotted that she could have offspring through her maidservant, Bilhah. Rachel gave Bilhah to her husband Jacob. Bilhah conceived and bore a son. Rachel named the child Dan, for she said, *"God has vindicated me."* And so we have this large company of Danites today."

Day Fourteen:
Justice Is Served

In an article titled "Justice, Law, and Legalism—Part 1," an Orthodox Jewish rabbi wrote the following:

"The purpose of justice within the kingdom is to ensure that each child of God receives every right and ounce of benefit for which the Lord Jesus Christ died. In order to accomplish this, the system of justice in the kingdom, much like in our secular justice systems, is supposed to set the law and standard of living and relating to one another…Law is a part of justice. Law is necessary for life; without law there is not a standard by which we live. Most importantly though, law does not equal legalism; law and legalism are not the same thing."[20]

In John 8:1-11, John tells the story of a woman caught in adultery. The woman was brought into the temple courts by the teachers of the Law and the Pharisees. They had the woman stand before Jesus, reminded Him of the Law to stone such a one, and asked Him what He would say about the matter. Jesus stooped down and began writing on the ground. There have been many ideas about what Jesus wrote. I don't know, but I'm sure it was very significant. Everything that Jesus did was significant. At any rate, the Pharisees and teachers continued to question Jesus. Eventually He rose and responded, instructing any who were without sin to cast the first stone. He then stooped down and continued writing. One by one, each of the accusers departed, until only Jesus was standing before the woman. He stood up once again and asked her if there were any accusers left, to which she responded, "No one, sir." *"Then neither do I condemn you," Jesus declared. "Go now and leave your life of sin."*

The woman's sin was brought into the light. The Pharisees saw that sin and were ready to meet it with legalism and condemnation. Jesus certainly knew the woman's sin, for He could see into her heart. Jesus, however, responded with love and mercy rather than condemnation. Surely He was not overlooking justice, for God is just. I rather believe that He was looking forward to His sin offering of Himself, the perfect spotless Lamb, on the cross He was

He Has Vindicated

to bear. *For God so loved the world that he gave his one and only Son, that whoever believes in him shall not perish but have eternal life. For God did not send his Son into the world to condemn the world, but to save the world through him* (John 3:16,17).

Jesus responded in the same way to the woman at the well. He saw her life, but did not use that discernment to condemn her. Rather, He offered her living water to meet the deep need of her heart. He offers us that same living water today. Come and drink!

> *Who will bring any charge against those whom God has chosen? It is God who justifies. Who is he that condemns? Christ Jesus who died—more than that, who was raised to life—is at the right hand of God and is also interceding for us* (Romans 8:33,34).

God, in Jesus Christ, sees our sin. He sees our lack, but rather than condemning us for our lack, He supplies to us what is lacking. Jesus Christ has brought our vindication, our justification, as our intercessor. God still remembered that "dead butterfly" that needed resurrection. Instead of seeing what we had become, He saw what we were created to be. He knew our potential if we could but connect once again with Him and receive His resurrection life, His breath in us. *God's heart's desire is not and never has been condemnation; His heart's desire is restoration!*

Jesus Christ is our justification. Jesus' sacrifice totally satisfied the claims of God's justice. But it doesn't stop there. Romans 4:25 in the Amplified Version reads *Who was betrayed and put to death because of our misdeeds and was raised to secure our justification—our acquittal, and to make our account balance, absolving us from all guilt before God.* Here the analogy of *"making our account balance"* helps us to see that it wasn't enough for God to simply do away with the sin, but something had to be deposited in its place. *God made him*

 Cocoon

who had no sin to be sin for us, so that in him we might become the righteousness of God (2 Corinthians 5:21).

We see this further stated in 2 Peter 1:3, which says, *His divine power has given us everything we need for life and godliness through our knowledge of him who called us by his own glory and goodness.* This *"knowledge of him"* is that intimate connection we have with Him in which He imparts to us what we were lacking.

> *We know very well that we are not set right with God by rule keeping but only through personal faith in Jesus Christ. How do we know? We tried it-and we had the best system of rules the world has ever seen! Convinced that no human being can please God by self-improvement, we believed in Jesus as the Messiah so that we might be set right before God by trusting in the Messiah, not by trying to be good* (Galatians 2:16 The Message).

Jesus Himself said that *There is only One who is good* (Matthew 19:17). Only in union with Him can we receive and experience that goodness. If you will look back at the original creation in the book of Genesis, you will find that God has pronounced what He created as good and especially on the sixth day when man was created *God saw all that he had made, and it was very good* (Genesis 1:31). God remembers that goodness and wants to bring it out again!

Jesus says, *"Do not think that I have come to abolish the Law or the Prophets; I have not come to abolish them but to fulfill them"* (Matthew 5:17).

Responding:

In Jesus' encounter with the Pharisees and teachers of the Law in their dealings with the woman caught in adultery, we see the tendency that we humans have of focusing on others' shortcomings

He Has Vindicated

and failures rather than our own. Jesus was quick to point them back to themselves. Matthew records Jesus' teaching in chapter 7 of his gospel:

Do not judge, or you too will be judged. For in the same way you judge others, you will be judged, and with the measure you use, it will be measured to you. Why do you look at the speck of sawdust in your brother's eye and pay no attention to the plank in your own eye? How can you say to your brother, 'Let me take the speck out of your eye,' when all the time there is a plank in your own eye? You hypocrite, first take the plank out of your own eye, and then you will see clearly to remove the speck from your brother's eye.

Perhaps the plank in our own eye is *condemnation*, and we need to replace it with *restoration*. Our heart motivation is so very important in our dealings with others. When our hearts are filled with love, we can then help our brothers and sisters by shining the light in their darkness.

Each of us has our own story that God is writing of our lives and that we are living out by His grace. We cannot write anyone else's story, and we really err when we try. On the shores of the Sea of Galilee after His resurrection, Jesus restored the apostle Peter in His love for him and His call to him. Following this encounter with Jesus, Peter turned and saw the apostle John and asked Jesus, *"Lord, what about him?" Jesus answered, "If I want him to remain alive until I return, what is that to you? You must follow me"* (John 21:21,22).

My husband and I had not seen an old friend for a number of years. We visited in his home, reminiscing about old times and catching up on where we were now. Our friend was not experiencing a closeness in his fellowship with the Lord at the time and we got into a discussion about the scriptures. We began to "argue" (in a friendly manner, of course) about the scriptures. Our friend instantly put up walls and resisted anything we were trying to share with him. The Holy Spirit nudged me, and I began to share what I had experienced in my own life relative to the scriptural truth we were discussing. I saw our friend's defenses fall and he was immediately more receptive to what we had to share.

Jesus is the *Word made flesh* (John 1:14). We are born again by that Word and that Word is deposited within us so that we can "flesh it out" also. *Therefore, there is now no condemnation for those who are in Christ Jesus, because through Christ Jesus the law of the Spirit of life set me free from the law of sin and death* (Romans 8:1). Jesus told His disciples and the other believers to wait in Jerusalem for the gift of the Father, a baptism of the Holy Spirit. Concerning this, He told them, *"But you will receive power when the Holy Spirit comes on you; and you will be my witnesses in Jerusalem, and in all Judea and Samaria, and to the ends of the earth"* (Acts 1:8). No one else but you can tell your story. Your story is also His story of His work in your life, the difference He has made. You are His witness as you testify of the things you have seen and heard in your walk with Him. What an opportunity we have to shine the light of Jesus!

Maybe there are those today waiting in the darkness for someone to shine a little light on their paths. Will you be that witness to them of who Christ is in your life? Remember, people don't need condemnation, but restoration. Let Christ fill you with His love and then pour it out on others who need that love. What an opportunity for folks lacking in their experience of the Lord in a particular area of their lives to find that Jesus has all they need to fill that void.

Maybe the Lord is bringing those to your mind and heart right now who need to experience more of Him. Begin to pray for them. Journal your impressions. As the Holy Spirit leads, you may share with them and with any others that may cross your path today.

He Has Vindicated

But the fruit of the Spirit is love, joy, peace, patience, kindness, goodness, faithfulness, gentleness and self-control. Against such things there is no law...Since we live by the Spirit, let us keep in step with the Spirit...Brothers, if someone is caught in a sin, you who are spiritual should restore him gently. But watch yourself, or you also may be tempted. Carry each other's burdens and in this way you will fulfill the law of Christ. If anyone thinks he is something when he is nothing, he deceives himself. Each one should test his own actions. Then he can take pride in himself, without comparing himself to somebody else, for each one should carry his own load (Galatians 5:22-6:5).

Day Fifteen: Horses

Horses are truly majestic creatures, aren't they? My husband loves to watch movies with horses in them, whether he's hearing the gallop of the posse in the old westerns, seeing the beautiful classic *Black Beauty*, or witnessing the power and strength of the modern day race horse. Throughout Israel's history, whenever they were faced with enemy armies, at times their kings would depend on the might of the horses of various allies to strengthen their defense. The Lord rebuked His people for depending on horses and chariots rather than on Him. David, in Psalm 20:7, wrote, *Some trust in chariots and some in horses, but we trust in the name of the LORD our God.*

Rachel looked at her own inability to conceive a child and cried out for her husband to do something about it. Jacob's response to her was, *"Am I in the place of God, who has kept you from having children?"* Then Rachel came up with her own plan to have a child through her maidservant. Might she have learned from her predecessor Sarah?

It is quite interesting to hear Jacob's blessing to his son, Dan, in Genesis 49:16,17: *Dan will provide justice for his people as one of the tribes of Israel. Dan will be a serpent by the roadside, a viper along the path, that bites the horse's heels so that its rider tumbles backward. I look for your deliverance, O LORD.*

One of the apostles Jesus called to follow Him was Philip. His name means *"lover of horses."* John's gospel gives us some insight into this apostle. On one occasion, a great crowd of people had followed Jesus. *When Jesus looked up and saw a great crowd coming toward him, he said to Philip, "Where shall we buy bread for these people to eat?" He asked this only to test him, for he already had in mind what he was going to do. Philip answered Him, "Eight months' wages would not buy enough bread for each one to have a bite!"*

Let's not be too hard on Philip. He was simply responding in a natural way. He was looking to *"horses"* for the provision, the natural means to provide. In the Bible, this is sometimes referred to as the "arm of flesh."

On another occasion, Jesus was speaking to His disciples.

> *Jesus answered, "I am the way and the truth and the life. No one comes to the Father except through me. If you really knew me, you would know my Father as well. From now on, you do know him and have seen him."*
>
> *Philip said, "Lord, show us the Father and that will be enough for us."*
>
> *Jesus answered: "Don't you know me, Philip, even after I have been among you such a long time? Anyone who has seen me has seen the Father. How can you say, 'Show us the Father'?"*

Once again, Philip needed to look a little closer. He needed to see beyond the natural, to look with the eyes of the spirit. He needed to surrender the "arm of the flesh" as empty and devoid of power and instead be infused with power from on high. *No eye has seen,*

He Has Vindicated

no ear has heard, no mind has conceived what God has prepared for those who love him" but God has revealed it to us by his Spirit (1 Corinthians 2:9,10).

The prophet Elisha and his servant were in Dothan. Israel was at war with Aram. Elisha was hearing from God about the plans of the enemy and alerting the king of Israel each time the enemy advanced so that he was prepared to meet them. The king of Aram grew frustrated and sent officers to find Elisha to capture him. Finding him in Dothan, the king sent a strong force of horses and chariots and surrounded the city.

> *"Oh, my lord, what shall we do?" the servant asked.*
> *"Don't be afraid," the prophet answered. "Those who are with us are more than those who are with them."*
> *And Elisha prayed, "O LORD, open his eyes so he may see." Then the LORD opened the servant's eyes, and he looked and saw the hills full of horses and chariots of fire all around Elisha* (2 Kings 6:15-17).

Needless to say, God had the last word in this situation. You can read about the whole story in 2 Kings 6.

Later on, Rachel did conceive and had two boys of her own. They were Joseph, his name meaning *may He add*, and Benjamin, his name meaning *son of my right hand*. In other chapters we will look at these two sons. God did add a son, even two sons, in His time. The *"right hand"* is referred to as *strength*. When we look to the Lord, He will supply His strength in our time of need. We can see this ultimately fulfilled in Jesus Christ in Revelation 19:11-16.

> *I saw heaven standing open and there before me was a white horse, whose rider is called Faithful and True. With **justice** he judges and makes war. His eyes are like blazing fire, and on his head are many crowns. He has a name written on him that no ones knows but he himself. He is dressed in a robe*

 Cocoon

> *dipped in blood, and his name is the Word of God. The armies of heaven were following him, riding on white horses and dressed in fine linen, white and clean. Out of his mouth comes a sharp sword with which to strike down the nations. "He will rule them with an iron scepter." He treads the winepress of the fury of the wrath of God Almighty. On his robe and on his thigh he has the name written: KING OF KINGS AND LORD OF LORDS* (emphasis added).

Jesus is riding the white horse. He alone can redeem the arm of flesh and cause it to be a vessel fit to serve the King of Kings and Lord of Lords. True justice comes from God in His time. We must rest in Him and wait upon His timing. He will make it right in the end!

Responding:

Are you trusting any "horses"?

There was a misunderstanding between our pastor and some of the folks in the church. I really wanted to be a "peacemaker" in the situation, and so I tried to talk to both sides and do what I could to help. I took the burden upon myself to bring forth the peace. Now there's nothing wrong with wanting to be a peacemaker, and sometimes God may work through us to accomplish that goal, but on this occasion, I was trying to do too much in my own strength and leaning too much on my own understanding. I was leaning on the "arm of flesh." That arm soon gave way, and I found myself almost ready for a nervous breakdown. I had never called my husband and asked him to come home from a ministry engagement, but I had to call him. For three days, I could not do even the menial tasks needed to tend to my two boys and my home responsibilities. My husband lovingly took up the slack, and I sought the Lord. My nerves were so fraught that I awakened in the night with my legs feeling numb. Kenny and I would get up out of bed and

He Has Vindicated

walk together around the room speaking the name of the Lord and praising Him. I needed to focus on the Lord once again. He needed to be the center of my life and bring everything back into balance. I could then rest in the Lord.

At the time, we had a little Pomeranian dog named Chuckles. (He was named by our two boys after a G.I. Joe figure.) I put Chuckles on a leash and walked him around the block so he could "take care of business." The Lord spoke to me so resolutely, "I just want to spend time with you just like you're spending time with your dog." If I had taken more time with Him instead of leaning on myself, He could have spoken to me and helped me "take care of business" in a far different manner, one much more fruitful for everyone involved. Leaning on the "arm of flesh" can cause you to be seriously wounded or possibly killed! Thanks be to God—He takes our mess and gives us His message and heals us.

It is sometimes interesting how God works in our lives to bring about our healing. One afternoon during this time, I turned on the TV and watched an episode of "Laverne and Shirley," trying to "lighten up" and get my mind onto something else. Something the girls from the 1950s sitcom said really hit me, caused me to laugh, and that laughter released healing in me. God works in and through everything!

Are there instances in your life in which you need to "come up higher" and trust in the Lord rather than your own understanding or effort? Ask the Lord to show you. Record what you hear in your journal. Give these things to Him and watch Him work in them.

Day Sixteen:
Our Redeemer

One of the amazing things about the Lord and His work in our lives is that no matter how big a mess we make, He can always redeem it and bring good out of it. No matter how bad things may look, He is still at work to bring forth His purposes of good for all. *And we know that in all things God works for the good of those who love him, who have been called according to his purpose. For those God foreknew he also predestined to be conformed to the likeness of his Son* (Romans 8:28,29). Even in such a situation as the birth of Dan, even though the perfect circumstances may not have surrounded his birth, God loved Dan and foreknew all the circumstances and released His work of redemption to bring Dan to be who He created him to be. And this is true of every child born—all the circumstances may not be perfect concerning every child's birth, but God loves that child. He is the one who created that child, and He has a plan and purpose for that child.

Even our adversary, Satan, is but a pawn in the hands of God. Just look at the story of Job. I know—Job's story is not the thriller that makes us feel good, at least not until the end. Who was this fellow?

> *In the land of Uz there lived a man whose name was Job. This man was blameless and upright; he feared God and shunned evil. He had seven sons and three daughters, and he owned seven thousand sheep, three thousand camels, five hundred yoke of oxen and five hundred donkeys, and had a large number of servants. He was the greatest man among all the people of the East* (Job 1:1-3).

Job was a "good" man, and bad things began to happen to him. We have the privilege and insight to see behind the scenes. Satan wanted to test Job and accuse him before God. (That's who he is, the accuser of the brethren.) God allowed Satan to test him but not to take his life. In the first test, all of Job's animals, his servants, and even his children were taken or killed. What was Job's response?

> *At this, Job got up and tore his robe and shaved his head. Then he fell to the ground in worship and said: "Naked I*

came from my mother's womb, and naked I will depart. The LORD gave and the LORD has taken away; may the name of the LORD be praised." In all this, Job did not sin by charging God with wrongdoing (Job 1:20-22).

The second test involved Job's own body, painful sores from head to toe. He was miserable. *His wife said to him, "Are you still holding on to your integrity? Curse God and die!"* It is especially hard for us to see others suffering and not be able to do anything that might help them. *He replied, "You are talking like a foolish woman. Shall we accept good from God, and not trouble?" In all this, Job did not sin in what he said* (Job 2:9,10).

Three of Job's friends came to see him, intending to sympathize with him and comfort him. They were so troubled by what they saw that they wept and sat with him for seven days and nights without even speaking. And as they sat, they attempted to find an answer to the age-old question, "Why?" And they came up with answers according to their own understanding (or lack thereof).

After everyone else had exhausted their insights, God spoke to Job. *Trust in the LORD with all your heart and lean not on your own understanding; in all your ways acknowledge him, and he will make your paths straight* (Proverbs 3:5,6). Notice how sometimes God doesn't really answer your question directly, but points you to what He wants you to focus on. Perhaps it's a matter of asking the right question. The right question was not "Why?" but rather "Who?" Who can I turn to when life is going absolutely crazy? Who can save me from any of this hell that is coming at me?

> *Then Job replied to the LORD: "I know that you can do all things; no plan of yours can be thwarted. You asked, 'Who is this that obscures my counsel without knowledge?' Surely I spoke of things I did not understand, things too wonderful for me to know. You said, 'Listen now, and I will speak; I will*

question you, and you shall answer me.' My ears had heard of you but now my eyes have seen you. Therefore I despise myself and repent in dust and ashes" (Job 42:1-6).

In the midst of all Job's pain, he saw God in a way he had not seen Him before. That revelation brought healing in his life and his body. Job's friends were called upon to repent of their wrong speaking. Job was called upon to pray for his friends. *After Job had prayed for his friends, the LORD made him prosperous again and gave him twice as much as he had before…The LORD blessed the latter part of Job's life more than the first* (Job 42:10,12).

We can say with Job, *"**I know that my Redeemer lives**, and that in the end he will stand upon the earth. And after my skin has been destroyed, yet in my flesh I will see God; I myself will see him with my own eyes—I and not another. How my heart yearns within me"* (Job 19:25-27 emphasis added.)

> *And those he predestined, he also called; those he called, he also justified; those he justified, he also glorified. What, then, shall we say in response to this? If God is for us, who can be against us? He who did not spare his own Son, but gave him up for us all—how will he not also, along with him, graciously give us all things? Who will bring any charge against those whom God has chosen? It is God who justifies. Who is he that condemns? Christ Jesus, who died—more than that, who was raised to life—is at the right hand of God and is also interceding for us. Who shall separate us from the love of Christ? Shall trouble or hardship or persecution or famine or nakedness or danger or sword? As it is written: "For your sake we face death all day long; we are considered as sheep to be slaughtered." No, in all these things we are more than conquerors through him who loved us. For I am convinced that neither death nor life, neither angels nor demons, neither the*

...rubs encircling an operating table. God was blowing His anointing from His hands down onto the group. This vision was my confirmation that I was to go ahead with the operation to remove the tumor.

Just before my scheduled surgery, some friends Kenny had met in Delaware invited us to spend a few days in their condo at the beach. While there, the couple shared their experience with his mother who had been diagnosed with a brain tumor. Before her surgery, her church prayed for her. When the doctors went in to remove the tumor, they found it floating, so it could be removed easily. She recuperated much sooner than they had anticipated, with no problems. This encouraging word, as well as a wonderful time of relaxation at the beach, was just the preparation I needed for what was ahead.

The day came to get rid of this thing that had invaded my body. When the anesthesiologist began sharing all that they would be doing, I trembled at the thought of it all, but we had taken care of that fear and I remembered the vision of the Lord's hands and my peace returned. The surgery lasted for eight hours. One of the nurses had brought a recording of Steve Green singing "To God and God Alone" in Spanish for Dr. Martinez, who was Spanish, to listen to in the operating room. Sometime during the surgery, the nurse came out and told Kenny that they were having revival in there. Kenny thought, "With my wife's head open?" But what an awesome presence of the Lord we experienced through the whole process. The doctor got all of the tumor, for which we were very grateful!

I spent two days in ICU. There was such a peace that I experienced. I remember it being a place of peaceful fluffy clouds where I seemed to be drifting. If I had gone on to be with the Lord it would have been fine, and if I came back it would have been fine— there was just so much peace! Moved into a private room, I con-

He Has Vindicated

tinued the healing process. I was not prepared for all that I had to deal with. My body had been affected as if I had suffered a stroke. My equilibrium was all out of balance. When I first tried to walk, it felt as if the whole room were spinning. Kenny was so good to me during this time. He even put on my makeup for me to try and help lift my spirits. One morning when he came into the room, he noticed that I was especially discouraged. He went into the hall and found the physician's assistant. She came and talked with us, sharing the physical information we needed and also prayed with us and encouraged us in the strength of the Lord. God was working at every turn! Every day I got stronger and stronger. I really felt as if I had found that *secret place* that the Bible talks about in Psalm 91. There was such a closeness to the Lord! God was doing a mighty work in me.

As Kenny drove me home, we listened to and sang along with the Brooklyn Tabernacle Choir singing "Praise Him." Tears of gratitude were streaming down both our faces. My recuperation took a little time even after I got home. It was not easy. There were days when I was very frustrated and depressed, but overall I experienced the faithfulness and strength of the Lord. We had moved back to my hometown and lived beside my sister and her family and right up the road from my mother and dad. During this time, my sister, a nurse, came over every day and cleaned my incision until it healed. My mother kept our clothes clean. The folks in our church, our families, and some wonderful friends kept us well fed and greatly encouraged. And Kenny and I grew closer than we had ever been as he remained right by my side through it all. I said to him, "I never knew God loves me so much; I never knew my friends and family love me so much; I never knew you love me so much." How wonderful it is to be loved!

God is so good! Through all this experience, my vision was expanded tremendously of Him and of His Body. I learned to rest in Him. I had always been the one who was busy, busy, busy doing for everyone else, but I didn't let others do for me. What a lesson I learned as so many were so kind in so many ways. I wouldn't want to go through this experience again, but the lessons I learned were certainly worth every minute of it all. When the Lord heals, He goes much deeper than just our physical bodies. He wants to restore us to wholeness in Him.

Are you or someone close to you experiencing a great trial in your life right now? Yield to the work of the Lord in the midst of it. Let Him do that great work in you that He desires to bring you into more wholeness in your life. Pray for others who are experiencing trials to receive that complete and deep healing that the Lord wants to minister to them. Within our cocoon, we may not understand all that is happening in our lives or the lives of others around us, but we can trust God and see Him in ways that we never have before. As we do, we will experience life in greater ways than ever before! Do you need to talk to the Lord about some of those experiences as you write in your journal today? Also record His responses. God desires restoration in our lives whenever we fall short of His abundant life for us. He does not condemn, but redeems and continues to make us whole. Even as I have written of my experiences once again, I sense even greater healing being released and I am reminded once again of God's great love and care for us. Bless you!

Chapter 11
My Struggle

Moses continued his discourse to the tribal leaders. "Rachel so wanted to continue to bring forth children for her husband, Jacob. Especially did she see her lack as she looked at the fruitfulness of her sister, Leah. And so she once again gave her servant, Bilhah, to Jacob. Bilhah conceived and bore Jacob another son. Rachel named this son, Naphtali, *my struggle*. Funny how we sense G-d's call on our lives and try to bring that forth in our own way. But He always has a better plan and a better way," spoke Moses, the man of G-d. "Indeed I tried to do the same. When I had learned that I was a Hebrew by birth rather than an Egyptian even though brought up in the palace of Egypt, things began to stir in me. I looked upon my people and saw their slavery to the Egyptians. I felt their pain, and I wanted to see them free. I could not believe that this was to be their lot in life. One day I saw an Egyptian beating one of the Hebrews. I could stand it no longer. A fierce anger rose in me. I killed the Egyptian and hid his body in the sand. I soon learned that this act had become known by others. Even the Pharaoh got wind of it. I was frightened and ran for my life. Some help I turned out to be. Out into this desert I ran, feeling the frustration of my soul. I had wanted to help my people, but here I was far from them. G-d had a different plan, however," continued Moses. "He was calling me to be a deliverer for my people, but in a far different way than I could have planned. His way was much more fruitful. Here we are this day on our way to the Promised Land. G-d indeed had a better plan for His people, Israel."

"Through Rachel's struggle, Jacob's family continued to grow larger," said Aaron.

"G-d is always at work in the midst of our struggles," responded Moses.

Day Seventeen:
Overcoming

Following the fall in the Garden of Eden, mankind was immediately thrown into a struggle. When we ate of the tree of the knowledge of good and evil, we began to experience that struggle.

A lot of the books we read and the movies we see are concerned with the age-old battle between good and evil—whether it's cowboys and villains in the old westerns or Darth Vader and Luke Skywalker in the *Star Wars* saga. From the beginning, God's enemy, Satan, has tried to get back at Him through His creation, mankind. Since we are His children, God's enemy is our enemy. And he definitely is a real enemy. Will we yield to the deception of this enemy as Adam and Eve did in the Garden of Eden, or will we resist him and remain true to God as Christ did in the Garden of Gethsemane? How we keep our garden will determine the fruit we bear.

In the final book of the Bible, Revelation 12:10-11, we see how the enemy is overcome.

> *Then I heard a loud voice in heaven say: "Now have come the salvation and the power and the kingdom of our God, and the authority of his Christ. For the accuser of our brothers, who accuses them before our God day and night, has been hurled down. They overcame him by the blood of the Lamb, and by the word of their testimony; they did not love their lives so much as to shrink from death.*

This scripture reveals three things that enable us to overcome the enemy, which are as follows:
1) the blood of the Lamb
2) the word of their testimony
3) they did not love their lives so much as to shrink from death.

Over the next few days, we will explore these three things. The first is the blood of the Lamb.

Nathanael (Bartholomew)—"God has given"

In John's gospel, we are given a glimpse of the disciple called Nathanael (also called Bartholomew).

> *Philip, like Andrew and Peter, was from the town of Bethsaida. Philip found Nathanael and told him, "We have found the one Moses wrote about in the Law, and about whom the prophets also wrote—Jesus of Nazareth, the son of Joseph."*
>
> *"Nazareth! Can anything good come from there?" Nathanael asked.*
>
> *"Come and see," said Philip.*
>
> *When Jesus saw Nathanael approaching, he said of him, "Here is a true Israelite, in whom there is nothing false."*
>
> *"How do you know me?" Nathanael asked.*
>
> *Jesus answered, "I saw you while you were still under the fig tree before Philip called you."*
>
> *Then Nathanael declared, "Rabbi, you are the Son of God; you are the King of Israel."*
>
> *Jesus said, "You believe because I told you I saw you under the fig tree. You shall see greater things than that." He then added, "I tell you the truth, you shall see heaven open, and the angels of God ascending and descending on the Son of Man"* (John 1:44-51).

This is the only personal glimpse we see of the disciple Nathanael, but much is said here. Jesus sees the sincere seeking of Nathanael after the things of God, for He says to him, *"Here is a true Israelite, in whom there is nothing false."* There is great significance that Jesus first saw Nathanael *"still under the fig tree."* If we look back into the Garden of Eden, we see fig leaves first mentioned as Adam and Eve attempted to cover their nakedness after their disobedience. The fig leaves were not a sufficient covering, and God made garments of animal skins to cover them instead. Obviously, He had to kill the animals to get their skins to use in this way. Blood was shed. To atone for the sin of mankind, blood was the only sacrifice that was sufficient. From the first mention of fig leaves in the garden, they have come to be understood as something standing for our religiosity, our own attempts to attain a right standing before God.

We are also reminded of Jesus cursing the fig tree because no fruit was found on it. Jesus saw Nathanael as a sincere seeker of God who had followed the ways taught to him as an Israelite. In response to Jesus' "word of knowledge" to him, Nathanael proclaimed, *"Rabbi, you are the Son of God; you are the King of Israel."* Though he did not understand this as of yet, something deep in Nathanael caught site of the hope that Jesus Christ who stood before him was indeed the one he had been seeking for the reality of true fulfillment and reconciliation to God. Jesus then assured him of a new revelation of gaining an entrance into those heavenly places of right standing before God.

Try as we might, the Word of God reminds us that our own righteousness is as "filthy rags." *All of us have become like one who is unclean, and all our righteous acts are like filthy rags; we all shrivel up like a leaf, and like the wind our sins sweep us away* (Isaiah 64:6). Nathanael's name means *God has given*. What we could not attain ourselves, God has given to us through His Son, Jesus Christ. *The reason the Son of God appeared was to destroy the devil's work* (1 John 3:8). The "accuser of the brethren" has been defeated.

The book of Hebrews is rich in proclaiming the new covenant we have in Christ. These excerpts further clarify what we are sharing:

> *When Christ came as high priest of good things that are already here, he went through the greater and more perfect tabernacle that is not man-made, that is to say, not a part of this creation. He did not enter by means of the blood of goats and calves; but he entered the Most Holy Place once for all by his own blood, having obtained eternal redemption. The blood of goats and bulls and the ashes of a heifer sprinkled on those who are ceremonially unclean sanctify them so that they are outwardly clean. How much more, then, will the blood of Christ, who through the eternal Spirit offered himself unblemished to God, cleanse our consciences from acts that lead to death, so that we may serve the living God!*
>
> *For this reason Christ is the mediator of a new covenant, that those who are called may receive the promised eternal inheritance—now that he has died as a ransom to set them free from the sins committed under the first covenant... In fact, the law requires that nearly everything be cleansed with blood, and without the shedding of blood there is no forgiveness... Therefore, brothers, since we have confidence to enter the Most Holy Place by the blood of Jesus, by a new and living way opened for us through the curtain, that is, his body and since we have a great high priest over the house of God, let us draw near to God with a sincere heart sprinkled to cleanse us from a guilty conscience and having our bodies washed with pure water. Let us hold unswervingly to the hope we profess, for he who promised is faithful* (Hebrews 9:11-15,22; 10:19-22).

Jesus spoke this to His disciples before His crucifixion: *"I will not speak with you much longer, for the prince of this world is coming. He has no hold on me, but the world must learn that I love the Father and that I do exactly what my Father has commanded me."* Jesus' blood was different from all other men. Remember, He was born of a virgin. Therefore, His inheritance did not come from Adam, who imparted a sinful nature to all mankind after him, but rather from His Father in heaven. Jesus knew no sin and He remained sinless throughout His life (2 Corinthians 5:21; Hebrews 4:15). Satan could find nothing in Christ, no sin that would give him legal grounds for entrance, no legal grounds for death, yet Christ gave Himself freely for our sins in our stead. His righteous blood paid the penalty for every sin ever committed or that will be committed. Jesus Christ's blood forgives our sins and sets us free from Satan's hold on us. His blood washes away our sin and allows us to receive His righteousness.

> *When you were dead in your sins and in the uncircumcision of your sinful nature, God made you alive with Christ. He forgave us all our sins, having canceled the written code, with its regulations, that was against us and that stood opposed to us; he took it away, nailing it to the cross. And having disarmed the powers and authorities, he made a public spectacle of them, triumphing over them by the cross* (Colossians 2:13-15).

> *Therefore, there is now no condemnation for those who are in Christ Jesus, because through Christ Jesus the law of the spirit of life set me free from the law of sin and death. For what the law was powerless to do in that it was weakened by the sinful nature, God did by sending his own son in the likeness of sinful man to be a sin offering. And so he condemned sin in sinful man, in order that the righteous requirements of the*

> *law might be fully met in us, who do not live according to the sinful nature but according to the Spirit* (Romans 8:1-4).

All that is required of us by the very just laws set in motion by our just Creator from the very beginning out of His perfect justice, God provides for the fulfillment. Jesus Himself said, in Matthew 5:17, *"Do not think that I have come to abolish the Law or the Prophets; I have not come to abolish them but to fulfill them."*

Responding:

Satan has legal entrance into our lives if we continue to sin. However, in our union with Christ as we have experienced the new birth in Him, we have His blood that is applied to the sin in our lives.

> *This is the message we have heard from him and declare to you: God is light; in him there is no darkness at all. If we claim to have fellowship with him yet walk in the darkness, we lie and do not live by the truth. But if we walk in the light, as he is in the light, we have fellowship with one another, and the blood of Jesus, his Son, purifies us from all sin. If we claim to be without sin, we deceive ourselves and the truth is not in us.* **If we confess our sins, he is faithful and just and will forgive us our sins and purify us from all unrighteousness** (1 John 1:5-9 emphasis added).

Have you been walking in darkness in any way? Ask God to reveal it to you, to allow His light to shine on you and dispel the darkness in your life. There is healing and wholeness in the light. Your "garden" needs the sunlight to grow and be fruitful. Confess your sins, the darkness you have been walking in, and receive His forgiveness. The light of the Son is a blazing fire, cleansing you and bringing you to purity.

Can you recall a time when you were working in a garden, perhaps a flower garden or a vegetable garden, or just working in the yard on a hot summer day? You were all covered with dirt and perspiration. How good it is to come in and take a refreshing shower! Clean feels good! Our cocoon is also a luxurious bath!

> *"There is a fountain filled with blood drawn from Immanuel's veins,*
> *And sinners plunged beneath that flood lose all their guilty stains."*[21]
>
> *They overcame him by the blood of the Lamb* (Revelation 12:11).

Day Eighteen: Hind's Feet

When Jacob blessed his sons before his death, he said of Naphtali, *"Naphtali is a doe set free that bears beautiful fawns"* (Genesis 49:21). Once again, we see God's redemption. As one yields to the Lord, he or she is set free to be all that he or she was created to be. Even our attempts to discover who we are and for what purpose we were created can be launching pads that propel us into our real fruitfulness and purpose.

David had been chosen as the new king of Israel by God and anointed by the prophet Samuel though David was not yet put into that position. King Saul was very jealous of David as the Lord began to raise him up. Saul, in his jealous rage, sought to kill David. David had to flee from Saul to preserve his life. A band of soldiers joined themselves to David. On one occasion, as Saul was pursuing David and drawing near to capture him, David had opportunity to sneak up on Saul and could have taken Saul's life had he chosen to do so. David, however, did not take matters into his own hands. Saul was God's anointed king for the present. He would not kill God's anointed king to open the way for his own release into his destiny. He would wait for God's way and God's timing to come into his kingdom. What an honorable man was David! God blessed this king as he ruled the nation of Israel.[22] In 2 Samuel 22 is recorded a psalm of David that he wrote in response to the Lord's deliverance from the hand of all his enemies and from the hand of Saul. Within that psalm, David wrote,

> *As for God, His way is perfect…It is God who arms me with strength and makes my way perfect.* **He makes my feet like the feet of a deer (KJV, hinds feet)**; *he enables me to stand on the heights. He trains my hands for battle; my arms can bend a bow of bronze. You give me your shield of victory; you stoop down to make me great. You broaden the path beneath me, so that my ankles do not turn…You have delivered me from the attacks of my people; you have preserved me as the head of nations. People I did not know are subject to me, and foreigners come cringing to me; as soon as they hear me, they obey me. They all lose heart; they come trembling from their strongholds. The LORD lives! Praise be to my Rock! Exalted be God, the Rock, my Savior! He is the God who avenges me, who puts the nations under me, who sets me free from my enemies. You exalted me above my foes; from violent men you rescued me. Therefore I will praise You, O LORD, among the nations; I will sing praises to your name. He gives his king great victories; he shows unfailing kindness to his anointed, to David and his descendants forever* (emphasis added).

This same psalm is also recorded in Psalm 18.

It is also very interesting that the prophet Habakkuk uses the same expression concerning the hind's feet in Habakkuk 3:19 in his song. In the book of Habakkuk, pointing to the seeming injustice and evil in the world, the prophet encourages those who serve the

Lord to remain faithful. He speaks of a vision that should be written and how that vision, though it tarries, *will* come to pass in the end. In the final chapter of the book, Habakkuk records his song in which he looks beyond what seems to be and looks to what is of far greater significance, to the one who will make everything turn out right in the end, His God, His Savior. *Though the fig tree does not bud and there are no grapes on the vines, though the olive crop fails and the fields produce no food, though there are no sheep in the pen and no cattle in the stalls, yet I will rejoice in the LORD, I will be joyful in God my Savior. The Sovereign LORD is my strength; he makes my feet like the feet of a deer, he enables me to go on the heights* (Habakkuk 3:17-19).

The hind is a female deer. It has a peculiar odyssey as it runs. Its rear feet fall into the same footprints its front feet have left as it runs. Our pathway we have traveled serves as a springboard for the path that lies ahead. Our life is a journey, one step at a time, with each step affecting in some way that which comes next. Nothing is wasted in our lives, even though it may seem that we have veered off course. Each step is a building block to lead us onward. Even when the step is a wrong choice, we can learn from our mistake. Our next step will then be even surer because of our experience and our yielding of it to the Lord to instruct us.[23]

In our cocoon, we are going through a great transition. Throughout this transition, God takes us from where we have walked in the past and moves us toward our final destination.[24] Simply going through this process evokes a struggle within. In the midst of the metamorphosis, we are not who we have been and not yet who we will become. We find ourselves somewhat frustrated in the process. Frustration doesn't have to be a bad thing. On the contrary, it can be a very good thing. We look at the Word of God and see the blessings that are there, and we look at ourselves and don't see ourselves walking in all that those blessings portray. Like

Rachel, we do not see a chance for fruitfulness in our own selves, and so we look elsewhere for help. However, unlike Rachel, we do not look to "the arm of flesh." Our frustration can lead us to press into the Lord more diligently, to pursue Him with a greater passion. As we draw near to Him in this way, we open our hearts to allowing His Spirit to work in us and through us in even greater measure. The result is more of the transformation taking place in us that we desire.

Going to the Other Side

Jesus had given the orders to cross to the other side of the lake of Galilee. He and His disciples got into a boat. As they were traveling across, a tempestuous storm rose up without warning. The waves rose so high that the disciples became frightened. Jesus was asleep in the boat, undisturbed by the fierce storm. His disciples woke Him, and after rebuking them, He turned and rebuked the storm so that it dissipated before their very eyes. Jesus' disciples were amazed at His authority over even the winds and waves (Matthew 8).

The many different types of storms that we encounter in our lives cause our doubts and our fears to be brought to the surface, and we are then forced to deal with them. Those things that we have suppressed or haven't even seen before are suddenly exposed in the light of Christ as we journey with Him. He *is* in our boat. The same light that exposes our darkness wants to burn away the dross and flood that part of our being with His healing presence. When we see our need and then give it to Jesus, He can fill that need with His provision. We are made whole as we yield to Him. When Jesus says, "Let's go to the other side," you can be sure that He is going to the other side. He will bring you through every transition as you journey onward.

When You Get There

When Jesus and His disciples reached the other side of the lake, who should be there waiting to meet them but two violent demon-possessed men coming from the tombs. Talk about going from the frying pan to the fire! But the same Jesus was with them on that side of the lake, and once again they saw Him at work in the situation with which they were faced. As we face the storm with Jesus in our boat, we know Him in a new, deeper way and a greater anointing is released in us to see others know Him in greater ways as well. We can comfort others with the same comfort that we ourselves have received (2 Corinthians 1:3,4).

Another possible translation for the verse concerning Naphtali is, *Naphtali is a doe set free; He utters beautiful words* (Genesis 49:21). As we go through things and learn from them, we can share what we have learned with others as a word of testimony. The God who calmed the raging wind and sea also calmed the storm within those two demon-possessed men. They were completely set free.

Once these two were taken care of, Jesus and His disciples got back into the boat and crossed the lake once again back to the side they had come from. The storms of our lives not only give opportunity for God to do a powerful work *in* us, but also for Him to work *through* us to touch others. Where sin abounded, grace does *much more abound*! There is always an abundant multiplication of fruit in God. *Naphtali is a doe set free that bears beautiful fawns.*

Responding:

If you were able to talk with the caterpillar, I am quite sure that at some point in its transformation from the worm to the butterfly it would be experiencing quite a lot of frustration. At this point, it's not a worm anymore, but it's not a butterfly yet either. Are you experiencing frustration in your life right now? Lord, I pray that

Your light shine on my friend and cause her or him to see the need in her or his life right now. How do You want her or him to grow? Lord, we lift up that need to You and ask You to fill it. We know that You alone are the one who can. You are our all in all. In You we live and move and have our being (Acts 17:28).

The storms in our lives can be of our own making or can be brought about by circumstances beyond our control. We especially have a hard time with the storms of our own making. The enemy tends to try and accuse us to bring condemnation. Christ has set us free from condemnation and given us victory by His blood. As we look at these storms we go through, what do we do with them once they have passed? I believe there are two very important things we must do with the storms in our lives to "clean up the damage." First, the apostle Paul encourages us to forget what is behind and press onward in Christ. ***Forgetting** what is behind, and straining toward what is ahead, I press on toward the goal to win the prize for which God has called me heavenward in Christ Jesus* (Philippians 3:13,14 emphasis added). Secondly, Asaph, in Psalm 77, was crying out to God in the midst of a struggle and responded.

> *Then I thought, "To this I will appeal; the years of the right hand of the Most High." I will **remember** the deeds of the LORD; yes, I will remember your miracles of long ago. I will meditate on all your works and consider all your mighty deeds. Your ways, O God, are holy; What god is so great as our God? You are the God who performs miracles; you display your power among the peoples. With your mighty arm you redeemed your people, the descendants of Jacob and Joseph. Selah* (Psalm 77:10-15 emphasis added).

You may be saying, "How can we forget and remember at the same time?" I believe that we are to forget our mistakes in the sense of not allowing them to bring condemnation to us but rather remembering how God brought us out, how He redeems even the stupid things that we do. God is so good to rescue us and to calm the storms in our lives! And remember that we are on a journey; we have not yet arrived at our destination. Copy this scripture passage from Psalm 84 to remind you of your journey. Then read the entire Psalm.

> *Blessed are those whose strength is in you, who have set their hearts on pilgrimage. As they pass through the Valley of Baca, they make it a place of springs; the autumn rains also cover it with pools. They go from strength to strength, till each appears before God in Zion* (Psalm 84:5-7).
>
> (Baca means "weeping.")

I got a telephone call from my son who was about fours hours away in Bible college. Things weren't going real well for him, and he was very discouraged and just about ready to come home. Kenny was traveling. The lot fell to me to drive the four hours and see if I could encourage our son. Before leaving, I gathered in the church office with my pastor and two other staff members as we prayed for Kevin and my journey to see him. At the conclusion of our prayer, Cleo got a word, "The anchor holds," and encouraged me to listen to that song, "The Anchor Holds" by Ray Boltz, as I traveled. I did.

When I got to the college campus, I searched for Kevin and found that he was still in class. I went to the class door and called him out. He stepped out into the hallway and invited me to join him in the class. It was a music class, and each of the students had been asked to prepare a song to sing to the class. When we went back into the class, would you believe what song was being sung? "The Anchor Holds!" God was indeed speaking something that we needed to hear!

I spent the rest of the afternoon with Kevin until he had to go to work. I encouraged him to "hang in there," really feeling that's

My Struggle

what the song was all about. Little did we know that the storm was only brewing in which that anchor would keep us all steady.

Within a short while, our son met the young woman who would become his wife. It seemed to be a good match though they "pushed the envelope" on becoming husband and wife by deciding to run off and tie the knot ahead of the planned date. After the first year of marriage, they had their first child. Two years later, another son joined the family, followed in another three years by their baby brother. Storm clouds had started forming throughout their relationship, and instead of dissipating as we had hoped, continued to build into a massive canopy of darkness, continuing to loom ominously overhead and unleash its fury. The marriage ended in divorce seven years after it had begun.

I believe that one reason the Lord hates divorce is that it is so devastating to those who experience it. We have all, especially our son and his family, gone through a very painful time as we have cried out to the Lord in our desperation. We know especially of the pain that our son has gone through because he has lived with us over the past several years. It has been reassuring to know throughout the process that Jesus was right there in the boat through the storm and that the hope He brings is our anchor. Even though there can be much devastation in the storm, the "Son" will shine again and there *is* restoration. Our son has learned much on this journey, and we see him being healed and coming into the plans that God has for him in his life. *"For I know the plans I have for you,"* declares the LORD, *"plans to prosper you and not to harm you, plans to give you hope and a future"* (Jeremiah 29:11).

Write in your journal a current storm story and what the Lord is doing in the midst of it or your remembrance of a past storm and how God brought His calm and redemption. Be alert this week of opportunities to share your story with someone else who may need to hear it.

 Cocoon

They overcame him…By the word of their testimony (Revelation 12:11).

Day Nineteen:
Strongholds

Naphtali was not the first child Rachel "conceived" through her servant Bilhah but the second. When we try something and it seems to work for us, we continue to follow that course. It then becomes a mindset, a way of thinking, and as we continue to think that way and live out of that thinking, a stronghold is established. Strongholds can be good or bad. If the Lord God and His ways are our stronghold, we are thinking and living in the path of life. However, if we establish other ways of thinking and living, even if they may seem to work for us, they keep us from God's highest and best. Once again, which of those trees are we eating of—the tree of the knowledge of good and evil or the tree of life? With what part of us are we making the choices in our lives—our spirit that has been born again or our soul, intended by God to be a servant of the spirit, to be its mode of expression?

When man was first created, he lived out of his spirit, the image of God. He had an intimate connection with God and His kingdom life. This was the highest plane on which to live. What we call "the fall" really was a fall, down to a lower level of existence. Instead of our spiritual senses being keen and alert and filtering everything through them, our body's senses became more keen and alert and everything filtered through them. Those senses are not always reliable, but rather shifting and changing, based on things that are themselves temporary. Our spiritual senses, however, are based on the eternal, in God, our Father.

How are we to live out of our spirits? Romans 12:1,2 gets us started and established in the journey. *Therefore, I urge you, brothers, in view of God's mercy, to offer your bodies as living sacrifices—this is your spiritual act of worship. Do not conform any longer to the pattern of this world, but be transformed by the renewing of your mind. Then you will be able to test and approve what God's will is— his good, pleasing and perfect will.*

The first thing we are exhorted to do is to offer our bodies as living sacrifices. Our bodies have served as an "antenna" by which we sense what is happening around us and to us. We must disable that antenna and instead raise the antenna of our spirit by which we can rightly discern. I believe that the antenna of our spirit is the cross. The cross was Christ's altar of sacrifice. In the Old Testament tabernacle of Moses, there was an altar of wood and bronze. On a wooden cross, Jesus was crucified with spikes of bronze. As the priest of the Old Covenant offered the sacrifice, first blood was shed on the brazen altar and then he washed in the laver before entering into the presence of the Lord. On the cross of Christ, the side of our new High Priest, Jesus, was pierced and out flowed the blood and water. 2 Corinthians 5:21 tells us what was happening. *God made him who had no sin to be sin* [or be a sin offering] *for us, so that in him we might become the righteousness of God.* Jesus said to His disciples then and continues to speak to us today, *"If anyone would come after me, he must deny himself and take up his cross and follow me"* (Matthew 16:24). This is God's pattern, not the pattern of the world.

A cross is formed when two beams of wood intersect one another. The cross is an intersection of heaven and earth, of heaven and hell, of God and man, of truth and deception. Will we take up our cross, denying ourselves and following Jesus in the pattern of the kingdom? Will we turn from the earthly and see the heavenly? Will we turn from heading toward hell to heading instead to heaven? Will we follow man or God? Will we live in the truth or be deceived? Jesus goes on to say, *"For whoever wants to save his life will lose it, but whoever loses his life for me will find it"* (Matthew 16:25). Jesus speaks this to His disciples just after He has an encounter with Peter. Let's look at it.

> *From that time on Jesus began to explain to his disciples that he must go to Jerusalem and suffer many things at the hands of the elders, chief priests and teachers of the law, and that he must be killed and on the third day be raised to life.*
> *Peter took him aside and began to rebuke him. "Never, Lord!" he said. "This shall never happen to you!"*
> *Jesus turned and said to Peter, "Get behind me, Satan! You are a stumbling block to me; you do not have in mind the things of God, but the things of men"* (Matthew 16:21-23).

God's ways are different than the ways of the world! How do we renew our minds to God's way of thinking? Hebrews 4:12 says, *For the word of God is living and active. Sharper than any double-edged sword, it penetrates even to dividing soul and spirit, joints and marrow; it judges the thoughts and attitudes of the heart.* The word of God speaks to us of God's ways. When our spirits hear the word of God, a fire is kindled within us. There is agreement. Our spirit within us that has been reborn reverberates to the truth. *Your word is a lamp to my feet and a light for my path* (Psalm 119:105). As Jesus was being tempted by the devil, He spoke the word in response. *Jesus answered, "It is written: 'Man does not live on bread alone, but on every word that comes from the mouth of God'"* (Matthew 4:4).

Even an honorable man finds himself facing temptation. King David's "antenna" caught sight of a beautiful woman bathing. As he continued to look, desire arose to have this woman, even though she was already married to another man. He had her brought to him, he knew her intimately, and she conceived. Upon learning that Bathsheba was with child while her husband was away in battle, David sought to cover up his fathering of the child. He had

Uriah brought home from the battlefront and thought surely Uriah would sleep with his wife. Then no one would know. Bathsheba's husband was far more honorable than David had been and refused to sleep with his wife while his fellow soldiers were still at war. Then David resorted to having Uriah killed in battle as if he were a casualty of war, and he took Bathsheba as his own wife.

James tells us how temptation turns to sin. *When tempted, no one should say, "God is tempting me." For God cannot be tempted by evil, nor does he tempt anyone; but each one is tempted when by his own evil desire, he is dragged away and enticed. Then, after desire has conceived, it gives birth to sin; and sin, when it is full-grown, gives birth to death* (James 1:13-15). It is interesting that James goes on to warn us in verses 16-18, *Don't be deceived, my dear brothers. Every good and perfect gift is from above, coming down from the Father of the heavenly lights, who does not change like shifting shadows. He chose to give us birth through the word of truth, that we might be a kind of first fruits of all he created.*

The enemy deceives us into thinking that what is tempting us will enrich our lives in some way, when in reality it will only rob us. Jesus Himself said, *"The thief comes only to steal and kill and destroy; I have come that they may have life, and have it to the full"* (John 10:10). Our perception becomes muddy when we depart from the word of the Lord. James further gives us some good advice in 1:21: *Therefore, get rid of all moral filth and the evil that is so prevalent and humbly accept the word planted in you, which can save you.* How do we get rid of the moral filth and evil? Present our bodies as a living sacrifice, taking up our cross and dying daily.

James 1:21 is a prayer that I constantly prayed for my boys as they were teenagers. I knew they had been taught the Word of the Lord throughout their lives. I prayed that they would receive that Word, that they would hear the Word of the Lord louder than all

the other voices calling out to them. They've been through their struggles, but they're both fine young men who are walking with the Lord today.

The "patterns of this world" are things that have become strongholds in our lives. We have chosen to live by them over and over. The Lord exhorts us to *"be transformed* [changed!] *by the renewing of your mind."* If we do have strongholds in our lives, how are they broken to allow God's word in to establish His patterns for our lives? 2 Corinthians 10:4,5 tells us, *The weapons we fight with are not the weapons of the world. On the contrary, they have divine power to demolish strongholds. We demolish arguments and every pretension that sets itself up against the knowledge of God, and we take captive every thought to make it obedient to Christ.*

Back in Chapter Five, "The Rhythm of the Process," I shared with you about David's five smooth stones representing our weapons—the name of the Lord, His word, His blood, the power of His Spirit, and His faith.

David used his weapon against Goliath. He did not use his weapon as he was tempted with Bathsheba. The enemy can be very subtle. The battlefield is our mind. The "fiery darts of the evil one" come at us continually, but what will we do with them? We must allow the light of Christ to identify them and then we must take those thoughts captive and submit them to His lordship.[25]

Responding:

David thought he had covered all his tracks in his affair with Bathsheba, but God knew and confronted him, speaking through the prophet Nathan. David repented of his sin, and we have his prayer recorded in Psalm 51. Let's pray that prayer for ourselves from our hearts.

Have mercy on me, O God, according to your unfailing love;

My Struggle

According to your great compassion blot out my transgressions.
Wash away all my iniquity and cleanse me from my sin.
For I know my transgressions, and my sin is always before me.
Against you, you only, have I sinned and done what is evil in your sight,
So that you are proved right when you speak and justified when you judge.
Surely you desire truth in the inner parts; you teach me wisdom in the inmost place.
Cleanse me with hyssop, and I will be clean;
Wash me, and I will be whiter than snow.
Let me hear joy and gladness; let the bones you have crushed rejoice.
Hide your face from my sins and blot out all my iniquity.
Create in me a pure heart, O God, and renew a steadfast spirit within me.
Do not cast me from your presence or take your Holy Spirit from me.
Restore to me the joy of your salvation and grant me a willing spirit, to sustain me.
Then I will teach transgressors your ways, and sinners will turn back to you.
Save me from bloodguilt, O God, the God who saves me, and my tongue will sing of your righteousness.
O Lord, open my lips, and my mouth will declare your praise.
You do not delight in sacrifice, or I would bring it; you do not take pleasure in burnt offerings.
The sacrifices of God are a broken spirit; a broken and contrite heart, O God, you will not despise.
In your good pleasure make Zion prosper; build up the walls of Jerusalem.

Then there will be righteous sacrifices, whole burnt offerings to delight you;
Then bulls will be offered on your altar.

On His cross, Jesus Christ's body was broken for our sins. On our cross, we must be broken over our sinfulness and *[as] we confess our sins, he is faithful and just and will forgive us our sins and purify us from all unrighteousness* (1 John 1:9).

Allow the broken places to be an entrance for the Word of God into your life. As you confess your sins and receive His forgiveness, ask Him to give you His word to put in this place in your heart. *I have hidden your word in my heart that I might not sin against you* (Psalm 119:11).

The major struggle we experience within our cocoon is simply being still and resting in God. The time will come when we will have totally surrendered to Christ and He will then allow us to flap our wings in His strength He has imparted to us to break free and fly.

Those who belong to Christ Jesus have crucified the sinful nature with its passions and desires (Galatians 5:24).

Count yourselves dead to sin but alive to God in Christ Jesus (Romans 6:11).

They did not love their lives so much as to shrink from death (Revelation 12:11).

Chapter 12
Good Fortune, or a Troop

Moses continued, "The battle was on. Each of these women was trying to outdo the other. When Leah stopped having children, she followed her sister's example by giving Jacob her maidservant Zilpah, who bore Jacob another son, Gad, *a troop*. Yes, Aaron, a troop was coming! Jacob's family just kept growing, and we have become quite a force to reckon with!"

Day Twenty:
Captain of the Hosts

Our God is a mighty warrior! He is the King of His Kingdom and leads the hosts of heaven in battle against the enemy who has captured the people of the Kingdom.

Joshua and the children of Israel had just crossed over the Jordan River into the Promised Land. They faced the city of Jericho.

> *Now when Joshua was near Jericho, he looked up and saw a man standing in front of him with a drawn sword in his hand. Joshua went up to him and asked, "Are you for us or for our enemies?"*
> *"Neither," He replied, "but as commander of the army of the LORD I have now come."*

 Cocoon

> *Then Joshua fell facedown to the ground in reverence, and asked Him, "What message does my Lord have for his servant."*
> *The commander of the LORD's army replied, "Take off your sandals, for the place where you are standing is holy." And Joshua did so* (Joshua 5:13-15).

And then the Lord gave the battle plan for capturing the city. Whenever the Israelites faced an enemy and carried out the battle as their commander instructed them, they experienced victory. The battle is the Lord's. We are but soldiers in His army. He will lead us to victory. *But thanks be to God, who always leads us in triumphal procession in Christ and through us spreads everywhere the fragrance of the knowledge of him* (2 Corinthians 2:14). The issue is not just about us, though the battles we face do shape us on the potter's wheel. The real issue is the advancement of the Kingdom of God in our lives, in other's lives and in the world.

Since Adam and Eve had left the Garden of Eden, God's people held onto a hope that a Messiah would come. Even amid the curses because of sin that were spoken to this first man and woman was the promise. The fullness of time came for this Messiah to come on the scene. He was born as was prophesied of a virgin, Mary. He grew up virtually in obscurity until He reached thirty years of age. As He began His public ministry, those who did believe that He was the Messiah had their own ideas of what that Messiah would look like. They envisioned a physical, political conquering king, who would overthrow the Romans that ruled over them during this time. Perhaps this was part of Judas Iscariot's thinking as he delivered Jesus into the hands of the authorities. Perhaps this would force Jesus' hands to rise up and take possession of His Kingdom. But as Jesus stood before Pilate, being questioned if He was the king of the Jews, He responded,

Good Fortune, or a Troop

> *"My kingdom is not of this world. If it were, my servants would fight to prevent my arrest by the Jews. But now my kingdom is from another place."*
> *"You are a king then!" said Pilate.*
> *Jesus answered, "You are right in saying I am a king. In fact, for this reason I was born, and for this I came into the world, to testify to the truth. Everyone on the side of truth listens to me"* (John 18:36,37).

> *"For my thoughts are not your thoughts, neither are your ways my ways," declares the LORD. "As the heavens are higher than the earth, so are my ways higher than your ways and my thoughts than your thoughts"* (Isaiah 55:8,9).

As the captain of the hosts and the champion of our salvation, Jesus Christ won His greatest victory, actually *our* greatest victory, on His cross. It seemed to be a great defeat. Here on a rugged cross raised to heaven hung the great Teacher who told of the Kingdom of God, the Healer who had touched many to make them well, the Deliverer who set many free from the demons that had enslaved them, the Messiah believed by some at least to be the very Son of God. As they lowered His limp body, beaten beyond recognition, dripping with blood and water, and laid it into the tomb, His followers were moved to despair. Who was this man? What had gone wrong? Their hopes were dashed as the stone was rolled to seal the entrance. The believers had disappeared into the darkness with so many unanswered questions.

On the third day, the day following the Sabbath, the women ventured out to anoint the body of our Lord. They didn't know how they would roll away the stone. However, when they reached the tomb, they found the stone rolled away and the Lord's body gone. Now, to add insult to injury, someone had stolen the body it seemed. But angels pointed them to the risen Lord. Christ Jesus had paid sin's penalty, defeated sin's mastery, and even bounded from sin's prison of death. He had overcome and was alive to extend that victory and freedom to everyone who would reach out and take it. Whoa! *For the message of the cross is foolishness to those who are perishing, but to us who are being saved it is the power of God* (1 Corinthians 1:18).

> *When you were dead in your sins and in the uncircumcision of your sinful nature, God made you alive with Christ. He forgave us all our sins, having canceled the written code, with its regulations, that was against us and that stood opposed to us; he took it away, nailing it to the cross. And having disarmed the powers and authorities, he made a public spectacle of them, triumphing over them by the cross* (Colossians 2:13-15).

> *But Christ has indeed been raised from the dead, the first fruits of those who have fallen asleep. For since death came through a man, the resurrection of the dead comes also through a man. For as in Adam all die, so in Christ all will be made alive. But each in his own turn: Christ, the first fruits; then, when he comes, those who belong to him. Then the end will come, when he hands over the Kingdom to God the Father after he has destroyed all dominion, authority and power. For he must reign until he has put all his enemies under his feet. The last enemy to be destroyed is death. For he "has put everything under his feet." Now when it says that "everything" has been put under him, it is clear that this does not include God himself, who put everything under Christ. When he has done this, then the Son himself will be made subject to him who put everything under him, so that God may be all in all* (1 Corinthians 15:20-28).

> *In putting everything under him, God left nothing that is not subject to him. Yet at present we do not see everything subject*

Good Fortune, or a Troop

> *to him. But we see Jesus, who was made a little lower than the angels, now crowned with glory and honor because he suffered death, so that by the grace of God he might taste death for everyone* (Hebrews 2:8,9).

Jesus, the King, ushered in His reign in His Kingdom. We exalt Him as Lord and King over all. He is the only one who has gone the distance to reign over all.

> *Lift up your heads, O you gates; be lifted up, you ancient doors that the King of glory may come in.*
> *Who is this King of glory? The LORD strong and mighty, the LORD mighty in battle.*
> *Lift up your heads, O you gates; lift them up, you ancient doors that the King of glory may come in.*
> *Who is he, this King of glory? The LORD Almighty, he is the King of glory. Selah* (Psalm 24:7-10).

Where is this King of glory? *Christ Jesus, who died—more than that, who was raised to life—is at the right hand of God and is also interceding for us* (Romans 8:34).

Responding:

I want to share with you a personal testimony of God's intervention in our lives. This happened when our boys were very young, before the days of car seats for children and seatbelt restrictions. We were driving from town back to our home in our red Pinto Rally, a very small car. As we were passing a small grocery store, a fellow driving a small station wagon pulled out into the road in front of us. Apparently, he had not seen us coming. Kenny was driving, and when he saw the car pull out into our path, he veered to the left so as not to hit it head-on. As he did, we were facing a large transport truck in the other lane coming toward us. There was a big ditch near the other side of the road. The truck driver had nowhere to go but to veer a little to his right to avoid hitting us head on. Kenny slammed on brakes. They locked and we sat there in the middle of the road after bouncing off of the two sets of tires on the trailer of the truck. It was miraculous that we did not go under the trailer. We believe that an angel had kept us from going underneath and being killed. We were very much in shock for several days but very grateful for the Lord's protection. We were all alright. The only injury sustained was a very small cut on our oldest son's head that did not even require stitches.

Just before this, a friend at church, Charlotte, had asked me if everything was okay with our family. She said that she had really had us on her heart and that she had really been praying for us. Our accident happened the following week, and we knew that God had prepared the way for our safety through Charlotte's prayers. He had dispatched angels to minister to us in our time of need. God still had plans for our lives. He wasn't finished with us yet. Thank you, Charlotte, and thank You, Lord!

Jesus is the Captain of the hosts. He will do whatever is necessary to bring victory in your life. Look to Jesus, the King of the Kingdom. Take it straight to the top. We have access into the Most Holy Place. He will give you the strategy to win the battle you are facing now. Remember, it's about God's Kingdom advancing in your life, in other's lives and in the world. What would He speak to you today concerning carrying out His battle plan for any situation you or those you love may be facing? Record it in your journal.

Day Twenty-one:
The Heavenly Host

All throughout the Bible, angels are identified as *ministering spirits sent to serve those who will inherit salvation* (Hebrews 1:14). The first angel recorded in scripture is in Genesis 3:24: *After he drove the man out, he placed on the east side (or placed in front) of the*

Good Fortune, or a Troop

Garden of Eden cherubim and a flaming sword flashing back and forth to guard the way to the tree of life. The Lord has been directing our paths since then by commissioning His angels to minister to us in many ways.

Abraham, the father of faith, was visited by angels sent to share God's plans. Abraham was a friend of God. Angels were sent to bring Lot and his family from the city doomed for destruction. The angels even took their hands and led them to safety as they hesitated leaving Sodom. Jacob dreamed of angels ascending and descending a ladder into heaven. Israel was led by an angel as they journeyed from Egypt to the Promised Land. Balaam was saved from death by his donkey who saw an angel with a drawn sword. The prophet Elijah was awakened by an angel and told to eat and drink God's provision to strengthen him for his journey. An angel touched Isaiah's mouth with a coal from the altar in heaven to take away his sin and guilt. An angel brought clarity concerning visions he had seen to Daniel. An angel foretold the birth of John the Baptist to his father, Zechariah, the priest. An angel appeared to Mary to tell her that she had been chosen by God to bring His Son into the world. Angels told shepherds in the field of Jesus' birth in Bethlehem. Angels warned Joseph in dreams about moving his family out of harm's way. Angels ministered to Jesus following his temptation in the desert. An angel told the women at the empty tomb of Jesus' resurrection. Angels spoke to the early believers as Jesus ascended into heaven. An angel led Peter out of a locked prison after loosing his chains. John tells of many angels in heaven worshipping God and carrying out His judgments.

The Kingdom of God transcends what our natural eyes can see. Frank Peretti does an excellent job in his two books, *This Present Darkness* and *Piercing the Darkness,* of opening our understanding to what may be happening in the supernatural, which influences what is happening in the natural.

Cocoon

One of the most vivid accounts of scripture that draws back the curtain for us to see into the supernatural is found in 2 Kings 6. We have looked at this story already, but let me draw your attention to it once again. Aram was at war with Israel. Every time Aram tried to attack Israel, the prophet Elisha was given a word of knowledge concerning their whereabouts. Elisha then sent word to the king of Israel so that he was on guard. The king of Aram became very frustrated and angry and was told that Elisha, the prophet, was the reason his plans were continually foiled. The king of Aram ordered his men to find Elisha and capture him. The men searched and found Elisha in Dothan. Under the cover of darkness, a strong force of soldiers surrounded the city with horses and chariots.

> *When the servant of the man of God got up and went out early the next morning, an army with horses and chariots had surrounded the city. "Oh, my lord, what shall we do?" the servant asked.*
> *"Don't be afraid," the prophet answered. "Those who are with us are more than those who are with them."*
> *And Elisha prayed, "O LORD, open his eyes so he may see." Then the LORD opened the servant's eyes, and he looked and saw the hills full of horses and chariots of fire all around Elisha* (2 Kings 6:15-17).

As the enemy came toward him, Elisha prayed and asked the Lord to strike them blind. God did. Elisha led them away to Samaria. Elisha prayed that their eyes be opened. When their eyes were opened, they were the ones surrounded. They were punished and sent away. Aram stopped raiding Israel.

There are angels all around us, working to bring about God's purposes and to protect and guide His people. Sometimes, like Elisha, God can allow us to see them. A prophet was also called a seer. There are many today as well whom God is allowing to see into the supernatural. We need to pay heed to what they may have to share with us. One of the gifts to the body of Christ is the prophet. Let me warn you, however, that the word of God also warns us of false prophets.

> *Do not let anyone who delights in false humility and the worship of angels disqualify you for the prize. Such a person goes into great detail about what he has seen and his unspiritual mind puffs him up with idle notions. He has lost connection with the Head, from whom the whole body, supported and held together by its ligaments and sinews, grows as God causes it to grow* (Colossians 2:18-19).

We need to pray for discernment. Jesus is the Head, the commander of all the heavenly hosts.

Responding:

Let's pray together. *Lord, I pray that you would open our eyes to see into the supernatural. Move us beyond our limited vision of just the earthly, but into a true vision of Your Kingdom. Thank you, Lord, for the ministry of angels to serve us in times of need. Amen.*

Listen to the Lord and wait on Him. Record anything that He would show you.

When my husband first started traveling in ministry, we lived in an old farmhouse out in the country. The boys were young. I had never stayed by myself much at night, and so when Kenny was gone, I was a little afraid. Every night I would take the Bible to bed with me and read Psalm 91, meditating on it over and over until I could see with my spiritual eyes angels positioned on the roof of our house as guards over us. They weren't just little cherubs that you've seen pictures of, but big men who were definitely able to take care of any situation.

 Cocoon

What about you? Do you have any angelic experiences that you'd like to remember and jot down in your journal today?

Day Twenty-two
The Army of the Lord

It is very interesting that when Joshua asked the Man before him, *"Are you for us or for our enemies?"* His reply was, *"Neither, but as commander of the army of the LORD I have now come."* God does not take sides with one person or group of persons against another. Rather, God is advancing His Kingdom in the lives of all. His army executes judgment on all that is contrary to His Kingdom. It is not as if God is demanding compliance because of some gigantic ego, but rather that His beautiful creation was brought into being out of His heart and His Kingdom and therein it finds its complete fulfillment. God really is a good God and desires good for us! The choices we make align us with the Lord or against Him. And that is where the battle lies—in our choices. When we choose God, His ways and His Kingdom, the armies of heaven join forces with us in the battle, and we are guaranteed victory. God is still God and no one has removed Him from His throne, nor will they ever. There is none like our God. In His great love, He purges us from sin to prepare us for the final judgment so that we will be able to stand on that day—in Him.

The book of Joel tells of an invasion of locusts and the complete devastation this plague brings. There is then a call to repentance. Sin has unleashed a ravaging force, eating away at all of creation like the destruction by the locusts. We can trace all of our problems ultimately to sin. This locust invasion is not the day of the Lord, but points ahead to the day of the Lord, when sin in the world will have reached its maximum and the Lord will bring judgment upon it. If we will repent in the day of the locusts' judgment, we will be ready for the day of the Lord. As we turn from our sin, we run to

Good Fortune, or a Troop

the Lord, crying out for His mercy and grace. *But where sin abounded, grace did much more abound* (Romans 5:20, KJV). Both John the Baptist and Jesus came bringing a call to repentance: *"Repent for the Kingdom of God is at hand."* As we repent, and turn to Christ, He can wash us clean from sin.

All of mankind and indeed all of creation is affected by sin and experiences judgment for sin. Even those of us who have received Christ and His forgiveness of sin have yet to deal with the influence of sin and the effects of sin in this world in which we now live. *For it is time for judgment to begin with the family of God; and if it begins with us, what will the outcome be for those who do not obey the gospel of God?* (1 Peter 4:17) After judgment and repentance comes restoration for God's people. (See Joel 2.) At the end of Joel 2, verses 28-32, a prophecy is given that was brought to fulfillment on the day of Pentecost. As the gift of the Father, the Holy Spirit, was poured out following Jesus' death, burial, resurrection, and ascension. Peter stood up and quoted this passage of scripture from Joel. How do we receive the restoration God desires for His people? Just as Peter told all those gathered on that day of Pentecost, he speaks to us as well, *"Repent and be baptized every one of you, in the name of Jesus Christ for the forgiveness of your sins. And you will receive the gift of the Holy Spirit"* (Acts 2:38).

Jesus foretold of the sending of the Spirit. *But I tell you the truth: It is for your good that I am going away. Unless I go away, the Counselor will not come to you; but if I go, I will send him to you. When he comes he will convict the world of guilt in regard to sin and righteousness and judgment...And in regard to judgment, because the prince of this world now stands condemned* (John 16:7,8,11).

The calling of the apostle Matthew is recorded in Luke's gospel, 5:27-31. Matthew was a tax collector and was also known as Levi. The scripture tells us that Matthew held a great banquet in his home for Jesus. There were many tax collectors and others eating with Him. The Pharisees complained to Jesus' disciples and asked, *"Why do you eat and drink with tax collectors and 'sinners'?"* Jesus answered them, *"It is not the healthy who need a doctor, but the sick. I have not come to call the righteous, but sinners to repentance"* (Luke 5:30,31).

Matthew records Jesus healing a demon-possessed man who was blind and mute. The Pharisees once again opposed Jesus and claimed that He drove out the demons by the power of Beelzebub, the prince of demons. In his answer to them, Jesus said, *"But if I drive out demons by the Spirit of God, then the Kingdom of God has come upon you. Or again, how can anyone enter a strong man's house and carry off his possessions unless he first ties up the strong man? Then he can rob his house"* (Matthew 12:28-29). It is interesting how Jesus continues the same conversation with the statement, *"He who is not with me is against me, and he who does not gather with me scatters"* (Matthew 12:30). There are only two sides to take—with Jesus or against Him. It is also interesting that He continues and warns against blasphemy of the Holy Spirit, which will not be forgiven. He further goes on to talk about a tree being either good or bad, and that it is recognized by its fruit. *For out of the overflow of the heart the mouth speaks* (Matthew 12:34).

To enter into the Kingdom of God, we must be born again by the Spirit (John 3:3-6). Our spirits are made alive by the Spirit of God. Therein is our entrance into the army of God and by His Spirit is the only way that we can do battle. In Luke 10:18, Jesus replied, *"I saw Satan fall like lightning from heaven. I have given you authority to trample on snakes and scorpions and to overcome all the power of the enemy; nothing will harm you. However, do not rejoice that the spirits submit to you, but rejoice that your names are written in heaven."* We must pay heed to the word of the Lord given to Zerubbabel in Zechariah's vision, *"Not by might nor by power, but by my Spirit," says the LORD Almighty* (Zechariah 4:6). As we exer-

Good Fortune, or a Troop

cise repentance from our own works, our own pride, and attempts at righteousness, He will give to us His righteousness and fill us with His Spirit. We will ride with Him in victory.

> *I saw heaven standing open and there before me was a white horse, whose rider is called Faithful and True. With justice he judges and makes war. His eyes are like blazing fire, and on his head are many crowns. He has a name written on him that no one knows but he himself. He is dressed in a robe dipped in blood, and his name is the Word of God. The armies of heaven were following him, riding on white horses and dressed in fine linen, white and clean. Out of his mouth comes a sharp sword with which to strike down the nations. "He will rule them with an iron scepter." He treads the winepress of the fury of the wrath of God Almighty. On his robe and on his thigh he has this name written: KING OF KINGS AND LORD OF LORDS* (Revelation 19:11-16).

"His eyes are like blazing fire." Continue to look into His eyes of love and allow the light to purify your life so that you walk in His righteousness. Allow His Holy Spirit within to bring conviction as needed to bring judgment to sin.

Notice in the book of Joel, chapter three, it is after the call to repentance and the pouring out of the Holy Spirit, after the offer that everyone who calls on the name of the Lord will be saved (Joel 2:32), that judgment comes. Peter tells us, [The Lord] *is patient with you, not wanting anyone to perish, but everyone to come to repentance* (2 Peter 3:9). The apostle Paul asks the question, *Do you show contempt for the riches of his kindness, tolerance and patience, not realizing that God's kindness leads you toward repentance?* (Romans 2:4) We see Jesus' heart further as He laments over Jerusalem, *"O Jerusalem, Jerusalem, you who kill the prophets and stone those sent to you, how often I have longed to gather your children together, as a hen gathers her chicks under her wings, but you were not willing"* (Luke 13:34).

In Revelation 21, following the final judgment of God, we see a glimpse of the new heaven and new earth. [God] *will wipe every tear from their eyes* (Revelation 21:4). Perhaps the first tears that are wiped away are God's own.

We are not to judge others, but to love them and extend God's kindness to them. We are to judge our own selves. *But if we judged ourselves, we would not come under judgment. When we are judged by the Lord, we are being disciplined so that we will not be condemned with the world* (1 Corinthians 11:31,32). That is the message of Joel in a nutshell: judgment comes on sin in the world. We experience its effects and are called to repentance by the kindness of God who desires that none should perish on that final judgment day. *But because of your stubbornness and your unrepentant heart, you are storing up wrath against yourself for the day of God's wrath, when his righteous judgment will be revealed* (Romans 2:5).

When we repent and change our thinking we find we are going in the wrong direction, so we turn around and go in the opposite direction. It's as if each of us is born with a magnet designed to connect with God, our Creator, but we've got the magnet turned around because of sin and instead of attracting to Him, we repel Him. All we need to do is turn around and we can be reconnected once again. We are either swimming upstream or going with the flow of God. We need to be like those little "bump and go" cars. You turn them on, set them on the floor to run, and whenever they bump into anything, they simply turn and go in another direction and keep on going. That's God's desire for us, that we continue to walk in the light. *The path of the righteous is like the first gleam of dawn, shining ever brighter till the full light of day* (Proverbs 4:18). We need to be willing to embrace the pain of letting go of those things that would hinder our walk with the Lord and moving ahead for greater glory to be experienced in Him.

Good Fortune, or a Troop

The LORD thunders at the head of his army; his forces are beyond number and mighty are those who obey his command. The day of the LORD is great; it is dreadful. Who can endure it? "Even now," declares the LORD, "return to me with all your heart, with fasting and weeping and mourning" (Joel 2:11,12).

The LORD will roar from Zion and thunder from Jerusalem; the earth and the sky will tremble. But the LORD will be a refuge for his people, a stronghold for the people of Israel (Joel 3:16).

Thy kingdom come; Thy will be done!
Are you walking in step in God's army, or do you find yourself opposing the army of the Lord? *Sing to the LORD, you saints of his; praise his holy name. For his anger lasts only a moment, but his favor lasts a lifetime; weeping may remain for a night, but rejoicing comes in the morning* (Psalm 30:4,5). What is He angry at? Sin and how it robs you!

Responding:

My two sons are just as different as night and day. Truly God has created each of us as unique individuals. And it is very fascinating to observe the differences.

I shared earlier with you about my experiences of healing from a tumor. During that process, my two sons reacted quite differently. I know they both cared about their mom; they just responded differently. My older son was going through some struggles of his own, and he chose to run. He didn't want to be around any more than he had to. Maybe he couldn't add any more pain to what he was already experiencing. My younger son spent the night with his dad in the hospital waiting room that first night. After I was moved into a private room, he would crawl up in bed with me

 *Cocoon*

and hang out, watching TV. He was there a lot. The surgery affected me as if I had experienced a stroke. My older son could hardly bear to look. My younger son never looked at me any differently, even though everyone else did.

Teenagers are constantly in "search mode," trying to find some answers to some pretty big questions. We almost always knew everything that was going on with our older son. He was wide open, out in full view. Our younger son, however, was a little more sneaky. You can imagine, then, our shock to receive a call from the office of the Christian school where our son was a senior in high school, telling us that he had been caught selling marijuana to a younger student. He had been sent home earlier that day. We didn't see him until later that night. Wisely, he had taken time to sort through his thoughts and allow us to do the same. The next day, we visited the school and discovered that the local authorities would not be brought in, but that our son would be expelled from school and could not graduate with his senior class. My husband and I grieved tremendously for him, but he had done wrong and had to suffer the consequences.

After wrestling a little more with his wrongdoing and with the consequences of it, he got his GED from the local community college, enrolled in college courses there, and then transferred to another college. During this time, he met the woman that he would marry. God has blessed him with a beautiful family and they continue to walk in God's grace for their lives. We are grateful for the grace of God and Kyle's response to His grace to choose to follow Him. As we allow God to purge us of our sin, we move on to experience greater glory in knowing Him even more.

My older son kept searching for a number of years and he, too, had many experiences with the grace of God through it all. In the past few years, he has had to come home and live with us for a season. God has helped him to find the answers to some of those questions, and he continues to seek, as do all of us. Kevin has a lot

Good Fortune, or a Troop

of talents and is exploring God's plan for his life. He has three wonderful boys. I had some special times with Kyle as he hung out with Mom, and recently I have had some special times with Kevin as well. God is so good. He is working in all of us to purge and prune us so that we will bear more fruit.

Are you now or have you been in a time of purging and pruning? Yield to the Master's loving hands. He sees the finished product—a beautiful butterfly. The light reflects many beautiful colors as it shines on the tiny scales of the intricate wings. What colors are you? Take time to journal any thoughts you may have in reference to this.

Day Twenty-three: Obedience

The most important lesson to be learned by anyone serving in an army is obedience to the commanding officer. Obedience to the Lord brings us in submission to Him and His purposes. It enables us to join together with other soldiers in harmony and unity of purpose.

The book of Judges tells us of the days following the death of Joshua, who had led the Israelites into their Promised Land. Time and time again, we see the same cycle. Moses had very explicitly and very eloquently expressed to the Israelites the choice they had to make as the people of God:

> *"See, I set before you today life and prosperity, death and destruction. For I command you today to love the LORD your God, to walk in his ways, and to keep his commands, decrees and laws; then you will live and increase, and the LORD your God will bless you in the land you are entering to possess.*
> *"But if your heart turns away and you are not obedient, and if you are drawn away to bow down to other gods and worship them, I declare to you this day that you will certainly be*

> *destroyed. You will not live long in the land you are crossing the Jordan to enter and possess.*
>
> *"This day I call heaven and earth as witnesses against you that I have set before you life and death, blessings and curses. Now choose life, so that you and your children may live and that you may love the LORD your God, listen to his voice, and hold fast to him. For the LORD is your life, and he will give you many years in the land he swore to give to your fathers, Abraham, Isaac and Jacob"* (Deuteronomy 30:15-20).

During the time of the Judges, Israel would turn away from following after God, opening the door for the oppression of its enemies. God would raise up a judge to lead them for a season. Deliverance would come. Then once again, the people would turn from following after God and find themselves in the same predicament of oppression by their enemies. God would again raise up a judge to bring deliverance. They would follow after God for a season, and the cycle would begin again over and over. Judges 17:6 sums it up for us. *In those days, Israel had no king; everyone did as he saw fit.* Left to our own devices, we quickly digress to the pig pen of sin.

The Why and How of Obeying

Proverbs 9:10 tells us that *the fear of the LORD is the beginning of wisdom.* But it doesn't stop there. *There is no fear in love. But perfect love drives out fear, because fear has to do with punishment. The one who fears is not made perfect in love.*

We love because he first loved us (1 John 4:18,19).

We don't obey the Lord out of fear of punishment. We obey because we love Him. (You might want to go back and read the story on Day Six.) Knowing his great love for us, we want to obey Him. Because the Lord loves us, we know that we can trust Him to lead us in paths of righteousness, in paths of blessing. Because

Good Fortune, or a Troop

He is all-wise and all-knowing, we can trust and obey. It is in our obedience that we are truly resting in the Lord. It is when we are walking in obedience that we are walking in faith.

Jesus said,

> *"As the Father has loved me, so have I loved you. Now remain in my love. If you obey my commands, you will remain in my love, just as I have obeyed my Father's commands and remain in his love. I have told you this so that my joy may be in you and that your joy may be complete. My command is this: Love each other as I have loved you. Greater love has no one than this, that he lay down his life for his friends. You are my friends if you do what I command. I no longer call you servants, because a servant does not know his master's business. Instead, I have called you friends, for everything that I learned from my Father I have made known to you. You did not choose me, but I chose you and appointed you to go and bear fruit—fruit that will last. Then the Father will give you whatever you ask in my name"* (John 15:9-16).

Even if I do love God and want to obey Him, can I? We say with the apostle Paul,

> *When I want to do good, evil is right there with me. For in my inner being I delight in God's law; but I see another law at work in the members of my body, waging war against the law of my mind and making me a prisoner of the law of sin at work within my members. What a wretched man I am! Who will rescue me from this body of death? Thanks be to God—through Jesus Christ our Lord…Therefore, there is now no condemnation for those who are in Christ Jesus, because through Christ Jesus the law of the Spirit of life set me free from the law of sin and death* (Romans 7:21-8:2).

For just as through the disobedience of the one man the many were made sinners, so also through the obedience of the one man the many will be made righteous (Romans 5:19). *And being found in appearance as a man, he humbled himself and became obedient to death—even death on a cross* (Philippians 2:8). Jesus Christ has fulfilled all obedience. I am in Christ. He enables me to be obedient.

The Goal of Obedience

God is not on some ego trip in which He has to order everyone around to prove that He is the head honcho. God is a loving Father. The goal of obedience is freedom. *To the Jews who had believed Him, Jesus said, "If you hold to my teaching, you are really My disciples. Then you will know the truth, and the truth will set you free"* (John 8:31,32). Jesus did not set us free from sin just so that we will not do sinful acts, all the while deep inside feeling miserable and desiring to do those things. No! *It is for freedom that Christ has set us free* (Galatians 5:1). The Lord goes deeper than just what we do or don't do. He reaches way down deep in our hearts and truly sets us free. He told us in the scripture quoted above from John 15, *"I have told you this so that My joy may be in you and that your joy may be complete."*

The old hymn is really true—*"Trust and obey, for there's no other way to be happy in Jesus than to trust and obey."* And—*"I sing because I'm happy; I sing because I'm free!"*

Responding:

Are you experiencing freedom in the Lord? If not, is there something that you haven't been obedient in? Why not talk to Him about it.

For though we live in the world, we do not wage war as the world does. The weapons we fight with are not the weapons of the world. On the contrary, they have divine power to demolish strongholds. We demolish arguments and every pretension that sets itself up against the

Good Fortune, or a Troop

knowledge of God, and we take captive every thought to make it obedient to Christ (2 Corinthians 10:3-5). This certainly doesn't mean that we need to stop thinking. We do, however, need to yield our thoughts to the Spirit of the Lord. He has told us that His thoughts are so much higher than ours. We cannot simply think and do what we want and then ask God to bless it. We must yield our ideas, our plans, our will to Him. Only as our thoughts are yielded to Christ, subject to His Lordship, can we walk in the freedom of His truth. Only as our thoughts are yielded to Christ, subject to His Lordship, can His will truly be done on earth as it is in heaven.

> *"You are a king, then!" said Pilate.*
> *Jesus answered, "You are right in saying I am a king. In fact, for this reason I was born, and for this I came into the world, to testify to the truth. Everyone on the side of truth listens to me"* (John 18:37).

> *I am the way and the truth and the life* (John 14:6).

Day Twenty-four: Unity

An army consists of many people. As each of us learns obedience to the Lord and commits to do the will of the Lord in our individual life we can then, because of each of us doing His will, come into a unity of purpose, a unity of heart and mind with the Lord and consequently with one another. Unity is a powerful thing.

In chapter 11 of Genesis, we find the story of the tower of Babel. At that time, all of mankind spoke the same language and so could understand each other very well. Men moved eastward and found a plain, later known as Babylonia, where they settled. The men agreed to work together to build a tower reaching to heaven, their purpose being to make a name for themselves so they wouldn't be scattered over all the face of the earth. God came down to investigate what these men were doing, which tells us that this was not His plan for them, but something they decided to do. It is interesting what the Lord said: *"If as one people speaking the same language they have begun to do this, then nothing they plan to do will be impossible for them. Come, let us go down and confuse their language so they will not understand each other"* (Genesis 11:6,7). And so they were scattered all over the earth, each different group speaking a different language. We don't need to build our own kingdoms. We have no truly righteous king to lead us.

During the days of Samuel the prophet, the children of Israel cried out for a king to lead them like the other nations. Samuel took their request to the Lord. His response can be found in 1 Samuel 8. *"Listen to all that the people are saying to you; it is not you they have rejected, but they have rejected me as their king...Now listen to them; but warn them solemnly and let them know what the king who will reign over them will do."* Samuel warned them that this king would require their sons and daughters to serve him, that they would actually become slaves to the king. But the people refused to listen and continued to cry for a king. And so, the Lord consented to give them a king.

Saul was chosen as the first king of Israel. He didn't fully obey the Lord, and he was succeeded by David. David was a good king—not perfect, but he loved the Lord and desired to follow Him fully. The nation of Israel prospered under the leadership of David. Next in line for the kingship was David's son Solomon. God was pleased that Solomon prayed for wisdom and discernment to govern the people of God, and so God gave him a great amount of wisdom. He was known all over the earth for his great wisdom. Solomon is considered to be the wisest man who ever lived, except for Jesus Christ. Solomon did many great things as King of Israel. He built a fabulous temple, which had been in the

Good Fortune, or a Troop

heart of his father David to build. He advanced the territory of Israel's boundaries and achieved many great civil accomplishments. He amassed great wealth, but his heart turned away from the Lord. His people were burdened with the heavy yoke of enslavement to carry out his great projects and fuel his great workforce, just as God had warned. Following his death, in accordance with the word of the Lord, as Solomon's son Rehoboam took the throne, the kingdom was divided. Even the wisest man on Earth was not a righteous king as is our God.

The prophet Isaiah prophesied of another King who would reign.

> *For to us a child is born, to us a son is given, and the government will be on his shoulders. And he will be called Wonderful counselor, Mighty God, Everlasting Father, Prince of Peace. Of the increase of his government and peace there will be no end. He will reign on David's throne and over his kingdom, establishing and upholding it with justice and righteousness from that time on and forever. The zeal of the LORD Almighty will accomplish this* (Isaiah 9:6-7).

On Golgotha's hill stood a cross. Above the man who hung on this cross was a sign that read: King of the Jews.

> *For the message of the cross is foolishness to those who are perishing, but to us who are being saved it is the power of God. For it is written: "I will destroy the wisdom of the wise; the intelligence of the intelligent I will frustrate." Where is the wise man? Where is the scholar? Where is the philosopher of this age? Has not God made foolish the wisdom of the world?...But we preach Christ crucified; a stumbling block to Jews and foolishness to Gentiles, but to those whom God has called, both Jews and Greeks, Christ the power of God and the wisdom of God.*

> *For the foolishness of God is wiser than man's wisdom, and the weakness of God is stronger than man's strength…It is because of him that you are in Christ Jesus, who has become for us wisdom from God—that is, our righteousness, holiness and redemption. Therefore, as it is written: "Let him who boasts boast in the Lord"* (1 Corinthians 1:18-30).

Jesus' Prayer for Unity

In John 17, in what is considered Jesus' priestly prayer before He offers Himself as our sacrifice, he prays for the unity of His believers with Him and with one another.

> *"My prayer is not for them alone. I pray also for those who will believe in me through their message, that all of them may be one, Father, just as you are in me and I am in you. May they also be in us so that the world may believe that you have sent me. I have given them the glory that you gave me, that they may be one as we are one: I in them and you in me. May they be brought to complete unity to let the world know that you sent me and have loved them even as you have loved me"* (John 17:20-23).

Prior to this, Jesus had commanded us to love one another. *"By this will all men know that you are my disciples, if you love one another"* (John 13:35). In my walk with the Lord, I am more and more made aware of the value of the contribution of each person within the Body of Christ to the whole. In what we know as the "Love Chapter," 1 Corinthians 13:9,12 says, *For we know in part and we prophesy in part, but when perfection comes, the imperfect disappears…Now we see but a poor reflection as in a mirror; then we shall see face to face. Now I know in part; then I shall know fully, even as I am fully known.* Paul goes on to tell us what our support posts are in this time of knowing in part, the things that remain to which we

Good Fortune, or a Troop

can tether ourselves: (verse 13) *And now these three remain: faith, hope and love. But the greatest of these is love.*

As we are transformed within our cocoon, we see Jesus Christ in whom we live and move and have our being, albeit not clearly. But Proverbs 4:18 says, *The path of the righteous is like the first gleam of dawn, shining ever brighter till the full light of day.* Our vision is getting clearer and clearer as we continue to look.

One of the ways we see Christ is in each other. *Now you are the body of Christ, and each one of you is a part of it* (1 Corinthians 12:27). We are warned, however, in the process to test the spirits. *Dear friends, do not believe every spirit, but test the spirits to see whether they are from God, because many false prophets have gone out into the world* (1 John 4:1). When we yield ourselves to the lordship of Jesus Christ and are led by His Spirit, He will lead us into all truth.

The Spirit Brings Unity

Following Jesus' resurrection and prior to His ascension into heaven, Jesus instructed His apostles, *"Do not leave Jerusalem, but wait for the gift my Father promised, which you have heard me speak about. For John baptized with water, but in a few days you will be baptized with the Holy Spirit"* (Acts 1:4,5).

In an upper room in Jerusalem on the day of Pentecost, the Father fulfilled His promise and poured out His Spirit on the believers who were gathered together waiting on Him as Jesus had instructed.

> *Suddenly a sound like the blowing of a violent wind came from heaven and filled the whole house where they were sitting. They saw what seemed to be tongues of fire that separated and came to rest on each of them. All of them were filled with the Holy Spirit and began to speak in other tongues as the Spirit enabled them. Now there were staying in Jerusalem God-fearing Jews*

> *from every nation under heaven. When they heard this sound, a crowd came together in bewilderment, because each one heard them speaking in his own language* (Acts 2:2-6).

Peter stood up and preached the gospel. The listeners were pricked in their hearts and asked what they were to do. *Peter replied, "Repent and be baptized, every one of you, in the name of Jesus Christ for the forgiveness of your sins. And you will receive the gift of the Holy Spirit. The promise is for you and your children and for all who are far off—for all whom the Lord our God will call"* (Acts 2:38,39).

The same tool that God had used to scatter the builders of the tower of Babel, He now used to bring together in unity His people in His Kingdom on the day of Pentecost. He restored a common speech to those in His Kingdom. How amazing it is that there is so much division in the Body of Christ over speaking in tongues. Here again, what seems to be foolishness to man, is indeed the wisdom of God. For when we pray with our spirits, in that heavenly language, we are not praying what our minds contrive from our own thoughts or reasoning, but we are praying the perfect will of God. We all need to be so filled with the Spirit of God, immersed totally in Him, so that what the Lord has implanted deep within us of His life would consume the old man and refine that new creation waiting to be released, that colorful butterfly to soar once again freely and victoriously.

Nevertheless,

> *There are different kinds of gifts, but the same Spirit. There are different kinds of service, but the same Lord. There are different kinds of working, but the same God works all of them in all men. Now to each one the manifestation of the Spirit is given for the common good...For we were all baptized by one Spirit into one body—whether Jews or Greeks, slave or free—and we were all given the one Spirit to drink...Now you are the body*

Good Fortune, or a Troop

of Christ, and each one of you is a part of it (1 Corinthians 12:4-7,13,27).

Make every effort to keep the unity of the Spirit through the bond of peace. There is one body and one Spirit—just as you were called to one hope when you were called—one Lord, one faith, one baptism; one God and Father of all, who is over all and through all and in all.

But to each one of us grace has been given as Christ apportioned it…It was he who gave some to be apostles, some to be prophets, some to be evangelists, and some to be pastors and teachers, to prepare God's people for works of service, so that the body of Christ may be built up until we all reach unity in the faith and in the knowledge of the Son of God and become mature, attaining to the whole measure of the fullness of Christ.

Then we will no longer be infants, tossed back and forth by the waves, and blown here and there by every wind of teaching and by the cunning and craftiness of men in their deceitful scheming. Instead, speaking the truth in love, we will in all things grow up into him who is the Head, that is, Christ. From him the whole body, joined and held together by every supporting ligament, grows and builds itself up in love, as each part does its work (Ephesians 4:3-7,11-16).

Responding:

Moses was overwhelmed with the responsibility of leading the children of Israel through the wilderness. Time and time again they expressed their discontent with God and His provision and their lust for other things. Moses cried out to the Lord,

"I cannot carry all these people by myself; the burden is too heavy for me…" The Lord said to Moses: "Bring me seventy

of Israel's elders who are known to you as leaders and officials among the people. Have them come to the Tent of Meeting, that they may stand there with you. I will come down and speak with you there, and I will take of the spirit that is on you and put the Spirit on them. They will help you carry the burden of the people so that you will not have to carry it alone..." So Moses went out and told the people what the LORD had said. He brought together seventy of their elders and had them stand around the Tent. Then the LORD came down in the cloud and spoke with him, and he took of the Spirit that was on him and put the Spirit on the seventy elders. When the Spirit rested on them, they prophesied, but they did not do so again.

However, two men, whose names were Eldad and Medad, had remained in the camp. They were listed among the elders, but did not go out to the Tent. Yet the Spirit also rested on them, and they prophesied in the camp. A young man ran and told Moses, "Eldad and Medad are prophesying in the camp." Joshua son of Nun, who had been Moses' aide since youth, spoke up and said, "Moses, my lord, stop them!" But Moses replied, "Are you jealous for my sake? I wish that all the LORD's people were prophets and that the LORD would put his Spirit on them!" (Numbers 11).

The Lord did just that on the Day of Pentecost!
Jesus had a similar experience.

"Teacher," said John, "we saw a man driving out demons in your name and we told him to stop, because he was not one of us."
"Do not stop him," Jesus said. "No one who does a miracle in my name can in the next moment say anything bad about me, for whoever is not against us is for us. I tell you the truth, anyone who gives you a cup of water in my name because you

Good Fortune, or a Troop

belong to Christ will certainly not lose his reward (Mark 9:38-41).

Are there people within the Body of Christ that you have cut off, that you have dismissed as having no value, those with whom you do not agree on some point of theology? Ask the Lord now to bring them to your mind. Repent of any judgment you have brought upon them. Release them to the power of God in their lives to bring about His wholeness. Journal your responses and any impressions the Lord gives you. On our journey to wholeness, we can all learn from each other, we can all pray for each other, and we can all love each other into the reality of God's Kingdom. We must!

Remember the story of Lazarus being raised from the dead? When Jesus called him forth out of the tomb, he came forth. However, he was still wrapped in grave clothes. Jesus spoke to those watching and said to them, *"Take off the grave clothes and let him go"* (John 11:44). We are a people who once were dead in our sins, but now are alive in Christ Jesus. Let's take off each other's grave clothes and release each other to be all that God has called us and created us to be. Yes, we have some grave clothes still on, but underneath is a beautiful resurrected Body!

We, as the Body of Christ, must learn to function together as a body. A body must work together for the good of the total person. Jesus has designed His Body to function in the unity of His Spirit, the oil that flows through the total Body, to cause it to work together smoothly and effectively. Only in that unity can we fully see His Kingdom come and His will be done. The Body of Christ is much bigger than each of our little fellowships. It is not limited by the denominational labels that churches have placed upon themselves. Its boundaries do not stop at our borders of nations. It is a body, a living organism, not an organization. A body is not rigid though it does have a skeletal frame, but is fluid as it moves, advancing the Kingdom of God. Jesus desires for His Body to carry

out the works He did in His earthly body and do even greater works.

Day Twenty-five:
Each Part Doing Its Work

As we saw yesterday, within the unified Body of Christ, each part has a particular job to do. To continue the analogy of the human body, there are many different systems, many different parts that work together for the function of the whole. The same is true of an army. An army consists of many people fulfilling many different roles, holding many different ranks. As each person marches in his assigned position, the entire army moves forward.

God has created each and every one of us to be unique. There is not another person who is exactly like you. And God has assigned a particular set of works for us to do within His Body, in service in His army. Nothing is unimportant. Each connects in some way to another to get the big job done, to reveal Jesus Christ, and to advance His Kingdom. *For we are God's workmanship, created in Christ Jesus to do good works, which God prepared in advance for us to do* (Ephesians 2:10).

Many times we hear of someone coming to know the Lord and then feeling they want to serve Him by going into a "traditional" preaching, pastoring, or evangelistic ministry. And God does call people into those places of service. But let's not limit the areas of service available to the Christian. Indeed, there are no limits to the ways and the places in which we can serve the Lord. He may call us to the worship place or to the marketplace. *And whatever you do, whether in word or deed, do it all in the name of the Lord Jesus, giving thanks to God the Father through him* (Colossians 3:17). *Whatever you do, work at it with all your heart, as working for the Lord, not for men, since you know that you will receive an inheritance from the Lord as a reward. It is the Lord Christ you are serving* (Colossians 3:23,24).

Good Fortune, or a Troop

In reality, it is most important that *who* we are defines *what* we do and *how* we do it.[26]

The Shepherd King

Throughout this chapter, we are seeing Jesus as our King and as the commander-in-chief of His army. But what kind of King is He? Yesterday's scripture included a portion from the book of Isaiah. *Of the increase of his government and peace there will be no end. He will reign on David's throne and over his Kingdom, establishing and upholding it with justice and righteousness from that time on and forever. The zeal of the LORD Almighty will accomplish this.*

David's throne?

The prophet Samuel was told by the Lord to fill his horn with oil. He was sending him to Jesse of Bethlehem. Samuel was to anoint one of Jesse's sons to become the next king of Israel. Samuel went to Bethlehem and invited Jesse and his sons to join him in sacrificing to the Lord. When they arrived at the place of sacrifice, Jesse had each of his seven sons pass before Samuel, but none of these were God's choice for king. Samuel asked Jesse,

> *"Are these all the sons you have?"*
> *"There is still the youngest," Jesse answered, "but he is tending the sheep."*
> *Samuel said, "Send for him; we will not sit down until he arrives."*
> *So he sent and had him brought in. He was ruddy, with a fine appearance and handsome features.*
> *Then the LORD said, "Rise and anoint him; he is the one."*
> *So Samuel took the horn of oil and anointed him in the presence of his brothers, and from that day on the Spirit of the LORD came upon David in power* (1 Samuel 16:11-13).

David was a shepherd king. He led his people with the heart of

God. God had rejected Israel's first king, who turned away from following Him. *But now your kingdom will not endure; the LORD has sought out a man after his own heart and appointed him leader of His people, because you have not kept the LORD's command* (1 Samuel 13:14). In Psalm 100, David compares God's people to sheep:

> *Shout for joy to the LORD, all the earth. Worship the LORD with gladness; come before him with joyful songs. Know that the LORD is God. It is he who made us, and we are his; we are his people, the sheep of his pasture. Enter his gates with thanksgiving and his courts with praise; give thanks to him and praise his name. For the LORD is good and His love endures forever; his faithfulness continues through all generations.*

In Psalm 23, David gives us a picture of the Lord as our Shepherd and shows us His care for us. Jesus Himself proclaimed,

> *"I am the good shepherd; I know my sheep and my sheep know me—just as the Father knows me and I know the Father—and I lay down my life for the sheep. I have other sheep that are not of this sheep pen. I must bring them also. They too will listen to my voice, and there shall be one flock and one shepherd. The reason my Father loves me is that I lay down my life—only to take it up again. No one takes it from me, but I lay it down of my own accord. I have authority to lay it down and authority to take it up again. This command I received from my Father"* (John 10:14-18).

Our Lord is a Shepherd King. Jesus can lead us as our Shepherd because He, too, is a Lamb. He doesn't drive us, but He leads us in paths of righteousness where He has already walked and gained the victory. He then parades us, His people, in those places of triumph.

Good Fortune, or a Troop

But thanks be to God, who always leads us in triumphal procession in Christ and through us spreads everywhere the fragrance of the knowledge of him (2 Corinthians 2:14).

Let us look with the apostle John into heaven as we view our King.

> *Then I saw in the right hand of him who sat on the throne a scroll with writing on both sides and sealed with seven seals. And I saw a mighty angel proclaiming in a loud voice, "Who is worthy to break the seals and open the scrolls?" But no one in heaven or on earth or under the earth could open the scroll or even look inside it. I wept and wept because no one was found who was worthy to open the scroll or look inside. Then one of the elders said to me, "Do not weep! See the Lion of the tribe of Judah, the Root of David, has triumphed. He is able to open the scroll and its seven seals."*
>
> *Then I saw a Lamb, looking as if it had been slain, standing in the center of the throne, encircled by the four living creatures and elders. He had seven horns and seven eyes, which are the seven spirits of God sent out into all the earth. He came and took the scroll from the right hand of him who sat on the throne. And when he had taken it, the four living creatures and the twenty-four elders fell down before the Lamb. Each one had a harp and they were holding golden bowls full of incense, which are the prayers of the saints. And they sang a new song:*
>
> *"You are worthy to take the scroll and open its seals, because you were slain, and with your blood you purchased men for God from every tribe and language and people and nation. You have made them to be a kingdom and priests to serve our God, and they will reign on the earth."*
>
> *Then I looked and heard the voice of many angels, numbering thousands upon thousands and ten thousand times ten thou-*

> *sand. They encircled the throne and the living creatures and the elders. In a loud voice they sang: "Worthy is the Lamb, who was slain, to receive power and wealth and wisdom and strength and honor and glory and praise!"*
>
> *Then I heard every creature in heaven and on earth and under the earth and on the sea, and all that is in them, singing: "To him who sits on the throne and to the Lamb be praise and honor and glory and power, for ever and ever!"*
>
> *The four living creatures said, "Amen," and the elders fell down and worshiped* (Revelation 5).

Responding:

As we see Jesus our Shepherd King, we cannot help but worship Him along with the heavenly hosts. He truly is worthy! He is high above all!

As you look at and to your Shepherd King, He wants to reveal to you who He has created you to be, what He has called you to do in His Kingdom, and He wants to place you in the green pastures in which you can feed and grow in Him, and lead you forth in triumph as you dwell in Him. Let's look at Psalm 23, speak it forth as our confession of faith, and trust the Lord to lead us.

> *The LORD is my shepherd, I shall not be in want. He makes me lie down in green pastures, He leads me beside quiet waters, He restores my soul. He guides me in paths of righteousness for His Name's sake. Even though I walk through the valley of the shadow of death, I will fear no evil, for you are with me; your rod and your staff, they comfort me. You prepare a table before me in the presence of my enemies. You anoint my head with oil; my cup overflows. Surely goodness and love will follow me all the days of my life, and I will dwell in the house of the LORD forever.*

Good Fortune, or a Troop

You may want to meditate on this Psalm and ask the Lord what He wants to show you today in it. You may want to ask the Lord about specific directions or understandings of who He has called you to be or where He has called you to be. Spend time with Him and record anything that He would show you.

Our cocoon is much larger than we ever thought possible. We are but a part of its contents. The many parts make up the whole. As God is working in us individually, He is also working in us collectively. Together, we are the Body, the Bride. Jesus unites us all.

Chapter 13
Happy

"Leah had yet another son by her servant Zilpah—Asher, meaning *happy*. She was a happy woman, surrounded by all her sons," said Moses. "I can remember the happiness of my own mother as I nursed at her breast. I felt such peace and contentment as she sang to me. I revel in the story of how I had been saved from death by being put into a basket and placed in the river. What a woman of such strong faith and trust in G_d!"

Day Twenty-six:
Going Deeper

We don't have a character study of Leah laid out for us in the Bible, but we get a little glimpse of her in the begetting of children and in her naming of them. Here it seems that at least to some degree Leah has found happiness. Perhaps she has drawn near to the Lord her Shepherd and He has begun to reveal to her who He created her to be and how much He loved her. Though I can't imagine that she understood her great role in helping to birth this nation of Israel, there must have been some sense of satisfaction down deep inside as she mothered all these sons. And so Leah is happy! Even if not fully, at least to some degree she turned away from the circumstances of her marriage, her seeming competition with her sister in vying for her husband's affections, and just dug down a little deeper than all of this to find happiness.

Jesus came preaching about the Kingdom of God. In the Kingdom of God, things were a lot different. He talked about it in chapters 5, 6, and 7 of Matthew, what we call the Sermon on the Mount. Whereas before, *actions* had been dealt with primarily by the laws God had given at Sinai, now *attitudes* were much more important. The Kingdom of God in our earth first begins as a place in our heart, our innermost being, our spirit, and then grows out from there, just like Jesus' illustration of the mustard seed, which is the smallest seed but grows into a big tree in which the birds can make nests.

As Jesus sat on the hillside overlooking the sparkling waters of the Sea of Galilee, a crowd continued to gather. Jesus began teaching His disciples who were there with Him,

> *"Blessed are the poor in spirit, for theirs is the kingdom of heaven. Blessed are those who mourn, for they will be comforted. Blessed are the meek, for they will inherit the earth. Blessed are those who hunger and thirst for righteousness, for they will be filled. Blessed are the merciful, for they will be shown mercy. Blessed are the pure in heart, for they will see God. Blessed are the peacemakers, for they will be called sons of God. Blessed are those who are persecuted because of righteousness, for theirs is the kingdom of heaven. Blessed are you when people insult you, persecute you and falsely say all kinds of evil against you because of me. Rejoice and be glad, because great is your reward in heaven, for in the same way they persecuted the prophets who were before you"* (Matthew 5:3-12).

Any need that we may have can only be filled properly with God. Jesus puts it even more simply as He continues to teach on the mountainside, *"But seek first his Kingdom and his righteous-*

ness, and all these things will be given to you as well" (Matthew 6:33).

Jesus and his disciples had to go through Samaria. They came to Jacob's well, where Jesus rested from His journey while His disciples went into town to buy food. A Samaritan woman came to the well to draw water. Jesus asked her for a drink of water. She was surprised at the request since He was a Jew and she was a Samaritan. The Jews did not usually associate with Samaritans. Jesus perceived the woman's own need and offered her living water. She drank and was satisfied, so satisfied that she was overflowing and ran to invite others to come and drink of that living water also. The disciples returned with food and urged Jesus to eat.

> *But He said to them, "I have food to eat that you know nothing about."*
> *Then his disciples said to each other, "Could someone have brought him food?"*
> *"My food," said Jesus, "is to do the will of him who sent me and to finish his work. Do you not say, 'Four months more and then the harvest'? I tell you, open your eyes and look at the fields! They are ripe for harvest. Even now the reaper draws his wages, even now he harvests the crop for eternal life, so that the sower and the reaper may be glad together"* (John 4:32-36).

When we have given ourselves to look beyond our natural circumstances and situations to seek first His Kingdom and His righteousness, when we have chosen to yield ourselves to do His will, we are filled with a deep, abiding fulfillment that nothing else can bring to us. We sense the Master's loving words of affirmation, "Well done, thou good and faithful servant," and experience a deep inner peace and contentment that wells up into pure joy. We are happy because He is happy.

Responding:

You have been in this cocoon for some time now. The work of transformation is a deep work being done in your life. God is doing a mighty work in you! Let me pray for you this prayer that Paul prayed for the Colossians. I believe that we need to pray this prayer continually for one another in the Body of Christ. I have taken the liberty to make it personal between us. The prayer is found in Colossians 1:9-12.

Lord, I pray for my friend, that you would fill him or her with the knowledge of Your will through all spiritual wisdom and understanding. I pray that he or she would live a life worthy of You, Lord, and that he or she may please You in every way, bearing fruit in every good work, growing in knowing You, being strengthened with all power according to Your glorious might so that he or she may have great endurance and patience, joyfully giving thanks to You, Father, who has qualified him or her to share in the inheritance of the saints in the kingdom of light.
I bless you, my friend, in the name of our Lord Jesus Christ. Amen.

Day Twenty-seven:
The Way

For forty long years they had journeyed. They had been at this juncture before. Just on the other side of the Jordan River lay their Promised Land. God had brought them out of the enslavement and bondage of Egypt, but they hadn't yet gone into the land of promise. This was a new generation. All of the former ones had died as they traveled through the wilderness, except for Joshua, their leader, and Caleb, the two who had brought back a good report and believed that God would give them the land. They weren't going to "blow it" this time. They camped by the river for three days, preparing themselves to cross over. The river was flooded as it was harvest time in the river valley. But they weren't going to look at those circumstances this time. They were going to trust their God.

Joshua sent the orders throughout the camp: "*When you see the ark of the covenant of the LORD your God, and the priests, who are Levites, carrying it, you are to move out from your positions and follow it. Then you will know which way to go,* **since you have never been this way before**" (Joshua 3:3,4 emphasis added). The people of God were about to embark on a new journey. Their father Abraham had begun the journey years ago as He believed God and followed Him into this new land. In covenant with the Lord, Abraham received the promise that his descendants would possess this land. When Abraham died, all that he possessed of this land was a burial plot for him and his wife, Sarah. And now that promise was being fulfilled.

Jesus tried to speak to His disciples about His going away from them. They just didn't understand.

> "*Do not let your hearts be troubled. Trust in God; trust also in me. In my Father's house are many rooms; if it were not so, I would have told you. I am going there to prepare a place for you. And if I go and prepare a place for you, I will come back and take you to be with me that you also may be where I am. You know the way to the place where I am going.*"
> *Thomas said to Him, "Lord, we don't know where you are going, so how can we know the way?"*
> ***Jesus answered, "I am the way*** *and the truth and the life*"
> (John 14:1-6 emphasis added).

The next time we see Thomas is after Jesus' resurrection. He had not been with the other disciples when Jesus suddenly appeared in their midst one week earlier. It is interesting that in John's relating of this, he makes it a point to say that on this occasion Jesus showed them His hands and side. They had told Thomas about seeing the Lord. *But he said to them, "Unless I see the nail marks in his hands and put my finger where the nails were, and put my hand into his side, I will not believe it"* (John 20:25).

On this day, Thomas was with them. Jesus appeared in their midst once again.

> *Then he said to Thomas, "Put your finger here; see my hands. Reach out your hand and put it into my side. Stop doubting and believe."*
> *Thomas said to Him, "My Lord and my God!"*
> *Then Jesus told him, "Because you have seen me, you have believed; blessed are those who have not seen and yet have believed"* (John 20:27-29).

Part of our walk with Jesus involves seeing Him and, because of what we see, choosing to follow. Another part of our walk with Jesus involves taking His hand even when we do not see and trusting Him to lead us. Just think of Ruth. She apparently saw enough of God in the family into which she married that she chose to leave her own country and go to Bethlehem with her mother-in-law with no promises for her future. God rewarded her journey of faith by bringing her to a husband and blessing her with a son. She and her son were in the lineage of the Messiah.

Think of Shadrach, Meshach, and Abednego. They had served the one true God. They determined to continue to serve the God they knew even in the face of the demands of King Nebuchadnezzar that they bow down and worship the golden image he had made. These three Hebrews found themselves before a blazing furnace, waiting to be cast into the fire. Their words to the king were, *"O Nebuchadnezzar, we do not need to defend ourselves before you in this matter. If we are thrown into the blazing furnace, the God we serve is able to save us from it, and he will rescue us from your hand, O king. But even if he does not, we want you to know, O king, that we will not serve your gods or worship the image of gold you have set up"* (Daniel 3:16-18). These boys had never been in a fiery furnace, but because they had learned to trust God prior to this, they were willing to trust Him in this new situation as well, regardless of the outcome. What happened? Jesus walked with them in the fire and not a hair on their heads was even singed! They didn't even smell of smoke! And…**God was exalted in Babylon**! In addition, they were promoted. What a mighty God we serve!

This walk is a walk of faith. *Now faith is being sure of what we hope for and certain of what we do not see* (Hebrews 11:1). This walk of faith enables us to grasp in the light the One who will walk with us in the dark, knowing that as He steps into the dark with us that it will no longer be dark, for He is the light!

It is believed that Thomas became a missionary to India where he was martyred for his faith. His vision of Jesus as he walked with Him for the three years of His earthly ministry and as he touched with his own fingers the Lord's hands and side following His resurrection was enough to propel him forward into the unknown territory of His missionary calling.

Responding:

My cousin was married to a really neat fellow. He was a very personable guy, a pleasure to be around. We didn't see him often, but when we did, he really made us feel that he was glad to see us, and we enjoyed his presence and his sharing with us. It was such a devastating blow to hear that he had cancer. We prayed for him, but he only grew worse until he could no longer live and so left his precious family and went on to his heavenly home—good for him, I'm quite sure, but not so good for those he left behind who still feel the emptiness of him no longer being with them.

The morning of the funeral, I read the scripture from John 14, in which Jesus tells Thomas, *"I am the way, the truth and the life."* Little did I know at that time how much I needed to eat that "daily bread" the Lord was feeding me. I went to my parents' home. They were also going to the funeral, along with my aunt, uncle, and sister. Mama and Daddy and my aunt and uncle went in one car, driven by my dad, while my sister and I went together in another car, following close behind. It was a beautiful day, and we saw lots of family, sharing in the grief and celebration of our loved one's life. We got back into our cars and headed back home, my sister and I again following our dad. What a journey we had!

My dad has always been "the driver." He always knew the way to any destination. He enjoyed traveling and did lots of it in his work as a real-estate appraiser and in social organizations he was involved with, as well as for family vacations. But something was different about this trip. We drove for quite some time, trying to get out of the city, only to find we had been going in circles. We finally got back on track and stopped for dinner. We discovered that it had taken us several hours to get to this place that should have taken twenty or thirty minutes. We all laughed about it and really kidded my dad. Though he didn't say so at the time, it really bothered him.

After dinner, we drove home. It had been a very long day, a very long drive. As we got closer home, my sister got in the car with my mom and dad and aunt and uncle. They traveled on toward their homes, and I headed toward mine. I even turned in a wrong direction, realized it pretty soon, and had to backtrack for a few minutes before heading in the right direction. Needless to say, we were all glad to get home that evening and were very perplexed about the day's journey. It turned out to be just the beginning of a new and difficult journey for all of us.

Not long after this trip, my dad went for a colonoscopy that revealed cancer. The doctors felt they could get all of it by surgically removing a small portion of his colon. My dad had always been very healthy and wasn't on any medications at this stage in his life. He did very well with the surgery. They believed that they had gotten all the cancer but wanted him to take chemotherapy treatments as a precaution just in case there had been any stray cells that had not been caught. He had undergone three treatments, which he handled very well. He was to take his fourth treatment. The morning of his fourth treatment, he was having difficulty getting dressed and ready. He couldn't tie his shoe. Something seemed very wrong. My sister, a nurse, was called, and then the rescue squad. He ended up in the hospital where tests determined he had experienced a stroke. There was also evidence he had experienced several smaller strokes prior to this one. (We believe that was why he experienced difficulty finding his way home from the funeral.) One side of Daddy's body had been particularly affected, and it was decided to transfer him to a rehabilitation facility to help get things working properly once again. Before he could be transferred, however, he developed a bowel blockage that had to be cleared up first. The blockage was taken care of, and he was transferred to rehab. He seemed to be making progress, though his mood was affected with all that was happening in his body.

We planned a birthday celebration in rehab, but when we got to the facility, he wasn't doing well. Upon further investigation, it was discovered that he had a blood clot in his lungs, a very serious situation. He was transferred to Duke Hospital. The doctors told us they could only give him medicine to thin his blood and wait for his body to fight the clot. He did have a procedure done to install a filter to prevent another clot in his leg from moving up in his body. This man who had lived a little over seventy years without having any major health problems was suddenly dealing with a lot. He was growing weary with the fight. My dad has a deep relationship with the Lord, and he began to talk about going on to see Him. I really think that he believed that his time was at hand. I remember one day in particular going to the hospital to sit with him to give my mother a much-needed rest and praying for him while he rested. I felt the battle he was experiencing and prayed fervently for his healing. There were many others who were praying for him also. He made it through once again, and the clot began to dissolve. His body continued to strengthen, although he was very weak from all that he had experienced. He was not strong enough to return to rehab just yet and so he was transferred to a nursing home temporarily, where he received physical and occupational therapy. Different medications were given to him to attempt to help with the healing. Their effects were often very difficult to deal with. He was very depressed at times. Little by little, he began to strengthen and finally the right combination of medicines were determined.

All of this was tremendously difficult for my mother. Not only did she have to stand by and watch helplessly as her husband went through one battle after another with his health, but she had to make decisions she had never had to make before. My dad had been a strong leader in our home and made most of the decisions about everything. Suddenly, everything was placed in her hands to handle. She was so overwhelmed at times, but I saw her reach out on many occasions to the Word of God where she found an anchor, though her boat was moored in a very tempestuous sea.

Day by day, step by step, both of them grew stronger. They have come through this time stronger, I am sure, because of all they have been through. My dad is doing well now. He is at home and able to get around well, especially if he knows he's going out to eat. My mom continues to take good care of him. They both seem to have grown closer, having weathered this storm together and made it to the other side.

Happy

It has been a scary journey, a very challenging journey, but we have found that as we have taken hold of the nail-scarred hands of Jesus, He has filled the darkness with His marvelous light. He *is* the Way. I wouldn't want to travel without Him.

Not only is He the Way in difficult times, but He leads us into new adventures with Him every day. A few years ago, the Lord spoke to my husband and me about a retreat center. As we prayed, we sensed we were to sell our home in town and move out into the county, purchasing a home on ten acres of land with other land available around us. It has been a very slow process in our eyes. We are being stretched tremendously, but we have come to know our God in truly awesome ways. This journey is only beginning, and we look forward to all that God has in store as we partner with Him in this venture in His Kingdom. The vision that the Lord gave my husband many years ago was of a lighthouse and troubled waters. As the light shone, the waters were stilled. He also saw an ulcerated stomach and the light shining upon it. The stomach was healed. God spoke to him and called him to shine the light of Jesus Christ into troubled lives to bring healing. He has done just that, and we continue to shine the light of Jesus to expel the darkness.

Jesus is the Way. I believe with all my heart that we as Christians can experience great adventures in the Kingdom of God. Dare to trust Him. As you have experienced Him in the light, so He will be with you in the unknown of your future. *"Blessed are those who have not seen and yet have believed."*

Many remember Thomas as a doubter. I believe that Thomas faced his doubts that day as he touched the Lord's hands and side. He chose to leave those doubts behind and move ahead in faith. He found once again that courage that he had expressed as the disciples warned Jesus about going back to Judea where some Jews had tried to stone Him previously. Jesus wanted to go to His friend, Lazarus.

Then Thomas (called Didymus) said to the rest of the disciples, "Let us also go, that we may die with him" (John 11:16). A doubter? For a moment, yes, but also a very courageous man. Jesus will do whatever we need to dispel our doubts. His love finds a way. Give Him your doubts today, and begin a new adventure with Him. The place that Jesus has prepared for us is a place of blessing. Every journey with Him ends in blessing. Look it up—blessed means happy!

Day Twenty-eight: Complete Joy

The real vitality of our Christian life hinges entirely on one thing—our union with our Savior and Lord Jesus Christ. In John 15, we have Jesus' teaching concerning this union available to us.

> *"Remain in me, and I will remain in you. No branch can bear fruit by itself; it must remain in the vine. Neither can you bear fruit unless you remain in me. I am the vine; you are the branches. If a man remains in me and I in him, he will bear much fruit; apart from me you can do nothing...As the Father has loved me, so have I loved you. Now remain in my love. If you obey my commands, you will remain in my love, just as I have obeyed my Father's commands and remain in his love. I have told you this so that my joy may be in you and that your joy may be complete. My command is this: Love each other as I have loved you"* (John 15: 4,5,9-11).

Joy goes beyond happiness. It is deep and abiding, rich and full. Jesus told us here that the secret to that complete joy is found in our union with Him.

In every generation, there are those who reach out a little further to go a little deeper with the Lord, and one such person was Rufus Mosley. He spoke much about our union with Christ. He

taught that there were different degrees of union and that there are basically three steps to union:
1) interchange;
2) interaction and partnership; and
3) integration or likeness.

In interchange, we come to God much like the prodigal son came home to his father. We bring our sin and receive His righteousness. We bring our weakness and receive His strength. We bring our folly and receive His wisdom. We bring our grief and sorrow and receive His joy. The prodigal son came home in his rags. In exchange, he received a robe. He came home with an appetite and received the fatted calf. What a wonderful exchange from our point of view—we bring our needs and He brings His provision for those needs.

In interaction and partnership, we join together with God to be laborers together in His Kingdom. We live and act in His name led by His Spirit. As the prodigal came home, he was celebrated and recognized once again as a son. He again worked with his father.

In integration or likeness, we become like Jesus. We watch Him and learn from Him; so much so that we actually begin to allow His thoughts to be our thoughts and get into His way of doing things. We live as an extension of who He is. The two are indeed becoming one, intertwined as the vine and the branch. In marriage, it is said that the longer two people live together, the more they begin to even look alike. They come to the point where they can finish each other's sentences—the two becoming one.

We are invited to come into the Kingdom of God and live in it by His grace, but there are aspects of our union with Him that we can never experience unless we enter more fully into doing His will as we release to Him those things that would hinder us from doing so.

 *Cocoon*

Jesus not only wants us to reconnect with Him and the Father, but He asks us to remain in Him, to dwell or live in Him continually. To stay in this union all the time, there are three considerations necessary. First of all, to be in union with Christ all the time, we have to love all the time. No one can abide in God unless he abides in His love. He is love. Love is the very atmosphere of His Kingdom. This is the new commandment that Jesus gives that we should love one another. Love begins with God. He pours out His love to us abundantly, extravagantly. He tells us in His Word that there is absolutely ***nothing*** that can separate us from His love. What we do or don't do does not change the truth that He loves us. He loves us unconditionally! Oh how difficult it is for us to grasp this truth! But it is so true! He loves you just as much on your worst day as He does on your best day. As a matter of fact, He loves you so much that on your worst day, He draws even closer to release to you all that you need of Him to overcome whatever it is that you're going through. Don't resist His love, but receive it. The only thing that changes concerning His love for us is our ability to receive it. He wants to heal us of our hurts so that we can receive His love in ever-increasing measure.

As His love pours into us, we fill up just like a pond filling with water. If we continue to fill and never allow an outflow of that love, we become a swamp. Swamp water turns sour and breeds mosquitoes. To keep the water fresh, we must have an outflow as well as an inflow. And so, as God pours in His love to us, we can pour it out to others. We don't have to manufacture this love. God gives it to us. It's not hard to take what someone has given you and pass it on to someone else.

Jesus taught us, *"Give, and it will be given to you. A good measure, pressed down, shaken together and running over, will be poured into your lap. For with the measure you use, it will be measured to you"* (Luke 6:38). Whatever we give out to others will be given back to us. If we give love, if we give heaven, that's what we'll get. If we give hell, we'll get hell back and that will be our experience. We can't give out something without going out into that ourselves. This is the battle we engage in as Christians. This is where we determine if we are remaining in Christ or not. As we encounter evil, will we meet it with good? As we encounter hate, jealousy, and fear, will we meet it with love? This is what the Lord asks of us and He gives us His love to meet every situation. The more we receive of His love, the more we rest in the security of His love, and are able to give out His love even in the most difficult of situations. We cannot refuse to love anybody. God's love is unconditional. None of us is worthy of it, but He gives it to us liberally just the same. Those who are difficult to love need His love all the more.

Jesus tells us, *"I am the gate; whoever enters through me will be saved. He will come in and go out, and find pasture. The thief comes only to steal and kill and destroy; I have come that they may have life, and have it to the full"* (John 10:9,10). What a joy to know that even when we wander off, He stands as the gate back into that sweet union with Him once again, that green pasture. As we realize that we're standing outside of fellowship with Him, we can repent and return to that sweet communion we once had. Jesus was speaking to the *church* in Laodicea when He said, *"Here I am! I stand at the door and knock. If anyone hears my voice and opens the door, I will come in and eat with him, and he with me"* (Revelation 3:20).

Secondly, to remain in union must be our major responsibility. In other words, if we'll look after the union, He'll look after us. Jesus put it this way, *"But seek first his kingdom and his righteousness, and all these things will be given you as well"* (Matthew 6:33). We are assured that if we seek, we shall find. *"Do not be afraid, little flock, for your Father has been pleased to give you the kingdom"* (Luke 12:32). Christ is Lord over all creation. We are in Him. We don't have to worry about anything. His yoke is easy, and His burden is light. As we rest in Him, we can accomplish what we could never do in our own effort apart from Him. Why, it's like trying to cut down a big forest with a little handsaw when He's sitting there with a big bulldozer. We might get the job done eventually, but by that time we'd be so worn out, sweaty, and stinky, and probably would have a bad attitude about the whole ordeal. Only in Him can we bear good fruit.

One of the things that can get us out of our sweet place of union is when we let other things that don't really matter get our attention. If we will seek Him who is the Highest of all, we will receive the highest and everything else will be added that we need. When Isaiah saw the Lord, He was *seated on a throne, high and exalted, and the train of his robe filled the temple* (Isaiah 6:1). We are the temple! His train fills us—an extension of all He is and has!

Thirdly, within this union, we are experiencing the new covenant relationship. The prophet Ezekiel looked ahead to this new covenant as he prophesied the word of the Lord, *"I will give you a new heart and put a new spirit in you; I will remove from you your heart of stone and give you a heart of flesh. And I will put my spirit in you and move you to follow my decrees and be careful to keep my laws* (Ezekiel 36:26,27). Hebrews 10 quotes from Psalm 40 concerning its fulfillment in Jesus, *Then I said, "Here I am, I have come—it is written about me in the scroll. I desire to do your will, O my God; your law is within my heart"* (Psalm 40:7,8). The King James Version uses the word *delight* rather than *desire*. In union with Him, we love to do what we should do. It becomes our delight. When it becomes our delight to do the will of God, then we will do it. Most of us do the things that we truly want to do. If we want to do His will, it will be a whole lot easier for us to actually do it.

Jesus encourages us to live in our union with Him. Our conduct doesn't always bear witness to this union. We come in and go out of the fellowship of this union, and so don't always experience the joy of it. However, Jesus paints a picture for us to see it in the vine and the branch. He wants us to experience this union in the same way that He experiences this union with the Father. He always enables us to do what He calls us to do. We are becoming children of God. *Yet to all who received him, to those who believed in his name, he gave the right to become children of God* (John 1:12). *The Spirit himself testifies with our spirit that we are God's children* (Romans 8:16).

Responding:

Jesus tells us, *"For where your treasure is, there your heart will be also"* (Matthew 6:21). Jesus Himself is our treasure. Picture Him as a treasure chest and yourself inside that treasure chest. The treasure you find there is far greater than material treasure. What is He showing you now about that treasure? Journal anything that He shows you or speaks to you about. Determine today to remain in Him and revel in the joy of this union. Pray that you will know His love and show His love. Pray that you will seek Him first. Pray that you will delight in Him. As you remain in Him, you will know complete joy—unspeakable and full of glory! Our cocoon is filled with joy.

Chapter 14
Reward

Moses had the undivided attention of all the leaders of the tribes, and so he continued his narrative. "Within this ongoing rivalry between the two wives of Jacob, they had one thing right. G_d desires us to be fruitful people. It was just amazing how they went about seeking that fruitfulness. Leah's firstborn son, Reuben, found some mandrakes and brought them to his mother. As you know, mandrakes are herbs that were believed to heal barrenness. Rachel, who had not conceived any children from her own womb as of yet, made a deal with Leah. If Leah would let her have the mandrakes, she could sleep with Jacob that night. Deal! And Leah cried out to G_d to bring forth the fruit of that night's liaison. Sure enough, along came Issachar, *reward*," said Moses.

Day Twenty-nine: Believe and Receive

We have already determined that our dead "butterfly" needed life imparted to it in order to fly once again. Leviticus 17:14 tells us that *the life of every creature is its blood.* God appeared to Abraham and desired to cut a blood covenant with him. As He came to him, He spoke to Abraham and said, *"Do not be afraid, Abram. I am your shield, your very great reward"* (Genesis 15:1). It is quite interesting that Abram's question immediately following this statement by God was concerning an heir. God responded to Abram's question by giving him His word on the matter and promising him a son that would come from his own body. He then took Abram out and had him to look up into the sky at all the stars. The number of the stars would be the number of his offspring, which Abram was unable to count. God had spoken to Abram when he had begun this journey to the land of Canaan:

> *"Leave your country, your people and your father's household and go to the land I will show you. I will make you into a great nation and I will bless you; I will make your name great, and you will be a blessing. I will bless those who bless you, and whoever curses you I will curse; and all peoples on earth will be blessed through you"* (Genesis 12:1-3).

Abram didn't just want to be blessed himself, but he wanted to pass on this blessing to others.

Following God's word to Abram about his offspring, Genesis 15:6 makes this statement: *Abram believed the LORD, and he credited it to him as righteousness.* Then God entered into a covenant relationship with Abraham and a new nation was born.

Abraham (his name had been changed as he covenanted with God) and his wife, Sarah, were past the childbearing age. They received God's promise of a son, yet took matters into their own hands as to how this son would come. Sarah gave her maidservant, Hagar, to her husband. Hagar gave birth to a son, Ishmael. But this was not God's provision. God brought forth His son of promise, Isaac, through Sarah, a miraculous conception and birth.

Years later, God spoke to Abraham to take this son of promise, his heir, and offer him as a burnt offering on Mount Moriah. Abraham was an old man. He could have easily given his own life, but that of his son? All around him, those who knew nothing of the one true God offered their sons to gods who were only idols. Did

Abraham love his God as much as these heathen loved their idols? Would he trust God and be obedient even in this? This was God's promised heir for him. How could he slay him? Abraham did not waver. He took two of his servants and his son and headed to the mountains. *On the third day Abraham looked up and saw the place in the distance. He said to his servants, "Stay here with the donkey while I and the boy go over there.* **We** *will worship and then* **we** *will come back to you"* (Genesis 22:5 emphasis added).

As Abraham and his son went on further, Isaac questioned him. *"The fire and the wood are here," Isaac said, "but where is the lamb for the burnt offering?" Abraham answered, "God himself will provide the lamb for the burnt offering, my son"* (Genesis 22:7,8).

When they reached the spot for the sacrifice, Abraham prepared the altar and bound his son, ready to carry out the Lord's request of him. Can you imagine the utter shock and confusion of Isaac? "What on earth is going on?" he must have wondered. The knife was poised in Abraham's trembling hand as the tears streamed down his face. And then the Angel of the Lord called out to him, *"Do not lay a hand on the boy,"* He said. *"Do not do anything to him. Now I know that you fear God, because you have not withheld from me your son, your only son* (Genesis 22:12). Abraham saw a ram caught in the thicket that he offered in the place of his son. *So Abraham called that place THE LORD WILL PROVIDE. And to this day it is said, "On the mountain of the LORD, it will be provided* (Genesis 22:14).

Hebrews 11:17-19 gives us more insight into Abraham's experience on Mount Moriah:

> *By faith Abraham, when God tested him, offered Isaac as a sacrifice. He who had received the promises was about to sacrifice his one and only son, even though God had said to him, "It is through Isaac that your offspring will be reckoned." Abraham reasoned that God could raise the dead, and figuratively speaking, he did receive Isaac back from death.*

Here we see a clear picture of Abraham's heart. Abraham did not put his trust in Isaac, but rather he put his trust in God. Nobody around him would have understood what he was about to do. This one whose miraculous birth brought joy to him in his old age and, from his own loins, an heir to all he possessed, could he now lay on the altar and slay? He didn't think about what others may have said. He didn't consider that some may even have thought he was backsliding in his faith to succumb to offering his son as a sacrifice just as the pagans did to their gods. Abraham knew his God. He knew he heard his God and proceeded to do the only thing he could do. He would obey though he did not understand. He knew that God had a bigger plan. And so, in this covenant relationship with our father Abraham, God looked ahead to that day when His Son would be sacrificed as the Lamb of God on that same mountain. Abraham had believed God. He had obeyed God though he did not understand. He had learned that he could not reason out and strategize the son of promise into being. Only God could bring him forth.

Trust in the LORD with all your heart and lean not on your own understanding; in all your ways acknowledge him, and he will make your paths straight (Proverbs 3:5,6). Abraham leaned his full weight on God and found him to be very trustworthy. We can trust God with anything we place in His hands. And as we give it all to Him, we receive more than we could have ever dreamed. We know our God in ways we never would have otherwise as we lean our total weight on Him. As we give Him our material goods, He provides us with eternal riches. As we give Him our houses and lands, He gives us the Kingdom in which we can live abundantly. As we give Him our loved ones, He gives us a huge, wonderful family filled with His incomprehensible love. As we give Him our lives, He gives us His.

A seed that is planted must first die to spring forth with new life. The new life that comes forth is a multiplication of the seeds sown. Jesus said of His upcoming death,

> *"I tell you the truth, unless a kernel of wheat dies, it remains only a single seed. But if it dies, it produces many seeds. The man who loves his life will lose it, while the man who hates his life in this world will keep it for eternal life. Whoever serves me must follow me; and where I am, my servant also will be. My Father will honor the one who serves me"* (John 12:24-26).

Each of us can and must say with the apostle Paul, *I have been crucified with Christ and I no longer live, but Christ lives in me. The life I live in the body, I live by faith in the Son of God, who loved me and gave himself for me* (Galatians 2:20).

> *Understand, then, that those who believe are children of Abraham. The Scripture foresaw that God would justify the Gentiles by faith, and announced the gospel in advance to Abraham: "All nations will be blessed through you." So those who have faith are blessed along with Abraham, the man of faith…The promises were spoken to Abraham and to his seed. The Scripture does not say "and to seeds," meaning many people, but "and to your seed," meaning one person, who is Christ…You are all sons of God through faith in Christ Jesus, for all of you who were baptized into Christ have clothed yourselves with Christ. There is neither Jew nor Greek, slave nor free, male nor female, for you are all one in Christ Jesus. If you belong to Christ, then you are Abraham's seed, and heirs according to the promise* (Galatians 3:7-9,16,26-29).

In Christ Himself is our inheritance as sons and daughters of God.

Responding:

Not a whole lot is known about the apostle James, son of Alphaeus. He is referred to as James the Less, possibly because he was younger or shorter than the other James who was also an apostle. Nevertheless, we are reminded of John the Baptist's words concerning Jesus, *"He must become greater; I must become less* (John 3:30). Some of John's disciples had come to him with a concern that more people were going to Jesus than to John to be baptized. John, however, knew his place in the Kingdom and reiterated that he was not the Christ, but found joy in pointing to the Christ. James was not known for anything particular he did while following Jesus as one of His disciples, but he was one of the twelve. He, too, answered the call to follow Jesus. He, too, learned at His side. He was faithful to remain with Jesus and with the twelve. Legends say that he preached the gospel in Persia where he was also crucified, but even in this there is no concrete evidence. James represents the faithful believer following God wherever He leads, not for any delusions of grandeur or aspirations of his own, but simply finding his reward in God alone.

My husband, Kenny, was called into full-time ministry while in college. He completed college, went on to seminary, was ordained into the ministry, and served in various churches as youth minister, associate pastor, and pastor. In 1982, God led him into an evangelistic ministry. He linked up with another minister, John Hobbs of Maranatha Ministries Unlimited. John and Betty Jo have been a tremendous blessing and wonderful friends to us. Kenny and John have been a dynamic duo in the Lord. They've done lots of camps, retreats, and revivals together over the past twenty-five years. Wherever they have gone, they have released the heart of the Father God into countless lives and seen God do amazing things.

Reward

During this time of ministry, as my husband was traveling, I was left behind to nurture our two sons as they grew. I was definitely not alone in this venture. Kenny was gone when he was gone, but he was home when he was home. In other words, when he was home, Kenny invested a lot of time into his family. As the boys grew older, I became more active in our church, teaching in children's church, leading a children's choir, and was very involved in the women's ministry, choir, and other activities. We were all growing tremendously in the Lord and having a great time in the process, even though we had our challenges as well. I have been blessed to have some wonderful friends throughout the years who have each imparted just a little more of the love and life of God into my life.

Our associate pastor was sent out with a different vision to begin another work in the area. We didn't go with him immediately, but we all kept in touch, and later on, we transferred into the new work, located in the heart of the city to reach all kinds of folks. We jumped in full force, very excited to see all that God was doing. I started helping organize some new ministries within our body and was loving my work. Eventually, I began teaching Sunday school and then Wednesday night Bible study, as well as helping oversee some of the ministries within the church. I was seeing lives touched in a wonderful way by the love of God in Christ. Pastor Howard asked me to become the associate pastor. After much prayer, I took that position and continued to grow in serving this wonderful body of believers. I could not ever have had such wonderful role models in ministry as Pastor Howard and Myrna. This couple is so full of the love of God and expressing that to others. They have never been moved by circumstances in their commitment to the Lord and in serving Him. They have followed Him faithfully.

Our boys grew up and married. I finally had some daughters! And then, the kicker, grandchildren came! Life was good. Kenny's ministry was going great, and even though I missed him tremendously when he was gone, there was a contentment in knowing that he was ministering to people so beautifully. I was experiencing such fulfillment in ministry at Life-Changing Christian Outreach. As I studied and taught the Word of God, I was getting to know Him so much better. As I sang with the praise team and even learned to play the drums a little (that's another story in itself!), I was experiencing such a joy in worshiping Him. And then the Lord began to stir the nest.

Kenny came home from a ministry trip and shared with me how God had put in his heart a vision for a Christian retreat center. We began to pray about it for some time and continued on in what we were doing. The Lord continued to stir our hearts until we knew it was time to make a move. We put our house up for sale and started looking for property out in the county that would give us some room to see this vision come to pass. We had seen a property we liked a great deal, but it was not zoned for what we had in mind. Well, our house sold very quickly and we had nowhere to go. The property we had seen and liked had been rented out, so we contacted the owner to see if it was possible to rent until we found something else to purchase. He agreed and we moved onto the property as renters. As Kenny rode with the owner to take some of his furniture to another location, the owner asked Kenny if we would still be interested in purchasing the property if the zoning could be changed. We took it to the Lord in prayer. God said, "Yes!" The zoning was changed. We were able to purchase the property, and that's where we are today.

In the next year, the Lord spoke to me to resign my position as associate pastor. I did. I knew this would cut our income and didn't know how we would make it, but we had to trust the Lord. We remained in the church for the rest of that year, and then, at the first of the new year, the Lord spoke to both Kenny and me separately at intercessory prayer one Thursday night, saying it was time for us to leave the church. We did. Kenny continued to travel, and I settled in at home, helping him with his secretarial tasks, but also spending lots of time with the Lord in prayer and in His Word. I began to walk over the land and pray for God's purposes to come forth. I had thought that our church would partner with us in this new venture, but the Lord had other plans. He wanted us to first get planted in Him above all else. People did not understand what we were doing, but they remained kind to us—just not as close because of our drawing away unto Him. It has been difficult to release some of the old, but I am so glad that we have desired to please Him. He Himself is our great reward! Knowing Him is worth all the pain of letting go of other things.

The Lord is continuing to call us deeper and deeper unto Himself, and in this process, He is bringing others who will be part of the team to minister at Yeshua's Vineyard. We are developing deep relationships with one another as together we are learning to trust the Lord and go where He leads.

I would encourage you today by challenging you to believe Him even when you don't understand. Knowing Him is worth it all! What is His word to you today? How will you respond? Will you believe Him and receive from Him? Journal your responses.

By now, we are learning more and more to trust the one who holds us in our cocoon. As we believe Him, we become more secure within Him, regardless of what is going on around us.

Day Thirty:
Seek and Find

One of my fondest memories of my childhood was playing hide and seek in our neighborhood. We'd wait until dusk. All the kids would gather around a big oak tree, and we'd choose who would be the lucky one to have to find everyone else, and then that person would close his eyes and count while everyone else scurried off in all different directions to hide. What fun it was to find my friends in their secret hiding places and tag them before they ran back to the big oak tree.

As a young girl, I also enjoyed reading mystery stories, trying to add up all the clues to solve the mystery. Now, lots of folks join me in becoming enthralled in the TV shows or movies, trying to unravel the plot of whodunits. Science labs all over the world are uncovering new tidbits of information as scientists delve into the human body or the earth's environment or many other intriguing quests to bring understanding. Astronauts are strapped into rocket ships designed to be propelled into outer space to learn just what's out there. There is something inborn in us that causes us to want to know more. I believe that something was put there by our Creator. Just as a loving grandchild hiding to elevate the anticipation of the find and being wrapped up in our arms, He waits for us to see Him more fully in all that He has created. Far beyond all the interesting information, He wants us just to know Him. We are all searching for God, whether or not we may want to admit it. Life must be more than what we can see at first glance—a whole lot more. And so in all the experiences of life, our search engine continues to spin, seeking out the answers to all our questions. Until we find Him, our hearts are not satisfied.

Jesus told the Pharisees, *"You diligently study the Scriptures because you think that by them you possess eternal life. These are the Scriptures that testify about me, yet you refuse to come to me to have life"* (John 5:39,40). The Pharisees were very religious people. They knew the scriptures inside and out. Yet, in all their knowing, they did not know the One about whom the scriptures taught.

Little children are always asked the question, "What do you want to be when you grow up?" And they have all kinds of answers. My mother tells me that when I was a little girl, I would get a Bible

Reward

and spread it open on the piano bench and then proceed to preach or teach my little heart out. I wish I knew what I said back then. Children are often more in touch with God than we adults. God has put things in us that often times get side-tracked or covered over because of trauma or the everyday experiences of life. We spend so much time training children in their ABCs, which is good, but we send them on a search for the plans for their lives without first sending them on a search for the Planner. He can put them in touch with the plans.

The prophet Jeremiah records the Lord's words to His people as they had lost a vision of His plans for them. They were about to be carried off from their homeland. In the midst of the turmoil, God spoke to draw them back to Him once again to find their "North Star." *"For I know the plans I have for you," declares the LORD, "plans to prosper you and not to harm you, plans to give you hope and a future. Then you will call upon me and come and pray to me, and I will listen to you. You will seek me and find me when you seek me with all your heart"* (Jeremiah 29:11-13). *"Call to me and I will answer you and tell you great and unsearchable things you do not know"* (Jeremiah 33:3). Jesus continues this invitation in the New Testament, *"Ask and it will be given to you; seek and you will find; knock and the door will be opened to you. For everyone who asks receives; he who seeks finds; and to him who knocks, the door will be opened"* (Matthew 7:7,8).

James tells us, *If any of you lack wisdom, he should ask God, who gives generously to all without finding fault, and it will be given to him* (James 1:5). But he also warns us, *But when he asks, he must believe and not doubt, because he who doubts is like a wave of the sea, blown and tossed by the wind. That man should not think he will receive anything from the Lord; he is a double-minded man, unstable in all he does* (James 1:6-8). God is always delighted to answer us and make Himself known to us when we come to Him with a sincere heart. In chapter 4, James goes on to say, *You do not have, because you do not ask God. When you ask, you do not receive, because you ask with wrong motives, that you may spend what you get on your pleasures* (James 4:2,3). We cannot have God fully if we are holding on to so many other things. He is a *big God!* He needs lots of room to rest in us and bring to us the fullness of Himself. We must make room for Him.

As Jesus is teaching the disciples how to pray, He tells them that the Father knows what they need before they ask Him. Yet, He taught them to ask. God does not force Himself on us, but waits to be invited, waits to be asked. He waits for our hunger to be aroused and then satisfies our hunger. He waits for our longing for Him to cause us to seek Him and then allows us to find Him. And that is our reward—that as we seek Him, we find Him.

Responding:

My closest friends have always been wonderful prayer partners, which has been a wonderful blessing. These powerful intercessors are too numerous to mention, but they will always hold a special place in my heart. For their prayers I am very grateful. Recently, I have learned about listening prayer.[28] I suppose I have skirted the fringes of this type of prayer as I have learned over the years to hear the voice of the Lord as I have come to Him. A friend has taught me in her gentle sweet surrender to the Lord how to wait on Him and hear what He would say or see what He would show as we ask Him, "Lord, what do you want to show us concerning this that is on our heart?" As we wait upon the Lord, we speak out anything we hear or see and continue to ask Him what He is speaking to us. It is amazing! We may see or hear something that seems totally off the subject of what we are praying about, but as we speak it forth and press on further in our conversation with the Lord, suddenly He reveals something previously hidden and we see Him in our midst with the answer to our questions. We can then repent as we

Reward

need to, give ourselves anew unto Him and move toward more and more of the wholeness in which He wants us to walk for our own lives and to share with others. I am in awe of the simplicity of seeking God and finding Him, and yet what a profound difference His presence and His answers make in our lives. And even after we see an area of need revealed to us, we must continue to rely on Him to work in and out the answer.

God is a good God! He has so much to share with us, so much to give us of Himself, but He is waiting for us to ask. For in asking, we get to know Him and share His presence with one another.

Beloved, ask and it *shall* be given unto you; seek and you *shall* find. *And without faith it is impossible to please God, because anyone who comes to him must believe that he exists and that he rewards those who earnestly seek him* (Hebrews 11:6). What pleases God? He delights in loving us and blessing us!

Draw near to Him now. I call your spirit to the forefront that you may connect with the Spirit of God and receive from Him. Lord, what would you say to my friend right now? Listen and respond to Him.

God should be the first one with whom we share our innermost thoughts and concerns. There are some things that should be kept between the two of us. He is working in us in those areas in deep personal ways, and we are leaning totally on Him. There are others times, after we have taken some matters to the Lord, that He would lead us to share these concerns with others and ask for their agreement for answers and insights. Prayer partners can help encourage us in wonderful ways. The power of agreement between a husband and wife or between trustworthy friends or ministers who honor our confidences can help thrust us over into victory as we deal with particular circumstances and situations or strongholds in our lives. What a blessing to be able to share with one another in our walk with the Lord.

It is absolutely mind boggling to think about all that the Lord wants to show us! Many times we become so accustomed to familiar surroundings that we begin to take things for granted and lose sight of all that is before us. Don't become so familiar with your cocoon that you miss out on all that the Lord wants to show you. Even as we know Him more, there is still much to be known about Him. There is still much mystery to be uncovered. Enjoy your discovery!

Day Thirty-one:
Sowing and Reaping

There is yet another principle involved with rewards, and that is the principle of sowing and reaping. There are several aspects of sowing and reaping. In giving to others, we receive in like kind as we give out. What we sow, we reap, good or bad.

> *Do not be deceived: God cannot be mocked. A man reaps what he sows. The one who sows to please his sinful nature, from that nature will reap destruction; the one who sows to please the Spirit, from the Spirit will reap eternal life. Let us not become weary in doing good, for at the proper time we will reap a harvest if we do not give up. Therefore, as we have opportunity, let us do good to all people, especially to those who belong to the family of believers* (Galatians 6:7-10).

In giving to God, however, we get into what I call *redemptive reaping*. As we give to the Lord, we receive better than we give. We talked about this in the previous chapter. We give the old and receive the new. We give our weakness and get His strength. Sometimes our giving to the Lord involves hurts from others. We give to Him that pain and disappointment, releasing forgiveness to those who have brought about the hurt. *Those who sow in tears will reap with songs of joy. He who goes out weeping, carrying seed to sow, will return with songs of joy, carrying sheaves with him* (Psalm 126:5,6).

There is a marked difference in life with the Lord.

> *The land you are entering to take over is not like the land of Egypt, from which you have come, where you planted your seed and irrigated it by foot as in a vegetable garden. But the land you are crossing the Jordan to take possession of is a land of mountains and valleys that drinks rain from heaven. It is a land the LORD your God cares for; the eyes of the LORD your God are continually on it from the beginning of the year to its end.*
>
> *So if you faithfully obey the commands I am giving you today—to love the LORD your God and to serve him with all your heart and with all your soul—then I will send rain on your land in its season, both autumn and spring rains, so that you may gather in your grain, new wine and oil. I will provide grass in the fields for your cattle, and you will eat and be satisfied* (Deuteronomy 11:10-15).

Spelled out in this passage, the difference is the rain of the Lord. In looking further into the Word of God, we understand more fully what God is saying.

> *As the rain and the snow come down from heaven, and do not return to it without watering the earth and making it bud and flourish, so that it yields seed for the sower and bread for the eater, "so is my word that goes out from my mouth: It will not return to me empty, but will accomplish what I desire and achieve the purpose for which I sent it. You will go out in joy and be led forth in peace; the mountains and hills will burst into song before you, and all the trees of the field will clap their hands. Instead of the thorn bush will grow the pine tree,*

and instead of briers the myrtle will grow. This will be for the LORD's renown, for an everlasting sign, which will not be destroyed (Isaiah 55:10-13).

The secret ingredient is the Word of God—BAM! In His love for us, the Lord releases His Word into our lives to make a difference. The analogy used in Ephesians 5:25-27 is that of a husband loving his wife. *Husbands, love your wives, just as Christ loved the church and gave himself up for her to make her holy, cleansing her by the washing with water through the word, and to present her to himself as a radiant church, without stain or wrinkle or any other blemish, but holy and blameless.*

Just as the fullness of our redemption in Jesus Christ is seen in His resurrection, so the fullness of our redemption will be seen in the resurrection of our bodies.

But some may ask, "How are the dead raised? With what kind of body will they come?" How foolish! What you sow does not come to life unless it dies. When you sow, you do not plant the body that will be, but just a seed, perhaps of wheat or of something else. But God gives it a body as he has determined, and to each kind of seed he gives its own body…So it will be with the resurrection of the dead. The body that is sown is perishable, it is raised imperishable; it is sown in dishonor, it is raised in glory; it is sown in weakness, it is raised in power; it is sown a natural body, it is raised a spiritual body…And just as we have borne the likeness of the earthly man, so shall we bear the likeness of the man from heaven.

I declare to you, brothers, that flesh and blood cannot inherit the kingdom of God, nor does the perishable inherit the imperishable. Listen, I tell you a mystery: We will not all sleep, but we will all be changed—For the trumpet will sound, the

Reward

dead will be raised imperishable, and we will be changed (1 Corinthians 15:35-38,42-44,49-52).

As the seed of God's Word is planted in our hearts, we become rooted and grounded in Christ and then the fruit can be born.

This will be the sign for you, O Hezekiah: "This year you will eat what grows by itself, and the second year what springs from that. But in the third year sow and reap, plant vineyards and eat their fruit. Once more a remnant of the house of Judah will take root below and bear fruit above. For out of Jerusalem will come a remnant and out of Mount Zion a band of survivors" (2 Kings 19:29-31; Isaiah 37:30-32).

The Father sowed His Son and is now receiving many sons. *For those God foreknew he also predestined to be conformed to the likeness of his Son, that he might be the firstborn among many brothers* (Romans 8:29).

On many occasions, Jesus taught about the Kingdom of God with parables, stories with everyday parallels to truths in the Kingdom of God. One such parable was the Parable of the Sower. Let's look at this story and Jesus' commentary on it as it is recorded in Luke 8.

"A farmer went out to sow his seed. As he was scattering the seed, some fell along the path; it was trampled on, and the birds of the air ate it up. Some fell on rock, and when it came up, the plants withered because they had no moisture. Other seed fell among thorns, which grew up with it and choked the plants. Still other seed fell on good soil. It came up and yielded a crop, a hundred times more than was sown...This is the meaning of the parable: The seed is the word of God. Those along the path are the ones who hear, and then the devil comes and takes away the word from their hearts, so that they may

not believe and be saved. Those of the rock are the ones who receive the word with joy when they hear it, but they have no root. They believe for a while, but in the time of testing they fall away. The seed that fell among thorns stands for those who hear, but as they go on their way they are choked by life's worries, riches and pleasures, and they do not mature. But the seed on good soil stands for those with a noble and good heart, who hear the word, retain it, and by persevering produce a crop."

One requirement for the sower is righteousness. We already know that Jesus has imparted to us His righteousness, but we must choose to walk in it. When we don't walk in righteousness, resulting in our lives being out of order, our sowing and reaping may be thwarted in the sense that what we sow is eaten up as soon as we reap. In warning about walking in disobedience, God instructs Moses, *You will plant seed in vain, because your enemies will eat it* (Leviticus 26:16).

The prophet Haggai had a very sobering word for the people of God who had been brought back into their land.

Now this is what the LORD Almighty says: "Give careful thought to your ways. You have planted much, but have harvested little. You eat, but never have enough. You drink, but never have your fill. You put on clothes, but are not warm. You earn wages, only to put them in a purse with holes in it." This is what the LORD Almighty says: "Give careful thought to your ways. Go up into the mountains and bring down timber and build the house, so that I may take pleasure in it and be honored, " says the LORD. "You expected much, but see, it turned out to be little. What you brought home, I blew away. Why?" declares the LORD Almighty. "Because of my house, which remains a ruin, while each of you is busy with

Reward

his own house... Then Zerubbabel son of Shealtiel, Joshua son of Jehozadak, the high priest, and the whole remnant of the people obeyed the voice of the LORD their God and the message of the prophet Haggai, because the LORD their God had sent him. And the people feared the LORD... This is what the LORD Almighty says: "In a little while I will once more shake the heavens and the earth, the sea and the dry land. I will shake all nations, and the desired of all nations will come, and I will fill this house with glory," says the LORD Almighty. "The glory of this present house will be greater than the glory of the former house," says the LORD Almighty. "And in this place I will grant peace," declares the LORD Almighty... "From this day on, for this twenty-fourth day of the ninth month, give careful thought to the day when the foundation of the LORD's temple was laid. Give careful thought: Is there yet any seed left in the barn? Until now, the vine and the fig tree, the pomegranate and the olive tree have not borne fruit. From this day on I will bless you" (Haggai 1:5-9,12; 2:6-9,18-19).

When we seek the Lord first, His Kingdom and His righteousness, all else that we need will be added. In giving to the Lord first, He tells us that He will "rebuke the devourer" for us.

"Bring the whole tithe into the storehouse, that there may be food in my house. Test me in this," says the LORD Almighty, "and see if I will not throw open the floodgates of heaven and pour out so much blessing that you will not have room enough for it. I will prevent pests from devouring your crops, and the vines in your fields will not cast their fruit," says the LORD Almighty. "Then all the nations will call you blessed, for yours will be a delightful land," says the LORD Almighty (Malachi 3:10-12).

The fruit of righteousness will be peace; the effect of righteousness will be quietness and confidence forever. My people will live in peaceful dwelling places, in secure homes, in undisturbed places of rest. Though hail flattens the forest and the city is leveled completely, how blessed you will be, sowing your seed by every stream, and letting your cattle and donkeys range free (Isaiah 32:17-19).

Responding:

The seed we need to sow is the Word of God, as seen in the parable of the sower. We were born again by opening our hearts to receive His Word. *For you have been born again, not of perishable seed, but of imperishable, through the living and enduring word of God* (1 Peter 1:23). The Lord continues to water that Word so that the fullness of the life contained therein can spring forth. His Word will accomplish all that He sends it to accomplish. Then we can walk it out in our lives. Ask the Lord today what Word you need to meditate on and plant in your heart. He has a Word to fit your circumstances and what He wants to do in the midst of them right now. Hear that Word and continue to plant it until it takes root. Record that Word in your journal. Speak it forth that you may continue to hear and cause faith to arise. He is the **Living Word.** *May God himself, the God of peace, sanctify you through and through. May your whole spirit, soul and body be kept blameless at the coming of our Lord Jesus Christ. The one who calls you is faithful and he will do it* (1 Thessalonians 5:23,24).

A friend shared a dream she had one night. In the dream, she was in a restaurant. She went and sat beside a girl and began to share with her concerning the things of God. The girl sent her away. Later, she went back to sit beside the girl again, and then she awoke from her dream. I believe that this dream illustrates something in the Kingdom of God. In our study today, we read the scripture from Deuteronomy 11:10-15. In it, the Lord spoke of the autumn and spring rains, or what we term the former and latter rains. The former rain is for the planting. The latter rain is for the seed to grow and be harvested. Even as we plant the seed of God in our own lives, we are also to scatter the seed for others to receive as well. It may fall on different soils, as in the parable of the sower. Oftentimes we cannot fully discern the soil. It may appear to be rocky or briar laden, but there may be just enough opening for the seed to fall through and be planted. The person may not respond right away, but as God waters the seed, it will grow and the harvest will come in its time.

Jesus had shared with the woman at the well. The disciples had gone into town to buy food. When they returned, Jesus did not appear hungry and they urged Him to eat. As He was responding to them, Jesus spoke these words:

"My food," said Jesus, "is to do the will of him who sent me and to finish his work. Do you not say, 'Four months more and then the harvest'? I tell you, open your eyes and look at the fields! They are ripe for harvest. Even now the reaper draws his wages, even now he harvests the crop for eternal life, so that the sower and the reaper may be glad together. Thus the saying 'One sows and another reaps' is true. I sent you to reap what you have not worked for, and you have reaped the benefits of their labor (John 4:34-38).

On another occasion, in Matthew's gospel, Jesus addressed this same subject: *Then He said to His disciples, "The harvest is plentiful but the workers are few. Ask the Lord of the harvest, therefore, to send out workers into his harvest field* (Matthew 9:37).

So we pray that the Lord would send laborers out into the harvest field. Perhaps you are one who would respond today just as the prophet Isaiah. As his sin was removed by the coal from the altar, he heard the Lord saying, *"Whom shall I send? And who will go for us?" And* [Isaiah] *said, "Here am I. Send me"* (Isaiah 6:8). The Lord sent him forth with His Word. He warned Isaiah that no one would listen. Isaiah remained faithful. Since that time, many have read the words of Isaiah and turned to the Lord. He saw no fruit in his lifetime, but oh the fruitfulness beyond his lifetime. His word speaks on into eternity, for it was the Word of the Lord. Be faithful, and God will bring forth fruit in its season.

There have been many seeds of faith sown throughout time; perhaps the time of harvest is nearing! There is an interesting principle at work as we remain in our cocoon. In his letter to Philemon, Paul shares this encouragement: *I pray that you may be active in sharing your faith, so that you will have a full understanding of every good thing we have in Christ* (Philemon 6). The more we speak the seed of the Word, the more that seed begins to bear fruit in our lives. Keep speaking the Word and watch for the harvest!

Chapter 15
Honor

Moses loved to share the stories of his ancestors. Though he grew up in the palace of Egypt, his delight was far greater in his own people, a people chosen by God with a special mission to bless the whole earth. An insatiable desire burned deep within him to lead these people on to the land of promise. He had come face to face with the one true God who held the highest place of honor within his heart.

"Leah bore yet one more son to Jacob," continued Moses. "She had perhaps given up on being loved by her husband in the same way as was her sister. Yet she found a special place of honor in his heart as the mother of six of his sons. That is indeed quite an honor among our people. She named this son, Zebulon, meaning *honor.*"

Day Thirty-two:
Honor God

> *Then the LORD said to Moses, "Tell the Israelites this: 'You have seen for yourselves that I have spoken to you from heaven: Do not make any gods to be alongside me; do not make for yourselves gods of silver or gods of gold. Make an altar of earth for me and sacrifice on it your burnt offerings and fellowship offerings, your sheep and goats and your cattle. Wherever I cause my name to be honored, I will come to you and bless*

you. If you make an altar of stones for me, do not build it with dressed stones, for you will defile it if you use a tool on it. And do not go up to my altar on steps, lest your nakedness be exposed on it" (Exodus 20:22-26).

God warned His people not to make any graven images to represent Him. A picture or other representation of someone is just not the same as the person himself. My husband loves to take photographs. We all cringe when he pulls out the camera. But later on it is quite a joy to pull out the pictures and remember the wonderful time we were having when the pictures were made. And the pictures are not just pretty scenery; the pictures he likes to take are of the people in his life. The pictures are only special because of the relationship that we have with the people in the pictures. God does not want us to focus on images that are an attempt to represent Him as we see Him in some way. These would be too limiting of who He is. It would not be an adequate picture. Rather, He wants us to come to know Him in relationship with Him. Many times we get a false picture of who God is because of our own self-centered mindset and our own shallow thinking. He tells us in Isaiah 55:8-9, *"For my thoughts are not your thoughts, neither are your ways my ways," declares the LORD. "As the heavens are higher than the earth, so are my ways higher than your ways and my thoughts than your thoughts."*

God is far bigger, more wonderful, more glorious than we can even imagine. But He invites us into relationship to know Him, to discover little by little (really there is nothing little in God!) more of His awesome character and nature. To honor someone is to recognize their value, to respect them for who they are, and consequently, to esteem them in high regard or reverence them. We honor God with our worship and praise, but these must come from our relationship with and discovery of Him to be genuine. As we know Him, in that relationship with Him, we yield to Him more and more in our lives.

Honor

In Exodus 20, we have just read how God instructed the people to build an earthen altar of stones to come before Him. God also instructed the Israelites to build a tabernacle that He might dwell among them, and He ordained priests to come into His presence and minister before Him.

> *Then Moses went up to God, and the LORD called to him from the mountain and said, "This is what you are to say to the house of Jacob and what you are to tell the people of Israel: You yourselves have seen what I did to Egypt, and how I carried you on eagles' wings and brought you to myself. Now if you obey me fully and keep my covenant, then out of all nations you will be my treasured possession. Although the whole earth is mine, you will be for me a kingdom of priests and a holy nation. These are the words you are to speak to the Israelites"* (Exodus 19:3-6).

Every part of this old covenant worship was a type and shadow of Jesus Christ. His is the reality of it all. He is the cornerstone of this altar of stone. He is the great high priest opening the way into the holy of holies.

> *As you come to him, the living Stone—rejected by men but chosen by God and precious to him—you also, like living stones, are being built up into a spiritual house to be a holy priesthood, offering spiritual sacrifices acceptable to God through Jesus Christ. For in Scripture it says, "See, I lay a stone in Zion, a chosen and precious cornerstone, and the one who trusts in him will never be put to shame."…But you are a chosen people, a royal priesthood, a holy nation, a people belonging to God, that you may declare the praises of him who called you out of darkness into his wonderful light* (1 Peter 2:4-6,9).

The greatest way that we can honor God is to live in vital relationship with Him, allowing our ever-widening, ever-deepening view of Him to transform us in His presence so that we walk out this new creation reality. Perhaps the reason that God wanted a kingdom of priests and now calls us a royal priesthood is that the priests were the ones who drew near to Him.

I have recently read one of the best books ever, *The Shack,* by William P. Young. I want to share with you from that book an awesome revelation pertaining to the Trinity.

> *"But what difference does it make that there are three of you, and you are all one God. Did I say that right?"*
>
> *"...It makes all the difference in the world!...We are not three gods, and we are not talking about one god with three attitudes, like a man who is a husband, father, and worker. I am God and I am three persons, and each of the three is fully and entirely the one....What's important is this: If I were simply One God and only One Person, then you would find yourself in this Creation without something wonderful, without something essential even. And I would be utterly other than I am."*
>
> *"And we would be without...?" Mack didn't even know how to finish the question.*
>
> *"Love and relationship. All love and relationship is possible for you only because it already exists within Me, within God myself...."*[29]

God experiences this relationship of love in the Father, Son, and Holy Spirit. He invites us to join Him in this relationship.

There is such an awesome description of the early church found in Acts 2:42-47.

> *They devoted themselves to the apostles' teaching and to the fellowship, to the breaking of bread and to prayer. Everyone*

was filled with awe, and many wonders and miraculous signs were done by the apostles. All the believers were together and had everything in common. Selling their possessions and goods, they gave to anyone as he had need. Every day they continued to meet together in the temple courts. They broke bread in their homes and ate together with glad and sincere hearts, praising God and enjoying the favor of all the people. And the Lord added to their number daily those who were being saved.

One of the important facets of this early church was fellowship. We are a part of a small group of believers here at Yeshua's Vineyard. I have to say that one of the most fun parts of our Sunday morning gatherings is our time of fellowship as we gather around the lunch table. This is something integral to the Body of Christ with which I feel we have lost touch. How often have we met together in impersonal services while wearing our superficial masks, not really relating to one another in the reality of life?! It's time to get real!

Responding:

Our eyesight is growing more keen as we live in our cocoon. We are seeing the Lord much clearer. He *is* worthy of honor!

I want to invite you to read chapters 4 and 5 of the book of Revelation and allow yourself to be transported to this heavenly place. While there, begin to exalt the Lord as holy, worship Him, and bring Him honor from your heart. We, too, can sing the new song to the Lamb: *You are worthy to take the scroll and to open its seals, because you were slain, and with your blood you purchased men for God from every tribe and nation. You have made them to be a kingdom and priests to serve our God, and they will reign on the earth* (Revelation 5:9-10).

We can join with every creature and sing: *To him who sits on the throne and to the Lamb be praise and honor and glory and power, forever and ever!* (Revelation 5:13).

Enjoy your time with Him!

Day Thirty-three:
Honor Your Father and Your Mother

One of what we call the Ten Commandments that Moses received on Mount Sinai tells us to *Honor your father and your mother, so that you may live long in the land the LORD your God is giving you* (Exodus 20:12). In Deuteronomy 5:16, this command is reiterated with another phrase added to it. *Honor your father and your mother, as the LORD your God has commanded you, so that you may live long and that it may go well with you in the land the LORD your God is giving you.* We are again reminded of this same command on several occasions in the gospels and in Paul's letter to the Ephesians. This Word tells us to do much more than just honor our birth mothers and fathers or the ones who reared us, although it includes that. We are to honor all those in the faith who have gone before us.

Throughout history, God has been releasing light to each new generation. Our forefathers were certainly not perfect people, but each generation has received and imparted understanding in a different facet of our life in Christ that propelled the Body of Christ further into its destiny as true mature sons of God. Jesus certainly gave us an example as He honored His Father. Hebrews 11 is a testimony to the faith of our forefathers. As we read this testimony, we are encouraged in our own walk of faith. The last two verses of this chapter attest to the progressive journey of this faith. *These were all commended for their faith, yet none of them received what had been promised. God had planned something better for us so that only together with us would they be made perfect* (Hebrews 11:39,40).

As we continue on into chapter twelve, we are encouraged as the saints who have gone before us are cheering us on. We honor all of those who have walked with God before us. Ephesians 2:11-22 speaks of this house of God that we are building.

> *Therefore, remember that formerly you who are Gentiles by birth and called "uncircumcision" (that done in the body by the hands of men)—remember that at that time you were separate from Christ, excluded from citizenship in Israel and foreigners to the covenants of the promise, without hope and without God in the world. But now in Christ Jesus you who once were far away have been brought near through the blood of Christ.*
>
> *For he himself is our peace, who has made the two one and has destroyed the barrier, the dividing wall of hostility, by abolishing in his flesh the law with its commandments and regulations. His purpose was to create in himself one new man out of the two, thus making peace, and in this one body to reconcile both of them to God through the cross, by which he put to death their hostility. He came and preached peace to you who were far away and peace to those who were near. For through him we both have access to the Father by one Spirit. Consequently, you are no longer foreigners and aliens, but fellow citizens with God's people and members of God's household, built on the foundation of the apostles and prophets, with Christ Jesus Himself as the chief cornerstone. In him the whole building is joined together and rises to become a holy temple in the Lord. And in him you too are being built together to become a dwelling in which God lives by his Spirit.*

I would encourage you to read about the lives of saints in past generations. Hear their testimonies of walking with the Lord and the revelations they have seen and heard along their journeys. Be grateful for what they can share with us. My youngest son will tell you that he learned a lot by watching his older brother! We can learn a lot by looking back, but at the same time, we should remember not to look for the same things to happen but rather to be open as those in the past have been to the new things that God wants to do in our midst. We are building a dwelling place for God. We are the lively stones that are set in place upon the ones before us!

Responding:

Our church employed a youth minister for the summer when I was a teenager. The first time I saw Brenda, I knew she was different. She sang in the morning worship service and was introduced to us. We began doing all kinds of fun activities. It was an awesome time in my life when the Lord continued to draw me closer to Him. Brenda took a group of us down to Spartanburg, South Carolina. A fellow by the name of Ken Callaham was an inner-city minister in Spartanburg. He had a big heart for young people. During the weekend, we participated in a crusade and I opened my heart to be filled with the Spirit of the Lord as I had never before experienced. I came home so hungry for the Lord. The *Good News for Modern Man* paraphrase of the New Testament had just come out. I purchased a copy and devoured it from cover to cover.

My love for the Word of God has never diminished. In my new-found zeal for the Lord, I lacked wisdom in that I thought those in my church who were not experiencing this new life in the way I was were hypocrites. I have had to repent of this attitude and judgment toward them. Recently, I had the opportunity to return to my home church and share with them on a women's ministry day. I had the opportunity to thank them for the foundation they provided me in the faith and share my journey with the Lord over the years. There are many godly examples in this church, as well as my own mother and father, grandparents, aunts, uncles, and good friends. I am truly grateful for their impact on my life.

I would encourage you to read Hebrews 11 to remember your spiritual heritage of faith. I would also encourage you to remember those who have touched your life in a special way because of their walk with the Lord. Write about them today in your journal. Choose to honor them as they blazed a trail before you. Follow that trail and then, cheered on by them, proceed forward as the Lord leads you ever onward.

Day Thirty-four: Zealous for His Honor

We don't know a lot about the apostle called Simon the Zealot, except for the clues given by the tag on his name, "the Zealot." Zealots were those Jews who desired to rise up and overthrow the Romans who ruled over them. As they began following Jesus, the disciples did not fully understand the kind of King He was and the nature of the Kingdom He ruled. They had hopes of a political king who would indeed overthrow those who ruled over them. Even as they followed Jesus to the Garden of Gethsemane on the night He was betrayed, some believe that Judas was attempting to force the Lord's hand to stand up and fight and enforce His Kingship. Peter, in his zeal for his Master, wielded his sword and cut off the ear of the Roman soldier, but Christ restored the soldier's ear. This was not God's way to establish His Kingdom. His Kingdom was far bigger than the boundaries of worldly empires. His rule was not one of forceful dominance but of love.

Nevertheless, zeal is a positive quality when directed correctly. I am sure that Simon, along with all the other apostles, realized the difference of King Jesus and His Kingdom rule following Christ's death, burial, resurrection, and ascension leading to the pouring out of the Holy Spirit on the Day of Pentecost. God had His own plan for extending His rule and reign. *"But you will receive power when the Holy Spirit comes on you; and you will be my witnesses in*

Jerusalem, and in all Judea and Samaria, and to the ends of the earth" (Acts 1:8).

On their journey toward the promised land, the children of Israel traveled to the plains of Moab. As they camped there, the Moabites were terrified of them. They had heard of how they had defeated the other kings and nations surrounding them. Because of their fear, they attempted to enlist Balaam to curse the Israelites. They found out that they could not curse what God had blessed. And so, they went to a more subtle plan, to seduce the Israelites to sexual immorality with the Moabite women, who led them to engage with them in worshiping their gods. This incited the Lord's anger against the Israelites. The Lord instructed Moses to kill those who had turned to these other gods. As Moses was speaking this to the leaders in Israel and they were weeping before the Tent of Meeting, an Israelite man brought a Midianite woman into his tent in plain view of them all. When Phinehas, grandson of Aaron the high priest, saw it, he took his spear, followed the Israelite into his tent, and drove the spear through both of them. The plague against the Israelites was stopped after 24,000 had died.

> *The LORD said to Moses, "Phinehas son of Eleazar, the son of Aaron, the priest, has turned my anger away from the Israelites; for he was as zealous as I am for my honor among them, so that in my zeal I did not put an end to them. Therefore tell him I am making my covenant of peace with him. He and his descendants will have a covenant of a lasting priesthood, because he was zealous for the honor of his God and made atonement for the Israelites* (Numbers 25:10-13).

Notice that Phinehas was *"zealous for my honor."* He was zealous for the honor of God among his people. He took up the cause of God and did what needed to be done to stop the spread of this evil. Isaiah prophesied of Jesus Christ and the zeal of the Lord. *Of the increase of his government and peace there will be no end. He will reign on David's throne and over his kingdom, establishing and upholding it with justice and righteousness from that time on and forever. The zeal of the LORD Almighty will accomplish this* (Isaiah 9:7).

For our offenses are many in Your sight, and our sins testify against us. Our offenses are ever with us, and we acknowledge our iniquities: rebellion and treachery against the LORD, turning our backs on our God, fomenting oppression and revolt, uttering lies our hearts have conceived. So justice is driven back, and righteousness stands at a distance; truth has stumbled in the streets, honesty cannot enter. Truth is nowhere to be found, and whoever shuns evil becomes a prey. The LORD looked and was displeased that there was no justice. He saw that there was no one, he was appalled that there was no one to intervene; so his own righteousness sustained him. He put on righteousness as his breastplate, and the helmet of salvation on his head; he put on the garments of vengeance and wrapped himself in zeal as in a cloak.

According to what they have done, so will he repay wrath to his enemies and retribution to his foes; he will repay the islands their due. From the west, men will fear the name of the LORD, and from the rising of the sun, they will revere his glory. For he will come like a pent-up flood that the breath of the LORD drives along [OR when the enemy comes in like a flood, the Spirit of the LORD will put him to flight].

"The Redeemer will come to Zion, to those in Jacob who repent of their sins," declares the LORD. "As for me, this is my covenant with them," says the LORD. "My Spirit, who is on you, and my words that I have put in your mouth will not depart from your mouth, or from the mouths of your children, or from the mouths of their descendants from this time on forever," says the LORD (Isaiah 59:12-21).

In the New Testament, we see a display of the zeal of the Lord as Christ drives out the sellers from the temple.

> *When it was almost time for the Jewish Passover, Jesus went up to Jerusalem. In the temple courts he found men selling cattle, sheep and doves, and others sitting at tables exchanging money. So he made a whip out of cords, and drove all from the temple area, both sheep and cattle; he scattered the coins of the money changers and overturned their tables. To those who sold doves he said, "Get these out of here! How dare you turn my Father's house into a market!"*
>
> *His disciples remembered that it is written: "Zeal for your house will consume me."*
>
> *Then the Jews demanded of him, "What miraculous sign can you show us to prove your authority to do all this?"*
>
> *Jesus answered them, "Destroy this temple, and I will raise it again in three days."*
>
> *The Jews replied, "It has taken forty-six years to build this temple, and you are going to raise it in three days?" But the temple he had spoken of was his body. After he was raised from the dead, his disciples recalled what he had said. Then they believed the Scripture and the words that Jesus had spoken* (John 2:13-22).

Jesus Christ is the standard that God raised to display His honor.

In seeing the zeal of Jesus aroused to drive out the temple merchants, let us take every caution not to use this as an occasion to excuse our anger, which can be aroused at times in similar display. As we have mentioned previously, the anger of God is different from our own. In his book *Anger: Handling a Powerful Emotion in a Healthy Way*, Gary Chapman gives good advice on dealing with anger. Anger itself does come from God. His anger comes from two aspects of His nature, His righteousness and His love. In light of this, Chapman shares,

> *"What about us? Because, as we have seen, we bear the image of God, each of us has on some level a concern for righteousness, fairness, and justice. Whenever we encounter that which we believe to be unrighteous, unkind, or unjust, we experience anger. I believe that in God's design this anger is to motivate us to take positive, loving action to seek to set the wrong right; and where there has been a relationship, to restore the relationship with the wrongdoer. Anger is not designed to stimulate us to do destructive things to the people who may have wronged us, nor does it give us license to say or do destructive things to our neighbors. Anger's fundamental purpose is to motivate us to positive, loving action that will leave things better than we found them."*[30]

It is imperative that we remember that it is about the honor of the Lord, not our own peeves or frustrations.

> *My dear brothers, take note of this: Everyone should be quick to listen, slow to speak and slow to become angry, for man's anger does not bring about the righteous life that God desires. Therefore, get rid of all moral filth and the evil that is so prevalent and humbly accept the word planted in you, which can save you. Do not merely listen to the word, and so deceive yourselves. Do what it says...If anyone considers himself religious and yet does not keep a tight rein on his tongue, he deceives himself and his religion is worthless* (James 1:19-26).

Remember, this cocoon we find ourselves in is lined with grace.

> *For the grace of God that brings salvation has appeared to all men. It teaches us to say "No" to ungodliness and worldly pas-*

sions, and to live self-controlled, upright and godly lives in this present age, while we wait for the blessed hope—the glorious appearing of our great God and Savior Jesus Christ, who gave himself for us to redeem us from all wickedness and to purify for himself a people that are his very own, eager to do what is good [KJV: *"a peculiar people, zealous of good works"*] (Titus 2:11-14).

The name *Simon* means *hearing*. Once again, we are hearing the Word of the Lord and choosing to walk in it.

The apostle Paul speaks of being zealous for God as he persecuted the Church. As he comes to Christ, however, he recognizes that his honor was displaced. He says of his Jewish brethren,

Brothers, my heart's desire and prayer to God for the Israelites is that they may be saved. For I can testify about them that they are zealous for God, but their zeal is not based on knowledge. Since they did not know the righteousness that comes from God and sought to establish their own, they did not submit to God's righteousness. Christ is the end of the law so that there may be righteousness for everyone who believes (Romans 10:1-4).

As we live in Christ Jesus, our righteousness, let us be zealous for the honor of our God.

Responding:

Today as we conclude our thoughts on honor, let us remember our Jewish roots and do as we are instructed in the Word of God: *pray for the peace of Jerusalem*. Let us pray that they may know Christ as the Messiah and rest in Him as their righteousness, the fulfillment of the law.

Let us not become weary in doing good, for at the proper time we will reap a harvest if we do not give up. Therefore, as we have oppor-

tunity, let us do good to all people, especially to those who belong to the family of believers (Galatians 6:9,10).

In this temporal world on this spiritual journey, let us take a stand to honor God in all we do and in all our relationships with others to seek their highest good, trusting God to work in all that we see now as incomplete, unjust, and needing Him.

The cocoon begins to crack, be it ever so slightly, as the butterfly nestled within twitches. Something *is* happening beneath the camouflaged cover.

Chapter 16
Justice

As the tribal leaders listened to the story of their beginnings, in the background they heard the sounds of life within the camp. The young children laughed and played with one another. The men spoke with one another of the hope of a new day in the land they had been promised by God as they tended the livestock. The women were busy preparing the manna for its consumption. And that ever-present cloud continued to surround them with an awesome presence, their G_d who was leading this journey.

There was no tribe named for the daughter that Leah bore to Jacob, but Moses spoke of her as well. "Leah concluded her birthing children by bringing forth a little girl, Dinah," Moses shared.

"Dinah had quite a lot to contend with, having all those brothers!" exclaimed Aaron.

"Yes, she did," laughed Moses. "Her name means *justice*. Her brothers sought justice for her after she had been violated by Shechem, a Hivite. Women are quite mysterious creatures, my brothers, are they not?"

"Here! Here!" they all responded.

Day Thirty-five:
A Suitable Helper

Moses was revealed part of the mystery of the woman as God

shared with him about her creation. Genesis 2:18-25 records the story.

> *The Lord God said, "It is not good for the man to be alone. I will make a helper suitable for him." Now the Lord God had formed out of the ground all the beasts of the field and all the birds of the air. He brought them to the man to see what he would name them; and whatever the man called each living creature, that was its name. So the man gave names to all the livestock, the birds of the air and all the beasts of the field. But for Adam no suitable helper was found. So the Lord God caused the man to fall into a deep sleep; and while he was sleeping, he took one of the man's ribs and closed up the place with flesh. Then the Lord God made a woman from the rib he had taken out of the man, and he brought her to the man. The man said, "This is now bone of my bones and flesh of my flesh; she shall be called 'woman,' for she was taken out of man." For this reason a man will leave his father and mother and be united to his wife, and they will become one flesh. The man and his wife were both naked, and they felt no shame.*

What is a suitable helper? Finis Jennings Dake says, "A help suitable to man intellectually, morally, and physically—as his counterpart."[31] The Hebrew word used here is *Ish shah*, the feminine form of *Ish*, "of man." It literally means she-man; womb-man; man with the womb; or female-man, because she was taken out of man. Dake also comments, "Woman is said not to have been taken out of man's head to be lorded over by him, nor from his feet to be trampled on by him, but from his side to be equal with him, from under his arm to be protected by him, and from near his heart to be loved by him."[32]

God's desire for the man and the woman is stated in the Genesis account as He proclaims that the two shall be one. There is not a competition between them, but a completion as they come together, in marriage and in the Body of Christ. We have talked about this oneness before and how it is modeled in the Trinity—Father, Son, and Spirit. We are to submit to one another in loving service.

> *Submit to one another out of reverence for Christ. Wives, submit to your husbands as to the Lord. For the husband is the head of the wife as Christ is the head of the church, his body, of which he is the Savior. Now as the church submits to Christ, so also wives should submit to their husbands in everything. Husbands, love your wives, just as Christ loved the church and gave himself up for her to make her holy, cleansing her by the washing with water through the word, and to present her to himself as a radiant church, without stain or wrinkle or any other blemish, but holy and blameless. In this same way, husbands ought to love their wives as their own bodies. He who loves his wife loves himself. After all, no one ever hated his own body, but he feeds and cares for it, just as Christ does the church—for we are members of his body. "For this reason a man will leave his father and mother and be united to his wife, and the two will become one flesh." This is a profound mystery—but I am talking about Christ and the church. However, each one of you also must love his wife as he loves himself, and the wife must respect her husband* (Ephesians 5:21-33).

In this passage of scripture, the concept of submission is modeled in Christ's relationship with His Church. The Church is to be submissive to Christ as its head (authority). This authority is one of love. Jesus stated and exhibited this: *Greater love has no one than this, that he lay down his life for his friends* (John 15:13).

Jesus further taught on this idea of authority in Mark 10:42-45. *Jesus called them together and said, "You know that those who are* regarded as rulers of the Gentiles lord it over them, and their high officials exercise authority over them. Not so with you. Instead, whoever wants to become great among you must be your servant, and whoever wants to be first must be slave of all. For even the Son of Man did not come to be served, but to serve, and to give his life as a ransom for many."

Jesus gave us a vivid picture of His servanthood as He girded Himself with a towel, filled a basin with water, and proceeded to wash His disciples' feet (John 13). In a book co-authored by Tommy Tenney and David Cape, *God's Secret To Greatness (The Power of the Towel)*, Tommy Tenney shares the following about our warfare in the Kingdom of God. I want to make it clear here that in talking about "weapons" I am not at all supposing there is a war between men and women! Au contraire! Rather, a weapon must be used on the enemy of our souls to combat his lies and perversions in our understanding one another and becoming one.

> *"Weapons are tools of influence that often represent the authority of a far greater power. The weapon of choice in the heavenly realm is obviously 'the sword of the Spirit,' but the weapon of choice in the earthly realm is a towel. Both weapons are effective—but only when each is used in the right realm…As misunderstood as it is, the secret to true authority on the earth is a towel and not a sword."*

He also shared further,

> *"I want to share something written by Gordon MacDonald (served as President of InterVarsity/Christian Fellowship) that makes a lot of sense: '[Jesus'] followers grew up in a culture that understood only one politic: power. The power of kings and armies—brute force. The power of a religious community—pronouncing or denying God's approval. The power of family, village, and tribal tradition—nailing people to mindless conformity to 'the way we do things.'*

> "Most of us still find it easier to relate to the sword than to the towel. We find it easier to point fiery fingers or righteous indignation at sinners and saints than to wash their feet, bind our brother's wounds, feed hungry stomachs or clothe naked bodies.
>
> "For some reason, we find it easier to preach in order to prod people into the Kingdom than to love them into God's presence. Perhaps that is because servant love gets messy. It requires us to strip off our hard-won religious robes and replace them with the garments of humility, naked vulnerability and servitude. MacDonald put it this way: 'Jesus' brand of servanthood means that everyone (child, leper, Gentile, opposite gender, sinner) is more important than me. Servanthood means that all I have and all I am is placed at your disposal if it will bring you into the presence of God. Servanthood is not about how I can add value to my life, but about how I add value to yours.'"[33]

This service is not just acts done for someone. It goes much deeper. Recall the story of Mary and Martha in Luke 10:38-42.

> *As Jesus and his disciples were on their way, he came to a village where a woman named Martha opened her home to him. She had a sister called Mary, who sat at the Lord's feet listening to what he said. But Martha was distracted by all the preparations that had to be made. She came to him and asked, "Lord, don't you care that my sister has left me to do the work by myself? Tell her to help me!"*
> *"Martha, Martha," the Lord answered, "you are worried and upset about many things but only one thing is needed. Mary has chosen what is better, and it will not be taken away from her."*

Often the ones around us need us more than they need the things we do. This submission is not one of duty but of giving oneself first. It is an attitude of the heart that then exhibits itself as actions of the life. It's not like the joke you've heard about the little boy who kept getting told to sit down by his teacher. Finally, he agreed to sit but had this comment: "I might be sitting down on the outside, but I'm standing up on the inside." Remember Jesus' warning to the Pharisees in Matthew 23:25-26, *"Woe to you, teachers of the law and Pharisees, you hypocrites! You clean the outside of the cup and dish, but inside they are full of greed and self-indulgence. Blind Pharisees! First clean the inside of the cup and dish, and then the outside also will be clean."* It may seem very challenging to be able to love others in the way that Jesus did, and indeed it is—except that He lives in us and *has poured out his love into our hearts by the Holy Spirit, who he has given us* (Romans 5:5).

And what is our job to do in the Kingdom? *God blessed them and said to them, "Be fruitful and increase in number; fill the earth and subdue it. Rule over the fish of the sea and the birds of the air and over every living creature that moves on the ground"* (Genesis 1:28). We are not to rule over each other, but together we are to advance the Kingdom of God to encompass the whole earth. We can be one with one another and with God as we serve one another and serve the Lord. *Two are better than one, because they have a good return for their work: If one falls down, his friend can help him up. But pity the man who falls and has no one to help him up! Also, if two lie down together, they will keep warm. But how can one keep warm alone? Though one may be overpowered, two can defend themselves. A cord of three strands is not quickly broken* (Ecclesiastes 4:9-12).

Responding:

My husband and I are just as different as night and day. Because of that, life has been very challenging over the years. God does perform a miracle in marriages, though, as He takes two individuals such as us and makes us one. There was a time when we both seemed to go in different directions, as he was on the road a lot in evangelism and I was at home with our boys and working in our home church. But God knew what He was doing all the time. He was working on us each individually to prepare us for what we would do together at this time. I have already shared with you about our venture together to build Yeshua's Vineyard. We are just beginning this new adventure, but already I can say with the wedding guests of Cana that the Lord has saved the best wine for last! He has changed the water into wine!

My prayer for you is that you truly experience this oneness with others, whether it be a husband or wife or co-workers in your calling and vision for life. Are you experiencing this now? If so, maybe you'd like to just thank God for His goodness. If not, maybe you'd like to talk to the Lord about his helper(s) for your life. Journal your prayer to Him. What a blessing to share in this walk with Christ and with others who are called alongside us!

Day Thirty-six: Violated

Now Dinah, the daughter Leah had borne to Jacob, went out to visit the women of the land. When Shechem son of Hamor the Hivite, the ruler of that area, saw her, he took her and violated her (Genesis 34:1,2). Shechem fell in love with Dinah and wanted to marry her. *Then Shechem's father Hamor went out to talk with Jacob. Now Jacob's sons had come in from the fields as soon as they heard what had happened. They were filled with grief and fury, because Shechem had done a disgraceful thing in Israel by lying with Jacob's daughter—a thing that should not be done* (Genesis 34:6,7). Jacob's sons plotted on how to handle the situation. They replied to Shechem and his father that they could not let Dinah marry him unless all their men agreed to be circumcised. The men agreed, and while the men were still in pain from the circumcision, Simeon and Levi attacked with their swords and killed all the men. Jacob's sons then plundered the city. *Then Jacob said to Simeon and Levi, "You have brought trouble on me by making me a stench to the Canaanites and Perizzites, the people living in this land. We are few in number, and if they join forces against me and attack me, I and my household will be destroyed." But they replied, "Should he have treated our sister like a prostitute?"* (Genesis 34:30, 31).

We all know the story of what happened in the Garden of Eden. God's perfect man and woman living in the perfect environment with everything they would ever need opened the door for sin and death by yielding to the serpent. The man and the woman ate of the fruit of the tree they had been warned about—rebellion against God. As the serpent was told of the consequences of this action, a promise was given that one day One would come who would crush his authority. *"And I will put enmity between you and the woman, and between your offspring and hers; he will crush your head, and you will strike his heel"* (Genesis 3:15). Since that awful day, this fallen angel who had tried to exalt himself over God and been cast down out of heaven has been attacking women. Woman had "fallen and couldn't get up." And every time she tried, this enemy worked overtime to knock her back down.

Things are continuing to improve for women throughout the world, but the following quotation is from a book written by Loren Cunningham (founder of one of the world's largest mission societies, Youth With A Mission) and David Hamilton (a dedicated student of the Word) and published in 2000, *Why Not Women? A Biblical Study of Women in Missions, Ministry, and Leadership.*

> *In countries based on biblical principles, however eroded, women fare much better than those in countries with little Christian heritage. But even in Europe and North America, women suffer more injustices than men. In the United States,*

Justice

women still earn only 74 percent of the salary that men earn for doing the same job. Many of these women are struggling to support themselves and their children, thanks to a spiraling divorce rate and "deadbeat dads" who don't pay child support. Add to this the fact that about 400,000 teenage girls will become mothers this year in the USA and will raise their babies without the help of the young man who fathered the child. These women are still better off than the more than 100,000 women who will be raped this year in the USA. Many more are molested as little girls—approximately one in every three girls is sexually abused before she grows to maturity.

No one knows whether wife abuse is on the increase or is simply being more accurately reported. But more than 800,000 women will be beaten by their husbands or boyfriends in America this year. More than 1,000 will not survive.

However bleak this picture seems, if you go to countries with little Christian heritage, it becomes even worse. According to World Vision:

* 450 million women are physically impaired due to childhood malnutrition. In many societies, girls and their mothers eat only after the men and boys are fed.

* Women make up half the world's population but own just 1 percent of its wealth. Seventy percent of the 1.3 billion living in poverty are women.

* A girl is twice as likely not to be educated as a boy.

* Two million girls, mostly in Africa and the Middle East, are mutilated through female circumcision to diminish their sexual desire. Little girls who survive the procedure grow up to face painful sex, possible infertility, and a greater chance of dying during childbirth.

> *According to Time magazine:*
> * *In Brazil, it is justifiable homicide to kill an unfaithful wife.*
> * *In Russia, a woman's office job can include having to sleep with the boss.*
> * *In India, a husband and his parents sometimes conspire to kill his young bride after they have collected her dowry, freeing the young man to marry again and get another dowry. There are six thousand cases of this a year, and growing....*
>
> *A few years ago, I found an article in a back section of the New York Times with the title "100 Million Are Missing." The article explained how demographic scientists can predict how many males and females will be born anywhere in the world. But recent statistics show that as many as 100 million little girls are missing in today's generation worldwide—killed by their families because of their gender. Many millions of these missing girls are from India or China, where mothers routinely have abortions when they learn they are carrying a girl...Other girl babies are carried to term, then left outside to die of exposure.*
>
> *According to the article, another reason for the 100 million missing girls is death by neglect. In many countries of the developing world, if a son gets sick, the family does everything possible to get medical help. If a little girl gets sick, she is often allowed to die.*[34]

But...*the reason the Son of God appeared was to destroy the devil's work* (1 John 3:8). Jesus came to restore God's original design and purposes for men and women. We see women in the spotlight during three of the greatest events of Jesus' life:
1) His birth;
2) His death; and
3) His resurrection, as well as throughout His ministry.

Justice

The seed of the woman was prophesied to be the one to crush Satan's head. No man was involved. The Holy Spirit overshadowed Mary, a virgin, who then gave birth to the Son of God, Jesus Christ. However, a human father was given Jesus to protect this mother and child as we read that Joseph had been instructed in dreams when and where to move in order to keep his young family safe. We don't hear much about the early years of Jesus until the day the family travels to Jerusalem when Jesus is twelve years old. At this time, we find Jesus remaining in the temple as his parents were traveling home. They recognized He was missing from them, returned to find Him, and He shared with them that it was right that He should be in His Father's house. We don't hear of Joseph anymore in the scriptures. We know that he taught Jesus the carpentry trade. Jesus did not begin His public ministry until the age of thirty. Prior to this, we assume that He was taking care of His family in the absence of Joseph.

As Mary and Joseph dedicated Jesus in the temple, both a man and a woman, Simeon and Anna, prophesied over Him and gave thanks for Him.

We have lots of examples of Jesus interacting with and ministering to women. There were no double standards with Him. When the men desired to stone the woman caught in adultery, He turned the tables and said, *"If any one of you is without sin, let him be the first to throw a stone at her"* (John 8:7). Adultery is not a sin someone can commit alone! It takes two to tango! Jesus healed women as well as men. He even healed a woman with an "issue of blood." Women were positioned in the rear of the synagogue in Jewish worship, but Jesus spotlighted a crippled woman, a "daughter of Abraham," and healed her right in front of everyone. This woman stood straight and tall that day in many ways! He even healed "foreign women" who desired to "eat of the crumbs of the table." In John 4, Jesus' conversation with the Samaritan woman is the longest recorded private conversation Jesus had with any individual. She was rejected by the Jews because she was a Samaritan. She was rejected by men (except for sexual services!) because she was a woman. (She must have had a powerful testimony and people must have seen a radical transformation in her life for all the people of her town to flock to Jesus at her word!) But Jesus did not reject her. He spoke to her with dignity and respect. He listened to her and answered her questions. He gave her of the His living water to quench her thirst.

Look at Jesus' relationship to Martha, Mary, and Lazarus. He was particularly close to Mary. [Martha] *had a sister called Mary, who sat at the Lord's feet listening to what he said* (Luke 10:39). The term "sit at the feet" of a teacher showed a mentoring relationship between a rabbi and his disciple. Luke is showing that Mary was taking the position of a rabbinic pupil. *"I (Paul) am indeed a Jew, born in Tarsus of Cilicia, but brought up in this city at the feet of Gamaliel, taught according to the strictness of our fathers' law, and was zealous toward God as you all are today"* (Acts 22:3 NKJV). Jesus did not send her to the kitchen with a rebuke, but rather applauded her choice to sit at His feet. And He certainly was not rebuking Martha for serving, for He told His disciples that the greatest in the Kingdom of God was the one who served. Serving, however, came from first sitting at His feet.

People in the Old Testament were ordained for ministry by anointing with oil. Who anointed Jesus prior to His death? A woman! (John 12:1-8; Matthew 26:6-13)

Many women followed Jesus during His public ministry, right up through His death on the cross, His burial and His resurrection. Women were the first to discover the empty tomb and to be commissioned by Jesus to proclaim the message that He had risen.

Women were also present in the upper room when the Holy Spirit was poured out and the word realized, *"In the last days, God says, I will pour out my Spirit on all people. Your sons and daughters will prophesy, your young men will see visions, your old men will dream dreams. Even on my servants, both men and women, I will pour out my Spirit in those days, and they will prophesy"* (Acts 2:17,18). Women were a very integral part of the young church that we see in the book of Acts.

Dorothy Sayers, in her book *Are Women Human?*, wrote:

> *"Perhaps it is no wonder that the women were first at the Cradle and last at the Cross. They had never known a man like this Man—there never has been such another. A prophet and teacher who never nagged at them, never flattered or coaxed or patronized; who never made arch jokes about them, never treated them as 'The women, God help us!' or 'The ladies, God bless them!'; who rebuked without querulousness and praised without condescension; who took their questions and arguments seriously; who never mapped out their sphere for them, never urged them to be feminine or jeered at them for being female; who had no axe to grind and no uneasy male dignity to defend; who took them as He found them and was completely unselfconscious. There is no act, no sermon, no parable in the whole Gospel that borrows its pungency from female perversity; nobody could possibly guess from the words and deeds of Jesus that there was anything 'funny' about woman's nature."*[35]

Under the Old Covenant, circumcision was a sign of entering into the covenant relationship. It was only observed by males. Under the New Covenant, however, the circumcision is one of the heart, and exhibited in baptism, observed by both men and women. *You are all sons of God through faith in Christ Jesus, for all of you who were baptized into Christ have clothed yourselves with Christ. There is neither Jew nor Greek, slave nor free, male nor female,*

 Cocoon

for you are all one in Christ Jesus. If you belong to Christ, then you are Abraham's seed, and heirs according to the promise (Galatians 3:26-29). In Christ Jesus, man and woman are once again restored to a unity and union of fellowship and purpose.

Responding:

In Christ, we are to elevate one another in love and respect as together we serve the Lord. How can you serve your mate today? How can you serve others in the Body of Christ? How can you join hands with one another and serve the Lord? Ask the Lord today what He would speak to your heart concerning this and how you should act on it. Record your thoughts and God's word to you in your journal.

I want to encourage you today, regardless if you are a man or woman, to know how valuable you are to the Lord. You are His unique creation. He loves you with an everlasting love. If you have been pressed down in any way in your life, take the hand of Jesus that He is reaching out to you today and allow Him to lift you up to the fullness of who He created you to be. And I pray that the Lord would show you in ways that would be so uniquely fashioned to you just how special you are to Him. It really is true as the old song says, "Everybody's beautiful in their own way!" You are beautiful, wonderful, awesome! *You really are!*

As God redeems your life, your past experiences only serve to enhance your beauty. These acts of redemption show the glory and love of God in magnificent display. What a beautiful butterfly you are becoming!

Day Thirty-seven: Womb-man

Remember the word used for the suitable helper God gave to the man? The Hebrew word used is *Ish shah,* the feminine form of

Ish, "of man." It literally means she-man; womb-man; man with the womb; or female-man, because she was taken out of man.

Speaking of the Holy Spirit to be poured out, Jesus stood up on the last day of the Feast of Tabernacles and proclaimed, *"He that believeth on me, as the scripture said, out of his belly shall flow rivers of living water* (John 7:38 KJV). According to *Vine's Expository Dictionary of New Testament Words,* the word for *belly* is *koilia.* "Koilia comes from the word *koilos,* 'hollow,' and denotes the entire physical cavity, but most frequently used to denote the womb. In John 7:38, it stands metaphorically for the innermost part of man, the soul, the heart. [This same word used elsewhere is translated womb (Matthew 19:12; Luke 1:15,41,42,44; 2:21; 11:27; 23:29; John 3:4; Acts 3:2; 14:8; Galatians 1:15).]"[36] The NIV uses the words *innermost being* instead of belly.

Dutch Sheets, in his book, *Intercessory Prayer,* says, "We are the womb of God upon the earth. We are not the source of life, but we are carriers of the source of life. We do not generate life, but we release, through prayer, Him who does."[37]

The Holy Spirit hovered over the waters in the beginning and as the Word was spoken, creation took shape. That same Spirit hovered over Sarah and enabled her previously barren womb to conceive a child. The Hebrew nation was born. The Holy Spirit hovered over, or overshadowed the virgin Mary to bring forth the Christ Child. In *A Greek-English Lexicon of the New Testament,* Joseph Henry Thayer says that *episkiazo* is used "of the Holy Spirit exerting creative energy upon the womb of the Virgin Mary and impregnating it."[38] This word is used only three times in the New Testament: Luke 1, of the Holy Spirit overshadowing Mary, Matthew 17:5, speaking of the transfiguration where the *"cloud of the Lord overshadowed them,"* and Acts 5:15, speaking of Peter's shadow falling on folks and their being healed.

Since the very beginning, God gave the man and the woman a mandate to be fruitful and multiply. Only in union with Christ Jesus, empowered by the Holy Spirit, is this possible. God could touch people and bring them to new life in Him, He could heal broken bodies and broken hearts, He could bring His new creation reality to our chaotic circumstances and situations all by Himself, but He has chosen to work in the earth in union with us, His people. What an awesome responsibility and power is at our disposal. Many times, instead of our waiting for God to move, He is waiting for us. Empowered by His Holy Spirit, we get to partner with God as we speak His Word and release His Spirit to see people born again, healed, and transformed into the sons and daughters of God that He has created us to be.

In the garden, when the man and the woman were first created, the scripture says that *the man and his wife were both naked, and they felt no shame* (Genesis 2:25). However, after the fall, they realized that they were naked and hid themselves because of their shame. The word *ashamed* is the word *buwsh (boosh),* and means "to pale, i.e., by implication, to be ashamed; also to be disappointed, or delayed: -(be, make, bring to, cause, put to, with, a-) shame (-d), be (put to) confounded (-fusion), become dry, delay, be long."

I believe that in the garden before the fall, Adam and Eve were not ashamed because they were covered with the glory of God. When they fell, the glory began to pale and so they saw their nakedness. When Moses spent time in the presence of the Lord on the mountain or in the tent of meeting, he would come forth from that encounter with his face shining brilliantly. God has designed us to live in the glory! And as we live in that glory, we can give out of what we live in. This New Covenant ministry is spoken of in 2 Corinthians 3:5-18.

> *Not that we're competent in ourselves to claim anything for ourselves, but our competence comes from God. He has made*

> us competent as ministers of a new covenant—not of the letter but of the Spirit; for the letter kills, but the Spirit gives life. Now if the ministry that brought death, which was engraved in letters on stone, came with glory, so that the Israelites could not look steadily at the face of Moses because of its glory, fading though it was, will not the ministry of the Spirit be even more glorious? If the ministry that condemns men is glorious, how much more glorious is the ministry that brings righteousness! For what was glorious has no glory now in comparison with the surpassing glory. And if what was fading away came with glory, how much greater is the glory of that which lasts!
>
> Therefore, since we have such a hope, we are very bold. We are not like Moses, who would put a veil over his face to keep the Israelites from gazing at it while the radiance was fading away. But their minds were made dull, for to this day the same veil remains when the old covenant is read. It has not been removed, because only in Christ is it taken away. Even to this day when Moses is read, a veil covers their hearts. But whenever anyone turns to the Lord, the veil is taken away. Now the Lord is the Spirit, and where the Spirit of the Lord is, there is freedom. And we, who with unveiled faces all reflect the Lord's glory, are being transformed into his likeness with ever-increasing glory, which comes from the Lord, who is the Spirit.

This ministry is for all of us, men and women alike. Together with the Lord, we ***can*** bear much fruit!

> For you did not receive a spirit that makes you a slave again to fear, but you received the Spirit of sonship. And by him we cry, "Abba, Father." The Spirit himself testifies with our spirit that we are God's children. Now if we are children, then we

are heirs—heirs of God and co-heirs with Christ, if indeed we share in His sufferings in order that we may also share in His glory.

I consider that our present sufferings are not worth comparing with the glory that will be revealed in us. The creation waits in eager expectation for the sons of God to be revealed. For the creation was subjected to frustration, not by its own choice, but by the will of the one who subjected it, in hope that the creation itself will be liberated from its bondage to decay and brought into the glorious freedom of the children of God.

We know that the whole creation has been groaning as in the pains of childbirth right up to the present time. Not only so, but we ourselves, who have the first fruits of the Spirit, groan inwardly as we wait eagerly for our adoption as sons, the redemption of our bodies. For in this hope we were saved. But hope that is seen is no hope at all. Who hopes for what he already has? But if we hope for what we do not yet have, we wait for it patiently.

In the same way, the Spirit helps us in our weakness. We do not know what we ought to pray for, but the Spirit himself intercedes for us with groans that words cannot express. And he who searches our hearts knows the mind of the spirit, because the Spirit intercedes for the saints in accordance with God's will.

And we know that in all things God works for the good of those who love him, who have been called according to his purpose. For those God foreknew he also predestined to be conformed to the likeness of his Son, that he might be the firstborn among many brothers. And those he predestined, he also called; those he called, he also justified; those he justified, he also glorified (Romans 8:15-30).

Responding:

Are there barren places in the lives of people around you that need to be filled with the glory of God? Yield yourself to Him. Allow His Holy Spirit to overshadow you and lead you as you speak forth the Word of the Lord in prayer to release His glory. List those who the Lord is inviting you to pray for today. Record any specific words He would have you to pray concerning them. We can't always see the answers to our prayers, but it is encouraging to note whenever we do see prayers being answered. Always remember to pray only the will of God for each person. Release each one to God's best for them. The Lord gives us each a free will to choose Him and His ways. We do not seek to control or manipulate others but to free them to hear the Lord, see Him, and understand His ways and purposes.

And the man and the woman are once again being enshrouded by a beam of glory, the presence of the Lord. His presence brings a newfound unity, the man and woman enfolding each other to see His Kingdom come. Male and female created He them—the woman from the man, the man from the woman, the two becoming one from God, the three in One.

Once again the cocoon rips a little more as the butterfly stretches within. The desire to spread its wings and fly is being released within this magnificent creature.

To him who sits on the throne and to the Lamb be praise and honor and glory and power, forever and ever! (Revelation 5:1).

Chapter 17
May He Add

Moses' voice became tender as he shared, "Then our dear Rachel, the one with whom Jacob's heart had united in love, the one for whom he worked diligently for fourteen years, was with child herself. G_d had remembered her, and as G_d touched her womb, she became fruitful. Rachel named the son of her womb Joseph, meaning *may He add*, recognizing that the Lord had added unto her this son. This son from his chosen bride held a special place in his father's heart. Jacob's other brothers were jealous of this relationship they shared. Because of their jealousy, they sold their brother into slavery, telling their father that he had been killed by wild animals. Jacob grieved greatly for his lost son. The brothers had plotted harm for Joseph, but God took the grievous circumstances and turned them around for good.

"Joseph ended up in Egypt, working for a captain of Pharaoh's guard, Potiphar. Potiphar's wife sought to seduce Joseph. In his purity and his honor for God, Joseph resisted her wooing. Not wanting to be rejected by him, Potiphar's wife accused him falsely of molesting her. Joseph had rendered excellent service to his master Potiphar and been elevated to a high position within his household. Nevertheless, at his wife's accusation, Potiphar had to put him in prison.

"In prison, Joseph found favor with the warden and rose to a high place of service once again. While in prison, Joseph interpreted the dreams of several of the king's officials. When Pharaoh dreamed several dreams and could find no one to interpret them, one of the officials who had been restored to his service to Pharaoh remembered Joseph and had him brought before Pharaoh. Joseph proclaimed that God would give him the interpretation of the dreams, and proceeded to share their meaning with Pharaoh. God was preparing Egypt for a great famine that would come upon all the land. He enlisted Joseph as second in command over all Egypt to prepare for the famine. God gave Joseph wisdom to store grain from the years of plenty to be a provision during the years of want.

"The famine became severe in all the land, reaching beyond Egypt and into the surrounding countries. They all came to Egypt to obtain grain for their sustenance, including Jacob's sons from Canaan. As Joseph's brothers came before him, he withheld his identity from them at first. He tested them and found that their hearts had changed. He revealed himself to his brothers, forgiving them for the past wrongdoing and seeing the plan of God at work in spite of their ill will. Jacob was restored to his son Joseph, and his household was brought to Egypt for provision during the famine.

"During his stay in Egypt, Joseph married Asenath and she bore him two sons, Manasseh and Ephraim. Before Jacob died, he blessed the two boys and received them as his very own. Today we have two tribes named for Joseph's sons, Manasseh and Ephraim, that we will count in the stead of the tribe of Levi, the priestly tribe not to be counted with the others."

Elishama, of the tribe of Ephraim spoke up, "Our forefather Joseph has come with us as we journey toward our land of promise. We carry his bones as we go."

"Yes," added Gamaliel of the tribe of Manasseh, "He knew of G_d's word to father Abraham to bring his people out of a strange country and into the land of promise. He wanted to receive that promise himself even if only his bones. He wanted to rest in the Promised Land."

"So do we all, my son," replied Moses, "so do we all."

Day Thirty-eight:
The Blessing of the Lord

As the children of Israel stood at the gate to the Promised Land, Moses gave his farewell speech, laying before them the blessings or the curses they could choose to walk in.

> *This day I call heaven and earth as witnesses against you that I have set before you life and death, blessings and curses. Now choose life, so that you and your children may live and that you may love the LORD your God, listen to his voice, and hold fast to him. For the LORD is your life, and he will give you many years in the land he swore to give to your fathers, Abraham, Isaac and Jacob* (Deuteronomy 30:19,19).

The wise king Solomon had this to say: *The blessing of the LORD makes one rich, And he adds no sorrow with it* (Proverbs 10:22 NKJV). Father Abraham was a very rich man. *Abram had become very wealthy in livestock and in silver and gold* (Genesis 13:2). But this was not the full extent of his wealth. He possessed a far richer store—God Himself. God had given Himself to Abraham. *"Do not be afraid, Abram. I am your shield, your very great reward* (Genesis 15:1). God had also spoken His word to Abraham, *"I will make you into a great nation and I will bless you; I will make your name great, and you will be a blessing. I will bless those who bless you, and whoever curses you I will curse; and all peoples on earth will be blessed through you* (Genesis 12:2,3). Abraham not only wanted to possess this blessing for himself but desired an heir to whom he could pass on all of his blessings. God gave him a son, Isaac.

Abraham gave this son back to God. God gave us His Son, through whom we are heirs.

> *If you belong to Christ, then you are Abraham's seed, and heirs according to the promise. What I am saying is that as long as the heir is a child, he is no different from a slave, although he owns the whole estate. He is subject to guardians and trustees until the time set by his father. So also, when we were children, we were in slavery under the basic principles of the world. But when the time had fully come, God sent his Son, born of a woman, born under law, to redeem those under law, that we might receive the full rights of sons. Because you are sons, God sent the Spirit of his Son into our hearts, the Spirit who calls out, "Abba, Father." So you are no longer a slave, but a son; and since you are a son, God has made you also an heir* (Galatians 3:29-4:7).

It is time for us to rise up as mature sons and daughters of God to walk in the fullness of our inheritance in Him. At the baptism of Jesus, the Spirit of God descended on Him like a dove. *And a voice from heaven said, "This is my Son, whom I love; with him I am well pleased"* (Matthew 3:17). We have already stated that this was a time when Jesus was stepping into partnership with the Father in His business as a mature Son. We can see the reality of baptism once again in the two sons of Joseph. Manasseh means *forget my father's house*. In baptism we are forgetting the old, dying to it, and leaving it behind. Ephraim means *doubly blessed*. We are rising into the newness of the life of God and all the blessings it contains.

We walk in faith as our father Abraham. *And without faith it is impossible to please God, because anyone who comes to him must believe that he exists and that he rewards those who earnestly seek him* (Hebrews 11:6). The word used here for pleasing God is rooted in the word meaning *agreeable*. In faith we come into agreement with

God. We align ourselves with Him. In doing so, we are coming into perfect alignment of our being—body, soul, and spirit. We rise up as mature sons and daughters of God, joint heirs with Jesus Christ, the Son.

As Moses met with God, he told the Lord, *"You have said, 'I know you by name and you have found favor with me.' If you are pleased with me, teach me your ways so I may know you and continue to find favor with you"* (Exodus 33:12,13). At the angels' proclamation of Jesus' birth to the shepherds on the Judean hillside, they praised God by saying, *"Glory to God in the highest, and on earth peace to men on whom his favor rests"* (Luke 2:14). When Jesus began His public ministry following His baptism and subsequent temptation in the desert, Jesus went into the synagogue in his hometown of Nazareth and read from the scroll of Isaiah (61:1,2): *"The Spirit of the Lord is on me, because he has anointed me to preach good news to the poor. He has sent me to proclaim freedom for the prisoners and recovery of sight for the blind, to release the oppressed, to proclaim the year of the Lord's favor."*

Then he rolled up the scroll, gave it back to the attendant and sat down. The eyes of everyone in the synagogue were fastened on him, and he began by saying to them, "Today this scripture is fulfilled in your hearing" (Luke 4:18-21).

Regarding Jesus' baptism, the apostle John gives this testimony of John the Baptist. *"I saw the Spirit come down from heaven as a dove and remain on him. I would not have known him, except that the one who sent me to baptize with water told me, 'The man on whom you see the Spirit come down and remain is he who will baptize with the Holy Spirit.' I have seen and I testify that this is the Son of God"* (John 1:32-34).

As Moses met with God, he asked of the Lord, *"Now show me your glory"* (Exodus 33:18). Within this passage of scripture in Exodus 33, we find two important aspects of the glory of God.

First of all, God's glory is His manifest presence. Moses wisely discerned that the presence of God among His people was their distinguishing factor. Only God's presence made the difference in their lives. Secondly, God hid Moses in the cleft of the rock and caused His goodness to pass by. God's glory is embodied in His character, His nature.

For I do not want you to be ignorant of the fact, brothers, that our forefathers were all under the cloud and that they all passed through the sea. They were all baptized into Moses in the cloud and in the sea. They all ate the same spiritual food and drank the same spiritual drink; for they drank from the spiritual rock that accompanied them, and that rock was Christ (1 Corinthians 10:1-4).

God hides us in the cleft of the Rock. *The Word became flesh and made his dwelling among us. We have seen his glory, the glory of the One and Only, who came from the Father, full of grace and truth* (John 1:14).

Moses' request was that he *continue to find favor*. When Jesus was baptized, the sign that John was to see was that the dove came down and *remained* on Him. We know that the dove was a symbol of the Holy Spirit. There are some interesting facts about doves. Doves make their nesting place in the cleft of the rocks. *My dove in the clefts of the rock, in the hiding places on the mountainside* (Song of Songs 2:14). Doves mate for life; they enter into a monogamous relationship. There is singleness of vision. *How beautiful you are, my darling! Oh how beautiful! Your eyes are doves* (Song of Songs 1:15). Doves are not hostile or aggressive toward other animals. They feed primarily on seeds and fruits. When sending the disciples out, Jesus said to them, *I am sending you out like sheep among wolves. Therefore be as shrewd as snakes and as innocent as doves* (Matthew 10:16). Doves are messengers, and are widely recognized as messengers of peace especially. As the flood waters were receding, Noah sent out a dove three different times. The first time, the dove went out and came back to him. There had been nowhere to light. When the dove returned from its second flight, *there in its beak was a freshly plucked olive leaf! Then Noah knew that the water had receded from the earth* (Genesis 8:11). The third time the dove flew out, it did not return. Noah knew that it was time to come out from the ark and begin to replenish the earth. Even in the world, the dove with the olive leaf has become a symbol of peace.

R.T. Kendall, renowned minister and author, was being interviewed on James Dobson's "Focus on the Family" radio program. He told a story of a British couple who went to Israel as missionaries. As they set up their home, a pair of doves nested in the top of their dwelling. They were very excited about their guests, taking it as a sign of approval by God for their mission work. The two noticed that the doves seemed quite content to remain as long as the atmosphere of their home was peaceful. However, whenever the couple had an argument and began to raise their voices and slam doors, disturbing the peace, the doves would fly away for a while and return only when the air had been cleared and settled. The man said to his bride, "We must either adjust to the doves or the doves will have to adjust to us."

The dove, as a symbol of the Holy Spirit, wants to remain on us, not just to visit, but to live with us and in us. We were created to live in this glory. In order to practice the manifest presence of God in our lives, that which truly makes the difference in our lives, we must not grieve the Holy Spirit. We must adjust to the dove.

Prior to His death, burial, and resurrection, Jesus spent a lot of time sharing deeply with His disciples. This special intimate time is recorded in John 13-17. Within this passage, Judas (not Judas Iscariot) questioned Jesus, *"But, Lord, why do you intend to show yourself to us and not the world?"* (John 14:22).

Jesus replied, "If anyone loves me, he will obey my teaching. My Father will love him, and we will come to him and make our home with him. He who does not love me will not obey my teaching. These words you hear are not my own; they belong to the Father who sent me. All this I have spoken while still with you. But the Counselor, the Holy Spirit, whom the Father will send in my name will teach you all things and will remind you of everything I have said to you. Peace I leave with you; my peace I give you. I do not give to you as the world gives. Do not let your hearts be troubled and do not be afraid...Remain in me, and I will remain in you. No branch can bear fruit by itself; it must remain in the vine. Neither can you bear fruit unless you remain in me. I am the vine; you are the branches. If a man remains in me and I in him, he will bear much fruit; apart from me you can do nothing (John 14:22-27; 15:4,5).

But the fruit of the Spirit is love, joy, peace, patience, kindness, goodness, faithfulness, gentleness and self-control (Galatians 5:22,23).

The Lord wants a resting place in our lives. Let the dove remain! As you do and consequently live in the glory of the Lord, people will smell the sweet fragrance of Christ in your life and be drawn to the fruit of His Spirit. *Surely goodness and love will follow* [you] *all the days of* [your] *life, and* [you] *will dwell in the house of the LORD forever* (Psalm 23:6).

Responding:

The cocoon has fallen away. The beautiful wings glisten as they reflect the rays of the Son. All the days of confinement as this amazing creature has gone through its transformation have proved fruitful. The tapestry of colors has been uniquely woven throughout the process. *My dove, my perfect one, is unique* (Song of Songs 6:9). The dazzling appendages seem rather small and

May He Add

limp. Can they cause this new creature to arise from its resting place to flights unknown? What grand and glorious adventures await?

What about you, oh beautiful new creature in Christ? You have seen His glory within your cocoon. You have nested in the warmth of His love. You have heard His voice, sometimes soft and gentle, other times loud and thunderous, yet always loving. Your new colors are shining, too, a beautiful tapestry woven as you have experienced life fresh and new and glorious each day you spend with Him. He has quenched your thirst with His living water. He has fed you with manna from His very bosom. His joy is your newfound strength. His love is your springboard to propel you into new adventures with Him. His peace is your resting place beneath His wings. Freedom unbounded awaits you as you lay aside the cocoon, yet ever take its impartation with you as you go. Will your new wings be integrated into the wings of the dove?

Arise, shine, for your light has come, and the glory of the LORD rises upon you (Isaiah 60:1).

I pray that you begin to rise up in all the strength of the Lord. Let go of all your fears and frustrations, your inhibitions and your insecurities. These things belong to you no more. You are a new creation in Christ Jesus. Let the dove remain on you as you stand as a mature child of God. I bless you in the name of Jesus Christ of Nazareth. May you be all God has created you to be and live in His blessings continually. Hear His voice say to you, "You are my beloved son (daughter), in whom I am well pleased." As you have been blessed, you can now go forth and be a blessing. Your beauty can be seen and enjoyed by all.

Flowers appear on the earth; the season of singing has come, the cooing of doves is heard in our land (Song of Songs 2:12).

Chapter 18
Son of My Right Hand

"Esau had been angry enough with his brother Jacob to kill him," Moses continued to tell the story. "Jacob had tricked him out of his birthright and then out of his blessing. Jacob had to flee. As he had left these many years ago, G_d had appeared to Jacob at Bethel. Jacob dreamed of a ladder that rested upon the earth and reached into heaven. He called that place, Bethel, *the house of G_d.* Jacob made a vow saying that if G_d would watch over him on his journey and bring him back safely to his father's house, the LORD would be his G_d.

"G_d sent Jacob back to Bethel. He had journeyed many miles. He now had eleven sons and a daughter. Jacob returned to Bethel and built an altar and worshiped the Lord. Rachel was great with child once again. As the family moved on from Bethel, Rachel began to give birth with great difficulty. Rachel died in childbirth, but before she died she was told she was birthing another son. With her last dying breath, Rachel named the son Ben-Oni, meaning *son of my trouble.* His father named the son Benjamin, *son of my right hand.*

"Jacob's beloved Rachel was buried on the way to Bethlehem. His family was now complete, the twelve sons the seedbed of the twelve tribes of Israel. This small band has grown exceedingly. We are the people of G_d surrounding this tabernacle enshrouded by

the cloud of His presence. I have called you here today to commission each of you to number your tribe as the Lord has requested. G_d has blessed us greatly. Count your blessings!" concluded Moses, the mighty man of G_d.

Day Thirty-nine: Victory in Jesus

Benjamin is the only son who was named by his father. Rachel had named him Ben-Oni, *son of my trouble.* Jacob named him Benjamin, *son of my right hand.*

The book of Hosea is a beautiful love story. *When the LORD began to speak through Hosea, the LORD said to him, "Go, take to yourself an adulterous wife and children of unfaithfulness, because the land is guilty of the vilest adultery in departing from the LORD"* (Hosea 1:2). As was often the case, God provided an object lesson to the children of Israel to woo them back unto Himself, to show them of His great love for them despite their wanderings. His call to them opened the door for a beautiful restoration. Let's read about it in Hosea 2:14-23:

> *"Therefore I am now going to allure her; I will lead her into the desert and speak tenderly to her. There I will give her back her vineyards, and will make the Valley of Achor a door of hope. There she will sing as in the days of her youth, as in the day she came up out of Egypt. In that day," declares the LORD, "you will call me 'my husband'; you will no longer call me 'my master.' I will remove the names of the Baals from her lips; no longer will their names be invoked. In that day I will make a covenant for them with the beasts of the field and the birds of the air and the creatures that move along the ground. Bow and sword and battle I will abolish from the land so that all may lie down in safety. I will betroth you to me forever; I will betroth you in righteousness and justice, in love and compas-*

Son of My Right Hand

sion. I will betroth you in faithfulness, and you will acknowledge the LORD. In that day I will respond," declares the LORD. "I will respond to the skies, and they will respond to the earth; and the earth will respond to the grain, the new wine and oil, and they will respond to Jezreel. I will plant her for myself in the land; I will show my love to the one I called 'Not my loved one.' I will say to those called 'Not my people,' 'You are my people'; and they will say, 'You are my God.'"

God said that He would *make the Valley of Achor a door of hope.* The word *Achor* means *trouble*. God can turn trouble into triumph! And that is just what He does in our lives. We see this at work in the life of Job of old. Even the devil is but a pawn in the hands of God and even he can only do what either we or God allows. And as we walk through the trials that come our way, like Job, when we come out on the other side if we remain steadfast in the Lord, we will realize greater victory than ever before. The devil gave his best attempt to kill the Son of God. Judas Iscariot was the disciple through whom he worked as Judas Iscariot betrayed his Master. He, too, played right into the hands of God to bring about God's ultimate triumph. The stone that the builders rejected has become the cornerstone (Psalm 118:22; 1 Peter 2:8). On this rock of the revelation of the Christ, the Son of the living God, is built His church, and *the gates of Hades will not overcome it* (Matthew 16:18). The closed door on the garden (Genesis 3:22-24) becomes the open door John sees (Revelation 4:1) as he hears the invitation of the Lord, *"Come up here."* **Who opened the door?** Jesus! *Therefore, brothers, since we have confidence to enter the Most Holy Place by the blood of Jesus, by a new and living way opened for us through the curtain, that is, his body, and since we have a great priest over the house of God, let us draw near to God with a sincere heart in full assurance of faith* (Hebrews 10:19-22). **Where is Jesus now?** *But when this priest had offered for all time one sacrifice for sins, he sat down at the* *right hand of God. Since that time he waits for his enemies to be made his footstool, because by one sacrifice he has made perfect forever those who are being made holy* (Hebrews 10:12-14). *For he must reign until he has put all his enemies under his feet. The last enemy to be destroyed is death* (1 Corinthians 15:25,26).

As John was caught away in the Spirit on the Isle of Patmos, he saw a vision of Jesus. *When I saw him, I fell at his feet as though dead. Then he placed his right hand on me and said: "Do not be afraid. I am the First and the Last. I am the Living One; I was dead, and behold I am alive for ever and ever! And I hold the keys to death and Hades* (Revelation 1:17,18).

> *Listen, I tell you a mystery: We will not all sleep, but we will all be changed—in a flash, in the twinkling of an eye, at the last trumpet. For the trumpet will sound, the dead will be raised imperishable, and we will be changed. For the perishable must clothe itself with the imperishable, and the mortal with immortality. When the perishable has been clothed with the imperishable, and the mortal with immortality, then the saying that is written will come true: "Death has been swallowed up in victory."*
>
> *"Where, O death, is your victory? Where, O death, is your sting?"*
>
> *The sting of death is sin, and the power of sin is the law. But thanks be to God! He gives us the victory through our Lord Jesus Christ* (1 Corinthians 15:51-57).
>
> *What, then, shall we say in response to this? If God is for us, who can be against us? He who did not spare his own Son, but gave him up for us all—how will he not also, along with him, graciously give us all things? Who will bring any charge against those whom God has chosen? It is God who justifies. Who is he that condemns? Christ Jesus, who died—more than*

Son of My Right Hand

that, who was raised to life—is at the right hand of God and is also interceding for us. Who shall separate us from the love of Christ? Shall trouble or hardship or persecution or famine or nakedness or danger or sword? As it is written: "For your sake we face death all day long; we are considered as sheep to be slaughtered." No, in all these things we are more than conquerors through him who loved us. For I am convinced that neither death nor life, neither angels nor demons, neither the present nor the future, nor any powers, neither height nor depth, nor anything else in all creation, will be able to separate us from the love of God that is in Christ Jesus our Lord (Romans 8:31-39).

Where are we? *And God raised us up with Christ and seated us with him in the heavenly realms in Christ Jesus, in order that in the coming ages he might show the incomparable riches of his grace expressed in his kindness to us in Christ Jesus. For it is by grace you have been saved, through faith—and this not from yourselves, it is the gift of God—not by works, so that no one can boast. For we are God's workmanship, created in Christ Jesus to do good works, which God prepared in advance for us to do* (Ephesians 2:6-9).

How are we seated in those heavenly places in Christ? We are overcomers. We have persevered through the process and gone the distance with Jesus. *To him who overcomes, I will give the right to sit with me on my throne, just as I overcame and sat down with my Father on his throne* (Revelation 3:21).

Soooo…*let your light shine before men, that they may see your good deeds and praise your Father in heaven* (Matthew 5:16). You go, girl! You go, boy! And as you go, *"make disciples of all nations, baptizing them in the name of the Father and of the Son and of the Holy Spirit, and teaching them to obey everything I have commanded you. And surely I am with you always, to the very end of the age"* (Matthew 28:19,20).

Cocoon

Responding:

The only way to respond to that is to thank God for what He's done and to do what He said to do. What are the good works that He has called you to do? Will you be His right-hand man or woman? By now, you have established a habit of journaling each day your experiences with the Lord. Continue to journal your journey as you travel onward. Record your prayers, your words from the Lord, and the God instances you experience daily.

I see those wings that have hung down now filling and beginning to open. Slowly they start to flutter and rise. New strength is realized in the stretching and pumping. There it is—the manifestation of the sons of God.

Chapter 19
The Butterfly

Day Forty

Now comes the time to release this new creation, a butterfly with beautiful colors glistening in the sunlight. Look with me into the mirror. What do you see? *I have been crucified with Christ and I no longer live, but Christ lives in me. The life I live in the body, I live by the faith of the Son of God, who loved me and gave himself for me* (Galatians 2:20). *Therefore, if anyone is in Christ, he is a new creation; the old has gone, the new has come* (2 Corinthians 5:17). Continue to release that new person that you are. The old self *is* crucified with Christ. Let the old man go as you have received the redemption from the old.

"I bless you with looking backward only until your vision is filled with the cross and you meditate on its effective work in your life."[39] Then, as the apostle Paul, *forgetting what is behind and straining toward what is ahead, [we] press on toward the goal to win the prize for which God has called [us] heavenward in Christ Jesus* (Philippians 3:13,14). That's right! *Therefore, since we are surrounded by such a great cloud of witnesses, let us throw off everything that hinders and the sin that so easily entangles, and let us run with perseverance the race marked out for us. Let us fix our eyes on Jesus, the author and perfecter of our faith* (Hebrews 12:1,2). You *are* a new creation.

You were taught, with regard to your former way of life, to put off your old self, which is being corrupted by its deceitful desires; to be made new in the attitude of your minds; and to put on the new self, created to be like God in true righteousness and holiness (Ephesians 4:22-24).

Christ Jesus has filled those wings with power to rise to new heights. He *is* the true vine and you are vitally connected to Him.

> *For in Christ all the fullness of the Deity lives in bodily form, and you have been given fullness in Christ, who is the head over every power and authority. In Him you were also circumcised, in the putting off of the sinful nature, not with a circumcision done by the hands of men but with the circumcision done by Christ, having been buried with him in baptism and raised with him through your faith in the power of God, who raised him from the dead. When you were dead in your sins and in the uncircumcision of your sinful nature (or your flesh), God made you alive with Christ* (Colossians 2:9-13).
>
> *Since, then, you have been raised with Christ, set your hearts on things above, where Christ is seated at the right hand of God. Set your minds on things above, not on earthly things. For you died and your life is now hidden with Christ in God. When Christ, who is your life, appears, then you also will appear with him in glory* (Colossians 3:1-4).

Yes, as you have been looking *at* Him, looking *to* Him, and looking *for* Him, a wonderful transformation has been taking place. It's becoming clearer and clearer everyday! *And we, who with unveiled faces all reflect the Lord's glory, are being transformed into his likeness with ever-increasing glory, which comes from the Lord, who is the Spirit* (2 Corinthians 3:18). *Now the Lord is the Spirit, and where the Spirit of the Lord is, there is freedom* (2 Corinthians 3:17).

So go ahead and flap those wings. Begin to rise on the wind of His Spirit. Rise higher and higher.

> *Do you not know? Have you not heard? The LORD is the everlasting God, the Creator of the ends of the earth. He will not grow tired or weary, and his understanding no one can fathom. He gives strength to the weary and increases the power of the weak. Even youths grow tired and weary, and young men stumble and fall; but those who hope in the LORD will renew their strength. They will soar on wings like eagles; they will run and not grow weary, they will walk and not be faint* (Isaiah 40:28-31).

As you're soaring, don't forget this: *"The only goal in life for an adult butterfly is to reproduce."*[40] *But you will receive power when the Holy Spirit comes on you; and you will be my witnesses in Jerusalem, and in all Judea and Samaria, and to the ends of the earth* (Acts 1:8). We can only say with Peter and John, *For we cannot help speaking about what we have seen and heard* (Acts 4:20). *He appointed twelve—designating them apostles—that they might be with him* **and** *that he might* **send them out** *to preach and to have authority to drive out demons* (Mark 3:14,15 emphasis added).

> *He said to them, "Go into all the world and preach the good news to all creation. Whoever believes and is baptized will be saved, but whoever does not believe will be condemned. And these signs will accompany those who believe: In my name they will drive out demons; they will speak in new tongues; they will pick up snakes with their hands; and when they drink deadly poison, it will not hurt them at all; they will place their hands on sick people, and they will get well* (Mark 16:15-18).

As you arise with your new wings you are lifting up Jesus. Lift Him up! *"But I, when I am lifted up from the earth, will draw all men to myself* (John 12:32).

> *I consider that our present sufferings are not worth comparing with the glory that will be revealed in us. The creation waits in eager expectation for the sons of God to be revealed. For the creation was subjected to frustration, not by its own choice, but by the will of the one who subjected it, in hope that the creation itself will be liberated from its bondage to decay and brought into the glorious freedom of the children of God* (Romans 8:18-21).

You are a son or daughter of God, one who hears His voice, who is attached to Him who is the true vine, one who gives Him praise because He has vindicated you. You are in His army and He has fought your battle and won. You are filled with His exceeding great joy. You are His treasure and He is yours. To Him be all honor and glory and power!

Soar as you abide in Him. *"The Holy Spirit will come upon you, and the power of the Most High will overshadow you. So the Holy One to be born will be called the Son of God…For nothing is impossible with God"* (Luke 1:35,37).

> *"Hallelujah! For our Lord God almighty reigns. Let us rejoice and be glad and give him glory! For the wedding of the Lamb has come, and his bride has made herself ready. Fine linen, bright and clean, was given her to wear" [fine linen stands for the righteous acts of the saints.]* (Revelation 19:6-8).
>
> *I saw the Holy City, the new Jerusalem, coming down out of heaven from God, prepared as a bride beautifully dressed for her husband. And I heard a loud voice from the throne saying, "Now the dwelling of God is with men, and he will live with them. They will be his people, and God himself will be with them and be their God. He will wipe every tear from their eyes. There will no more death or mourning or crying or pain, for the old order of things has passed away." He who was*

The Butterfly

seated on the throne said, "I am making everything new!" Then he said, "Write this down, for these words are trustworthy and true." He said to me: "It is done. I am the Alpha and the Omega, the Beginning and the End. To him who is thirsty I will give to drink without cost from the spring of the water of life. He who overcomes will inherit all this, and I will be his God and he will be my son...One of the seven angels who had the seven bowls full of the seven last plagues came and said to me, "Come, I will show you the bride, the wife of the Lamb." And he carried me away in the Spirit to a mountain great and high, and showed me the Holy City, Jerusalem, coming down out of heaven from God. It shone with the glory of God, and its brilliance was like that of a very precious jewel, like a jasper, clear as crystal. It had a great, high wall with twelve gates, and with twelve angels at the gates. On the gates were written the names of the twelve tribes of Israel. There were three gates on the east, three on the north, three on the south and three on the north, three on the south and three on the west. The wall of the city had twelve foundations, and on them were the names of the twelve apostles of the Lamb (Revelation 21:2-14).

You are a very real part of that new Jerusalem being prepared by Jesus, the Holy City, the home of the Bride, the wife of the Lamb. You are shining with the glory of God, your wings reflecting the light of His being. Under His wings, you are resting in Him, your cocoon of transformation. Any day now your transformation will be complete as you respond to the heavenly trumpet call—"Oh when the saints go flyin' in...." Until then, beautiful butterfly, spread your wings and fly in the garden He has placed you in. That garden has a great potential of transformation also. Perhaps Eden is being restored—here, there, everywhere—when eternity dawns. And when eternity dawns, we have only just begun.

And they sung a new song, saying, Thou art worthy to take the book, and to open the seals thereof; for thou wast slain, and hast redeemed us to God by thy blood out of every kindred, and tongue, and people, and nations; And hast made us unto our God kings and priests: and we shall reign on the earth (Revelation 5:9,10 KJV).

Bibliography

[1] All of the information herein concerning the butterfly and moth and its life stages were gleaned from a website of The Butterfly Farm in Costa Rica, c.2002 The Butterfly Farm S.A., Selected by the SciLinks program, a service of National Science Teachers Association. c. 2001. 2008.<http:// www.butterfly farm.co.cr/>

[2] Ibid.

[3] Ibid.

[4] Ibid.

[5] From Wade Taylor's article, "Two Ways." 2008.< www.wadetaylor.org>

[6] Spirit-Filled Life Bible. Copyright 1991 by Thomas Nelson, Inc.

[7] Two really awesome worship CDs entitled "Cloud By Day" and "Fire by Night" with Joann McFatter really bring out this interesting insight.

[8] *The Interpreters Bible*, Vol. VIII (New York/Nashville: Abingdon Press, 1952) p. 472, 473.

[9] I would strongly recommend that you obtain this teaching from the Dick Rueben Evangelistic Association.

10 *Melanie & Mike say... Take Our Word For It*, an endeavor of the *Institute for Etymological Research and Education*. C.1995-2008 TIERE. Last updated 4/13/08, 12:20 PM. 2008. <http://www.takeourword.com>

11 2008.< www.minnesotapublicradio.org/display/web/2006/08/15/butter/>

12 Lewis L. Dunnington, *The Inner Splendor* (New York: The Macmillan Company, 1955) p. 1-5.

(W. L. Stidger, *There Are Sermons in Stories* (Nashville, TN: Abingdon-Cokesbury Press, 1942) p. 106-107.)

13 From *Blessing Your Spirit* by Arthur Burk and Sylvia Gunter c. 2005 by Sylvia Gunter, The Father's Business, P. O. Box 380333, Birmingham, AL 35238, <http://www.thefathersbusiness.com> or E-mail FathersBiz@cs.com

14 Arthur Burk, *Gift of Mercy: The Redemptive Gifts of Individuals*. These teachings were obtained on audio CD and are available at www.plumblineministries.com.

15 NKJV Greek-English Interlinear New Testament, translated by Farstad, Hodges, Moss, Picirilli and Pickering. Published 1994 by Thomas Nelson Nashville, p. 663.

16 *The Interpreter's Bible*, Vol. VIII (New York/Nashville: Abingdon Press, 1952) p. 485, 486.

17 Signa Bodishbaugh, *The Journey to Wholeness in Christ: A Devotional Adventure to Becoming Whole* (Mobile, AL: Journey Press, 1997) p. 70,71.

18 Dutch Sheets, *Intercessory Prayer* (Ventura, CA: Regal Books, A Division of Gospel Light, 1996) p. 64-66.

19 J.R. Mosely, *Manifest Victory* (New York: Harper & Brothers Publishers, 1941 & 1947) p. 131, 133.

Bibliography

[20] An Orthodox Jewish Rabbi, "Justice, Law, and Legalism—Part 1," *The Morning Star Journal: Vol. 17—Life in the Spirit, No. 4—Bringing Heaven to Earth*, p. 13.

[21] Hymn—"There Is A Fountain Filled With Blood" by William Cowper.

[22] Read *A Tale of Three Kings* by Gene Edwards for more insight into this matter.

[23] Read the classic *Hinds' Feet on High Places* by Hannah Hurnard.

[24] For an excellent reading pertaining to this transition, read *Permission Granted To Do Church Differently in the 21st Century* by Gary Goodall and Graham Cook.

[25] For further study, I recommend: *Breaking Free* by Beth Moore, *The Victory Over the Darkness, The Bondage Breaker*, and *Steps to Freedom in Christ* by Neil Anderson, and *The Three Battlegrounds* by Francis Frangipane.

[26] I would highly recommend that you study Arthur Burk's teachings on the redemptive gifts of individuals and the different niche anointings that he has observed in the Body of Christ. It is so exciting to hear of how Christians are discovering who they are and what their callings are within the Body of Christ and in the world today. For more information go to www.plumblineministries.org.

[27] Suggested reading: *A Shepherd Looks at Psalm 23* by W. Phillip Keller

[28] For a better understanding of "listening prayer," read Leanne Payne's book, *Listening Prayer: Learning to Hear God's Voice and Keep a Prayer Journal*.

[29] William P. Young, *The Shack* (Los Angeles, CA: Windblown Media, 2007) p. 101.

[30] Gary Chapman, *Anger: Handling a Powerful Emotion in a Healthy Way* (Chicago, IL: Northfield Publishing, 1999, 2007) p. 26, 27.

[31] *Dake's Annotated Reference Bible* (Lawrenceville, GA: Dake Bible Sales, Inc., 1963)

[32] Ibid.

[33] Tommy Tenney and David Cape, *God's Secret To Greatness (The Power of the Towel)* (Ventura, CA: Regal Books, a division of Gospel Light, 2000).

[34] Loren Cunningham and David Hamilton, *Why Not Women? A Biblical Study of Women in Missions, Ministry, and Leadership* (Seattle, WA: YWAM Publishing, 2000) p. 17, 18, 20, 21.

[35] Dorothy L. Sayers, *Are Women Human?* (Grand Rapids: William B. Eerdmans Publishing Co., 1971).

[36] W.E. Vine, *Vine's Expository Dictionary of New Testament Words* (McLean, VA: MacDonald Publishing Co.)

[37] Dutch Sheets, *Intercessory Prayer* (Ventura, CA: Regal Books, a division of Gospel Light, 1996) p. 116.

[38] Joseph H. Thayer, *Thayer's Greek-English Lexicon of the New Testament* (Hendrickson Publishers, 1996)

[39] From *Blessing Your Spirit* by Arthur Burk and Sylvia Gunter c. 2005 by Sylvia Gunter, The Father's Business, P. O. Box 380333, Birmingham, AL 35238, <http//www.thefathersbusiness.com>or E-mail FathersBiz@cs.com, p. 97.

[40] <www.butterflyfarm.co.cr/>